Table of Contents

Preface

Don't let people fool you into believing that Ruby on Rails is easy to learn. It is not! It's probably the best and most effective framework to develop web applications but it is hard to understand in the beginning. The worst mistake of all is to not learn Ruby before diving into Ruby on Rails. To avoid it this book starts with the basics of Ruby. You will not become a Ruby guru after reading it but you'll understand the basic ideas and that is important.

I wrote this book for developers who learn best by following clean examples. I don't like the idea of coding one big single application throughout a book but prefer smaller stand-alone code examples. Therefore you can skip a couple of pages or even complete chapters without losing context.

Shameless plug: Please contact me by e-mail to stefan.wintermeyer@amooma.de if you need Ruby on Rails consulting or training.

Have fun with Ruby on Rails!

Stefan Wintermeyer

PS: I post updates about this book and Rails in general at https://twitter.com/wintermeyer

Ruby Basics

Introduction

This book requires basic knowledge of HTML, plus the reader - you, in other words - should also have a basic understanding of programming.

 The beginning of this chapter is going to be a bit boring.   Bear with me. It's worth it.

> It is easy to program in Ruby, but Ruby is not a simple language.

—— Yukihiro Matsumoto

This chapter is a tightrope walk between oversimplification and a degree of detail that is unnecessary for a Rails newbie. After all, the objective is not becoming a Ruby guru, but understanding Ruby on Rails. I am going to elaborate on the most important points. The rest is then up to you. If you would like to know more about Ruby, then I recommend the book "The Ruby Programming Language" by David Flanagan and Yukihiro Matsumoto.

The command `ruby -v` will print the current running Ruby version:

```
$ ruby -v
ruby 2.3.0p0 (2015-12-25 revision 53290) [x86_64-darwin15]
$
```

Hello World

Ruby is a scripting language. So it is not compiled and then executed, but read by an interpreter and then processed line by line.

A simple Ruby program `hello-world.rb` consist of the following line:

hello-world.rb

```
puts 'Hello World!'
```

Use your favorite editor to open a new file with the filename `hello-world.rb` and insert the above line into it. You can then execute this Ruby program in the command line as follows:

```
$ ruby hello-world.rb
Hello World!
$
```

A program line in a Ruby program does not have to end with a semicolon. The Ruby interpreter is even so intelligent that it recognizes if a program line was split over two or more lines for the sake of readability. I will spare you the corresponding examples and am only mentioning this so you don't say or think later, "is it okay like this?"

Indenting code is also not necessary. But it does make it much easier to read for human beings!

puts and print

If you go looking for examples on Ruby on the Internet, you will find two typical ways of printing text on the screen:

- `puts` prints a string, followed by a newline.
- `print` prints a string (without newline).

Example program (an extension of the program `hello-world.rb`):

hello-world.rb

```ruby
puts 'Hello World!'
puts
puts 'zzz'
print 'Hello World!'
print
puts 'zzz'
```

On the screen, you will see this:

```
$ ruby hello-world.rb
Hello World!

zzz
Hello World!zzz
```

Comments

A comment in a Ruby program starts with a #-sign and ends with a newline. As an example, I can add a comment to the `hello-world.rb` above:

hello-world.rb

```ruby
# Program for displaying "Hello World!"
# by Stefan Wintermeyer

puts 'Hello World!'
```

A comment can also follow a program line:

hello-world.rb

```ruby
# Program for displaying "Hello World!"
# by Stefan Wintermeyer

puts 'Hello World!'  # output
```

A #-sign within strings in inverted commas is not treated as the start of a comment. Example program:

hello-world.rb

```ruby
# Example program
# by Stefan Wintermeyer

puts 'Hello World!'
puts '###########'
puts
puts '1#2#3#4#5#6#'  # Comment on this
```

Help via ri

When programming, you do not always have a Ruby handbook available. Fortunately, the Ruby developers thought of this and provided a built-in help feature in form of the program ri (of course only if you have installed the documentation which is the default).

This is a typical chicken and egg situation. How can I explain the Ruby help feature, if we are only just getting started with Ruby? So I am going to jump ahead a little and show you how you can search for information on the class String:

```
$ ri String
  [...]
$
```

If we are looking for information on a specific method (chicken-egg!), then we can also use ri. Let's take gsub as an example. This is a method for replacing parts of a String (that is useful now and again).

```
$ ri String.size
= String.size

(from ruby site)
------------------------
  str.size      -> integer

------------------------

Returns the character length of str.
```

The program ri always prints the output in the pager program defined by the shell (for example less). You can also use the command option -T to output everything directly to STDOUT.

irb

irb stands for Interactive Ruby and is a kind of sandbox where you can play around with Ruby at your leisure. irb is launched by entering irb on the shell and ends if you enter exit.

An example is worth a thousand words:

```
$ irb
>> puts 'Hello World!'
Hello World!
=> nil
>> exit
$
```

 I use IRB.conf[:PROMPT_MODE] = :SIMPLE in my .irbrc config   file to generate shorter irb output. You can do the same by   using irb --simple-prompt.

Ruby is Object-Oriented

Ruby only knows objects. Everything is an object (sounds almost like Zen). Every object is an instance of a class. You can find out the class of an object via the method .class.

An object in Ruby is encapsulated and can only be reached from the outside via the methods of the corresponding object. What does this mean? I cannot change any property of an object directly from the outside. The corresponding object has to offer a method with which I can do so.

Please do not panic if you have no idea what a class and an object is. I won't tell anyone and you can still work with it just fine without worrying too much. This topic alone could fill whole volumes. Roughly speaking, an object is a container for something and a method changes something in that container.

Please go on reading and have a look at the examples. The puzzle will gradually get clearer.

Methods

In other programming languages, the terms you would use for Ruby methods would be: functions, procedures, subroutines and of course methods.

Here we go with the oversimplification. We can not compare non-Object oriented programming languages with OO ones. Plus there are two kinds of methods (class methods and instance methods). At this point, I do not want to make it too complicated and am simply ignoring this "fine" distinctions for now.

At this point you start looking for a good example, but all I can think of are silly ones. The problem is the assumption that we are only allowed to use knowledge that has already been described previously in this book.

So let's assume that we use the following code sequence repeatedly (for whatever reason):

```
$ irb
>> puts 'Hello World!'
Hello World!
=> nil
>> puts 'Hello World!'
Hello World!
=> nil
>> puts 'Hello World!'
Hello World!
=> nil
>> exit
$
```

So we want to output the string "Hello World!" three times in a row. As this makes our daily work routine much longer, we are now going to define a method (with the meaningless name three_times), with which this can all be done in one go.

Names of methods are always written in lower case.

```
$ irb
>> def three_times
>>    puts 'Hello World!'
>>    puts 'Hello World!'
>>    puts 'Hello World!'
>> end
=> :three_times
>> three_times
Hello World!
Hello World!
Hello World!
=> nil
>>
```

When defining a method, you can define required parameters and use them within the method. This enables us to create a method to which we pass a string as parameter and we can then output it three times.

```
>> def three_times(value)
>>    puts value
>>    puts value
>>    puts value
>> end
=> :three_times
>> three_times('Hello World!')
Hello World!
Hello World!
Hello World!
=> nil
>>
```

Incidentally, you can omit the brackets when calling the method.

```
>> three_times 'Hello World!'
Hello World!
Hello World!
Hello World!
=> nil
>>
```

Ruby gurus and would-be gurus are going to turn up their noses on the subject of "unnecessary" brackets in your programs and will probably pepper you with more or less stupid comments with comparisons to Java and other programming languages.

There is one simple rule in the Ruby community: the fewer brackets, the cooler you are! ; -)

But you won't get a medal for using fewer brackets. Decide for yourself what makes you happy.

If you do not specify a parameter with the above method, you will get the error message: wrong number of arguments (0 for 1):

```
>> three_times
ArgumentError: wrong number of arguments (0 for 1)
    from (irb):1:in 'three_times'
    from (irb):6
    from /usr/local/bin/irb:11:in '<main>'
>> exit
$
```

You can give the variable value a default value and then you can also call the method without parameter:

```
$ irb
>> def three_times(value = 'blue')
>>    puts value
>>    puts value
>>    puts value
>> end
=> :three_times
>> three_times('Hello World!')
Hello World!
Hello World!
Hello World!
=> nil
>> three_times
blue
blue
blue
=> nil
>> exit
```

Classes

For now you can think of a class as a collection of methods. The name of a class always starts with an upper case letter. Let's assume that the method belongs to the new class This_and_that. It would then be defined as follows in a Ruby program:

```
class This_and_that
  def three_times
    puts 'Hello World!'
    puts 'Hello World!'
    puts 'Hello World!'
  end
end
```

Let's play it through in irb:

```
$ irb
>> class This_and_that
>>   def three_times
>>     puts 'Hello World!'
>>     puts 'Hello World!'
>>     puts 'Hello World!'
>>   end
>> end
=> :three_times
>>
```

Now we try to call the method three_times:

```
>> This_and_that.three_times
NoMethodError: undefined method `three_times' for This_and_that:Class
    from (irb):8
    from /usr/local/bin/irb:11:in `<main>'
>>
```

This results in an error message, because This_and_that is a class and not an instance. As we are working with instance methods, it only works if we have first created a new object (a new instance) of the class This_and_that with the class method new:

```
>> abc = This_and_that.new
=> #<This_and_that:0x007fc6f306bd70>
>> abc.three_times
Hello World!
Hello World!
Hello World!
=> nil
>> exit
$
```

I will explain the difference between instance and class methods in more detail in the section called "Class Methods and Instance Methods". Another chicken and egg problem.

Private Methods

Quite often it makes sense to only call a method within its own class or own instance. Such methods are referred to as private methods (as opposed to public methods), and they are listed below the keyword private within a class.

irb example:

```
$ irb
>> class Example
>>   def a
>>     puts 'a'
>>   end
>>   private
>>   def b
>>     puts 'b'
>>   end
>> end
=> :b
>> abc = Example.new
=> #<Example:0x007fbb3383b1e8>
>> abc.a
a
=> nil
>> abc.b
NoMethodError: private method `b' called for #<Example:0x007fbb3383b1e8>
  from (irb):13
  from /usr/local/bin/irb:11:in `<main>'
>> exit
$
```

Method initialize()

If a new instance is created (by calling the method new), the method that is processed first and automatically is the method initialize. The method is automatically a private method, even if it not listed explicitly under private.

irb example:

```
$ irb
>> class Room
>>   def initialize
>>     puts 'abc'
>>   end
>> end
=> :initialize
>> kitchen = Room.new
abc
=> #<Room:0x007fba8b050350>
>> exit
$
```

The instance kitchen is created with Room.new and the method initialize is processed automatically.

The method new accepts the parameters specified for the method initialize:

```
$ irb
>> class Example
>>   def initialize(value)
>>     puts value
>>   end
>> end
=> :initialize
>> abc = Example.new('Hello World!')
Hello World!
=> #<Example:0x007f8389040088>
>> exit
$
```

return

puts is nice to demonstrate an example in this book but normally you need a way to return the result of something. The return statement can be used for that:

```
$ irb
>> def area_of_a_circle(radius)
>>   pi = 3.14
>>   area = pi * radius * radius
>>   return area
>> end
=> :area_of_a_circle
>> area_of_a_circle(10)
=> 314.0
>> exit
```

But it wouldn't be Ruby if you couldn't do it shorter. You can simply skip return:

```
$ irb
>> def area_of_a_circle(radius)
>>   pi = 3.14
>>   area = pi * radius * radius
>>   area
>> end
=> :area_of_a_circle
>> area_of_a_circle(10)
=> 314.0
>> exit
```

You can actually even skip the last line because Ruby returns the value of the last expression as a default:

```
$ irb
>> def area_of_a_circle(radius)
>>   pi = 3.14
>>   area = pi * radius * radius
>> end
=> :area_of_a_circle
>> area_of_a_circle(10)
=> 314.0
>> exit
```

return is sometimes useful to make a method easier to read. But you don't have to use it in case you feel more comfortable with out.

Inheritance

A class can inherit from another class. When defining the class, the parent class must be added with a < (smaller than) sign:

```
class Example < ParentClass
```

Rails makes use of this approach very frequently (otherwise I would not be bothering you with it).

In the following example, we define the class Abc and which contains the methods a, b and c. Then we define a class Abcd and let it inherit the class Abc and add a new method d. The new instances example1 and example2 are created with the Class-Methods new and show that example2 has access to the methods a, b, c and d but example1 only to a, b and c.

```
$ irb
>> class Abc
>>   def a
>>     'a'
>>   end
>>   def b
>>     'b'
>>   end
>>   def c
>>     'c'
>>   end
>> end
=> :c
>> class Abcd < Abc
>>   def d
>>     'd'
>>   end
>> end
=> :d
>> example1 = Abc.new
=> #<Abc:0x007f827b958a30>
>> example2 = Abcd.new
=> #<Abcd:0x007f827b931610>
>> example2.d
=> "d"
>> example2.a
=> "a"
>> example1.d
NoMethodError: undefined method `d' for #<Abc:0x007fc73a0731c8>
    from (irb):19
    from /usr/local/bin/irb:11:in `<main>'
>> example1.a
=> "a"
>> exit
$
```

 It is important to read the Error-Messages. They tell you what happened and where to search for the problem. In this example Ruby said that there is an undefined method for #<Abc:0x007fb463023928>. With that information you know that the Class Abc is missing the method which you were trying to use.

Class Methods and Instance Methods

There are two important kinds of methods: class methods and instance methods.

You now already know what a class it. And an instance of such a class is created via the class method new. A class method can only be called in connection with the class (for example, the method new is a class method). An instance method is a method that only works with an instance. So you cannot apply the method new to an instance.

Let's first try to call an instance method as class method:

```
$ irb
>> class Knowledge
>>    def pi
>>      3.14
>>    end
>> end
=> :pi
>> Knowledge.pi
NameError: uninitialized constant Knowledge
  from (irb):6
  from /usr/local/bin/irb:11:in `<main>'
```

So that does not work. Well, then let's create a new instance of the class and try again:

```
>> example = Knowledge.new
=> #<Knowledge:0x007fce04039bf0>
>> example.pi
=> 3.14
>> exit
$
```

Now we just need to find out how to define a class method. Hardcore Rails gurus would now whisk you away into the depths of the source code and pick out examples from ActiveRecord. I will spare you this and show an abstract example:

```
$ irb
>> class Knowledge
>>    def self.pi
>>      3.14
>>    end
>> end
=> :pi
>> Knowledge.pi
=> 3.14
>>
```

And the proof to the contrary:

```
>> example = Knowledge.new
=> #<Knowledge:0x007ffda3050980>
>> example.pi
NoMethodError: undefined method 'pi' for #<Knowledge:0x007ffda3050980>
  from (irb):7
  from /usr/local/bin/irb:11:in '<main>'
>> exit
$
```

There are different notations for defining class methods. The two most common ones are self.xyz and class
<< self:

```
# Variant 1
# with self.xyz
#
class Knowledge
  def self.pi
    3.14
  end
end
```

```
# Variant 2
# with class << self
#
class Knowledge
  class << self
    def pi
      3.14
    end
  end
end
```

The result is always the same.

Of course you can use the same method name for a class and an instance method. Obviously that doesn't
make code easier to understand. Here is an example with pi as a class and an instance method:

```
$ irb
>> class Knowledge
>>   def pi
>>     3.14
>>   end
>>   def self.pi
>>     3.14159265359
>>   end
>> end
=> :pi
>> Knowledge.pi
=> 3.14159265359
>> example = Knowledge.new
=> #<Knowledge:0x007fa5c28890b8>
>> example.pi
=> 3.14
>> exit
$
```

List of All Instance Methods

You can read out all defined methods for a class with the method `instance_methods`. We try it out with the class `Knowledge` (first we create it once again in the irb):

```
$ irb
>> class Knowledge
>>   def pi
>>     3.14
>>   end
>> end
=> :pi
>> Knowledge.instance_methods
=> [:pi, :instance_of?, :public_send, :instance_variable_get, :instance_variable_set,
:instance_variable_defined?, :remove_instance_variable, :private_methods, :kind_of?,
:instance_variables, :tap, :is_a?, :extend, :define_singleton_method, :to_enum, :enum_for, :<=>,
:===, :=~, :!~, :eql?, :respond_to?,
:freeze, :inspect, :display, :send, :object_id, :to_s, :method, :public_method,
:singleton_method, :nil?, :hash, :class,
:singleton_class, :clone, :dup, :itself, :taint, :tainted?,
:untaint, :untrust, :trust, :untrusted?, :methods,
:protected_methods, :frozen?, :public_methods, :singleton_methods,
:!, :==, :!=, :send, :equal?, :instance_eval, :instance_exec,
:id]
>>
```

But that is much more than we have defined! Why? It's because Ruby gives every new class a basic set of methods by default. If we only want to list the methods that we have defined, then we can do it like this:

```
>> Knowledge.instance_methods(false)
=> [:pi]
>> exit
$
```

Variables

You already know that everything in Ruby is an object. So a variable must also be an object.

Naming Conventions

Normal variables are written in lower case. Constants start with an upper case letter.

A constant can also be overwritten with a new value in Ruby 2.3 (but you will get a warning message). So please do not rely on the constancy of a constant.

```
$ irb
>> Pi = 3.14
=> 3.14
>> Pi = 123
(irb):2: warning: already initialized constant Pi
(irb):1: warning: previous definition of Pi was here
=> 123
>> puts Pi
123
=> nil
>> exit
```

You are on the safe side if you are using only ASCII symbols. But with Ruby 2.3 and the right encoding, you could also use special characters (for example German umlauts) more or less without any problems in a variable name. But if you want to be polite towards other programmers who probably do not have those characters directly available on their keyboards, it is better to stick to pure ASCII.

Strings

Let's experiment a little bit in the irb. The method .class tells us which class we are dealing with.

```
$ irb
>> a = 'First test'
=> "First test"
>> a.class
=> String
```

That was easy. As you can see, Ruby "automagically" creates an object of the class String. We could also do this by explicitly calling the method new:

```
>> b = String.new('Second test')
=> "Second test"
>> b.class
=> String
```

If we call String.new without a parameter, this also creates an object of the class String. But it is an empty String:

```
>> c = String.new
=> ""
>> c.class
=> String
>> exit
$
```

Single and Double Quotations Marks

Strings can be defined either in single quotes or double quotes.

 If we mention single or double quotation marks in the context of strings, we do not mean typographically correct curly quotation marks (see wikipedia.org/wiki/Quotation_mark), but the ASCII symbols referred to as *apostrophe* (') or *quotation mark*(").

There is a special feature for the double quotes: you can integrate expressions with the construct #{}. The result is then automatically inserted in the corresponding place in the string.

Example:

```
$ irb
>> a = 'blue'
=> "blue"
>> b = "Color: #{a}"
=> "Color: blue"
>> b.class
=> String
>> exit
$
```

If the result of the expression is not a string, Ruby tries to apply the method to_s in order to convert the value of the object into a string.

Integers

Fixnum and Bignum

Fixnum and Bignum are Integer classes. A Fixnum is an Integer that can be saved in a Word. If a Fixnum gets bigger, it automatically becomes a Bignum. Here is an example where a becomes larger and by that becomes a Bignum.

```
$ irb
>> 20.class
=> Fixnum
>> a = 20
=> 20
>> a.class
=> Fixnum
>> a = a * 5555555555
=> 111111111100
>> a.class
=> Fixnum
>> a = a * 5555555555
=> 617283950493827160500
>> a.class
=> Bignum
>> exit
$
```

Floats

Float is a class for real numbers ("floating point numbers"). The decimal separator is a point.

```
$ irb
>> a = 20.424
=> 20.424
>> a.class
=> Float
>> 42.2.class
=> Float
>> exit
$
```

Simple Calculations

Adding two integers will result in an integer. Adding an integer and a float will result in a float:

```
$ irb
>> a = 10
=> 10
>> b = 23
=> 23
>> a + b
=> 33
>> (a + b).class
=> Fixnum
>> (a + 3.14).class
=> Float
>> exit
```

Boolean Values and nil

For boolean values (true and false) and for nil (no value) there are separate classes:

```
$ irb
>> true.class
=> TrueClass
>> false.class
=> FalseClass
>> nil.class
=> NilClass
>> exit
$
```

nil (no value) is, by the way, the contraction of the Latin word *nihil* (nothing) or, if you look at it in terms of programming history, the term derives from "*not in list*" from the legacy of the programming language Lisp (the name is an acronym of *List Processing*).

Scope of Variables

Variables have a different scope (or "reach") within the Ruby application and therefore also within a Ruby on Rails application.

 You need to keep this scope in mind while programming. Otherwise you can end up with odd effects.

Local Variables (aaa or _aaa)

Local variables either start with a lower case letter or an underscore (_). Their scope is limited to the current environment (for example the current method). The following example defines two methods which use the same local variable radius. Because they are local they don't interact with each other:

```
$ irb
>> def area(radius)
>>    3.14 * radius * radius
>> end
=> :area
>> def circumference(radius)
>>    2 * 3.14 * radius
>> end
=> :circumference
>> area(10)
=> 314.0
>> circumference(1)
=> 6.28
>> exit
$
```

Global Variables ($aaa)

A global variable starts with a $-sign and is accessible in the entire programm. Example:

```
$ irb
>> $value = 10
=> 10
>> puts $value
10
=> nil
>> def example
>>    $value = 20
>> end
=> :example
>> puts $value
10
=> nil
>> example
=> 20
>> puts $value
20
=> nil
>> exit
$
```

Global variables are used very rarely! You wouldn't harm yourself by forgetting that they exist right now.

Instance Variables (@aaa)

Instance variables ("*A*ttributes", hence the @) only apply within a class, but everywhere in it – a mini version of global variables, so to speak. Unlike global variables, you will find instance variables all over the place in a Rails application. Let's tackle them in form of an example program with the name color.rb:

```ruby
class Wall
  def initialize
    @color = 'white'
  end

  def color
    @color
  end

  def paint_it(value)
    @color = value
  end
end

my_wall = Wall.new
puts my_wall.color

my_wall.paint_it('red')
puts my_wall.color
```

If you start this program, the following output will appear:

```
$ ruby color.rb
white
red
$
```

In the method `initialize` we set the instance variable `@color` to the value "white". The method `paint_it(value)` changes this instance variable.

With the method `color` we can access the value of `@color` outside of the instance. This kind of method is called a setter method.

Methods Once Again

In order to keep the amount of chicken and egg problems in this chapter at a manageable level, we need to go back to the topic Methods and combine what we have learned so far.

Getters and Setters

As instance variables ("attributes") only exist within the relevant instance, you always need to write a "getter" method for exporting such a variable. If we define a class `Room` that has the instance variables `@doors` and `@windows` (for the number of doors and windows in the room), then we can create the getter methods `doors` und `windows` (example program `room.rb`):

room.rb

```ruby
class Room
  def initialize
    @doors   = 1
    @windows = 1
  end

  def doors
    @doors
  end

  def windows
    @windows
  end
end

kitchen = Room.new

puts "D: #{kitchen.doors}"
puts "W: #{kitchen.windows}"
```

The execution of the program:

```
$ ruby room.rb
D: 1
W: 1
$
```

As this scenario – wanting to simply return a value in identical form – is so common, there is already a ready-made getter method for it with the name attr_reader, which you would apply as follows in the program room.rb:

room.rb

```ruby
class Room
  def initialize
    @doors   = 1
    @windows = 1
  end

  attr_reader :doors, :windows
end

kitchen = Room.new

puts "D: #{kitchen.doors}"
puts "W: #{kitchen.windows}"
```

attr_reader is a method which is called on the Room class. That is the reason why we use Symbols (e.g. :doors and :windows) instead of variables (e.g. @doors and @windows) as parameter.

 attr_reader is a good example for meta programming in Ruby. When working with Rails, you will frequently come across meta programming and be grateful for how it works automagically.

If you want to change the number of doors or windows from the outside, you need a "setter" method. It can be implemented as follows:

room.rb

```ruby
class Room
  def initialize
    @doors   = 1
    @windows = 1
  end

  attr_reader :doors, :windows

  def doors=(value)
    @doors = value
  end

  def windows=(value)
    @windows = value
  end
end

kitchen = Room.new

kitchen.windows = 2

puts "D: #{kitchen.doors}"
puts "W: #{kitchen.windows}"
```

The corresponding output is this:

```
$ ruby room.rb
D: 1
W: 2
$
```

As you can probably imagine, there is of course also a ready-made and easier way of doing this. Via the setter method `attr_writer` you can simplify the code of room.rb further:

room.rb

```ruby
class Room
  def initialize
    @doors   = 1
    @windows = 1
  end

  attr_reader :doors, :windows
  attr_writer :doors, :windows
end

kitchen = Room.new

kitchen.windows = 2

puts "D: #{kitchen.doors}"
puts "W: #{kitchen.windows}"
```

And (who would have thought!) there is even a method `attr_accessor` that combines getters and setters. The code for `room.rb` would then look like this:

room.rb

```
class Room
  def initialize
    @doors   = 1
    @windows = 1
  end

  attr_accessor :doors, :windows
end


kitchen = Room.new

kitchen.windows = 2

puts "D: #{kitchen.doors}"
puts "W: #{kitchen.windows}"
```

Built-In Methods for String

Most classes already come with a bundle of very useful methods. These methods are always written after the relevant object, separated by a point.

Here are a few examples for methods of the class `String`.

```
$ irb
>> a = 'A dog'
=> "A dog"
>> a.class
=> String
>> a.size
=> 5
>> a.downcase
=> "a dog"
>> a.upcase
=> "A DOG"
>> a.reverse
=> "god A"
>> exit
$
```

With `instance_methods(false)` you can get a list of the build in methods:

```
$ irb
>> String.instance_methods(false)
=> [:<=>, :==, :===, :eql?, :hash, :casecmp, :+, :*, :%, :[], :[]=, :insert, :length,
:size, :bytesize, :empty?, :=~, :match, :succ, :succ!, :next, :next!, :upto, :index,
:rindex, :replace, :clear, :chr, :getbyte, :setbyte, :byteslice, :scrub, :scrub!,
:freeze, :to_i, :to_f, :to_s, :to_str, :inspect, :dump, :upcase, :downcase,
:capitalize, :swapcase, :upcase!, :downcase!, :capitalize!, :swapcase!, :hex, :oct,
:split, :lines, :bytes, :chars, :codepoints, :reverse, :reverse!, :concat, :<<,
:prepend, :crypt, :intern, :to_sym, :ord, :include?, :start_with?, :end_with?,
:scan, :ljust, :rjust, :center, :sub, :gsub, :chop, :chomp, :strip, :lstrip, :rstrip,
:sub!, :gsub!, :chop!, :chomp!, :strip!, :lstrip!, :rstrip!, :tr, :tr_s, :delete,
:squeeze, :count, :tr!, :tr_s!, :delete!, :squeeze!, :each_line, :each_byte,
:each_char, :each_codepoint, :sum, :slice, :slice!, :partition, :rpartition,
:encoding, :force_encoding, :b, :valid_encoding?, :ascii_only?, :unpack, :encode,
:encode!, :to_r, :to_c, :unicode_normalize, :unicode_normalize!, :unicode_normalized?]
>> exit
$
```

If you are not sure what one of these methods does you can use ri to look it up:

```
$ ri String.size
= String.size

(from ruby site)
---------------------------
    str.size     -> integer

---------------------------

Returns the character length of str.
```

Method Chaining

You may not think of it straight away, but once you have got used to working with Ruby, then it makes perfect sense (and is perfectly logical) to chain different methods.

```
$ irb
>> a = 'A dog'
=> "A dog"
>> a.upcase.reverse
=> "GOD A"
>> exit
$
```

Converting from One to the Other: Casting

There is a whole range of useful instance methods for converting ("casting") objects from one class to another. First, let's use the method .to_s to convert a Fixnum to a String.

```
$ irb
>> a = 10
=> 10
>> a.class
=> Fixnum
>> b = a.to_s
=> "10"
>> b.class
=> String
>> exit
$
```

 Incidentally, that is exactly what puts does if you use puts   to output a Fixnum or a Float
(for non-strings, it simply   implicitly adds the method .to_s and outputs the result).

Now we use the method .to_i to change a Float to a Fixnum.

```
$ irb
>> c = 10.0
=> 10.0
>> c.class
=> Float
>> d = c.to_i
=> 10
>> d.class
=> Fixnum
>> exit
$
```

Method to_s for Your Own Classes

Integrating a to_s method is often useful. Then you can simply output a corresponding object via puts (puts
automatically outputs an object via the method to_s).

Here is an example:

```
$ irb
>> class Person
>>   def initialize(first_name, last_name)
>>     @first_name = first_name
>>     @last_name = last_name
>>   end
>>   def to_s
>>     "#{@first_name} #{@last_name}"
>>   end
>> end
=> :to_s
>> person1 = Person.new('Stefan', 'Wintermeyer')
=> #<Person:0x007ffeaa84af98 @first_name="Stefan", @last_name="Wintermeyer">
>> puts person1
Stefan Wintermeyer
=> nil
>> exit
$
```

Is + a Method?

Why is there also a plus symbol in the list of methods for String? Let's find out by looking it up in ri:

```
$ ri -T String.+
String.+

(from ruby site)
----------------------------------
  str + other_str   -> new_str


----------------------------------


Concatenation---Returns a new String containing other_str
concatenated to str.

  "Hello from " + self.to_s   #=> "Hello from main"
```

hmmm ... Let's see what it says for Fixnum:

```
$ ri -T Fixnum.+
Fixnum.+

(from ruby site)
----------------------------------
  fix + numeric  -> numeric_result


----------------------------------


Performs addition: the class of the resulting object depends on the class of
numeric and on the magnitude of the result.
```

Let's have a go and play around with this in irb. So we should be able to add the + to an object, just as any other method, separated by a dot and add the second number in brackets as parameter:

```
$ irb
>> 10 + 10
=> 20
>> 10+10
=> 20
>> 10.+10
=> 20
>> 10.+(10)
=> 20
>> exit
$
```

Aha! The plus symbol is indeed a method, and this method takes the next value as parameter. Really we should put this value in brackets, but thanks to Ruby's well thought-out syntax this is not necessary.

Can I Overwrite the Method +?

Yes, you can overwrite any method. Logically, this does not make much sense for methods such as +, unless you want to drive your fellow programmers mad. I am going to show you a little demo in irb so you will believe me.

The aim is overwriting the method + for Fixnum. We want the result of every addition to be the number 42.

```
$ irb
>> 10 + 10
=> 20
>> class Fixnum
>>   def +(name, *args, &blk)
>>     42
>>   end
>> end
=> :+
>> 10 + 10
=> 42
>> exit
$
```

First we perform a normal addition. Than we redefine the method + for the class Fixnum, and after that we do the calculation again. But this time, with different results.

if-Condition

An abstract if-condition looks like this:

```
if expression
   program
end
```

The program between the expression and end is executed if the result of the expression is not false and not nil.

You can also use a then after the expression:

```
if expression then
   program
end
```

The construct for a simple if-branch in a Ruby program looks like the following example program:

```
a = 10

if a == 10
   puts 'a is 10'
end
```

 The == is used to compare two values.   Please don't mix it up with the single =.

You can try an *expression* really well in irb:

```
$ irb
>> a = 10
=> 10
>> a == 10
=> true
>> exit
$
```

Shorthand

A frequently used shorthand notation of an if-condition can be found in the following code:

```
a = 10

# long version
#
if a == 10
  puts 'a is 10'
end

# short version
#
puts 'a is 10' if a == 10
```

else

You can probably imagine how this works, but for the sake of completeness, here is a little example:

```
a = 10

if a == 10
  puts 'a is 10'
else
  puts 'a is not 10'
end
```

elsif

Again, most programmers will know what this is all about. Example:

```
a = 10

if a == 10
  puts 'a is 10'
elsif a == 20
  puts 'a is 20'
end
```

Loops

There are different ways of implementing loops in Ruby. The iterator variation is used particularly often in the Rails environment.

while and until

An abstract while loop looks like this:

```
while expression do
   program
end
```

The do that follows the expression is optional. Often you will also see this:

```
while expression
   program
end
```

Here is an irb example:

```
$ irb
>> i = 0
=> 0
>> while i < 3 do
?>   puts i
>>   i = i + 1
>> end
0
1
2
=> nil
>> exit
$
```

Until loops are built similarly:

```
until expression
   program
ends
```

Again, here is the corresponding irb example:

```
$ irb
>> i = 5
=> 5
>> until i == 0
>>   i = i - 1
>>   puts i
>> end
4
3
2
1
0
=> nil
>> exit
$
```

Blocks and Iterators

"Block" and "iterator" are some of the favorite words of many Ruby programmers. Now I am going to show you why.

In the loop

```
5.times { |i| puts i }
```

i is the iterator and puts i is the block.

You can also express the whole thing in the following syntax:

```
5.times do |i|
  puts i
end
```

Iterators

Iterators are just a specific type of method. As you probably know, the word "*iterate*" means to repeat something. For example, the class Fixnum has the iterator times() Rubytimes. Let's see what help r i offers us:

```
$ ri -T Fixnum.times
Fixnum.times

(from ruby site)
Implementation from Integer
--------------------------------------------
  int.times {|i| block }  -> self
  int.times               -> an_enumerator
--------------------------------------------

Iterates block int times, passing in values from zero to int -
1.

If no block is given, an enumerator is returned instead.

  5.times do |i|
    print i, " "
  end

produces:

  0 1 2 3 4
```

And it also gives a nice example that we are going to try out in irb:

```
$ irb
>> 5.times do |i|
?>    puts i
>> end
0
1
2
3
4
=> 5
>> exit
$
```

There is also a single-line notation for small blocks:

```
$ irb
>> 5.times { |i| puts i }
0
1
2
3
4
=> 5
>> exit
$
```

By the way, an iterator does not necessarily have to pass a variable to the block:

```
$ irb
>> 5.times { puts 'example' }
example
example
example
example
example
=> 5
>> exit
$
```

Blocks

A block is the code that is triggered by an iterator. In the block, you have access to the local variable(s) passed by the iterator.

Method upto

Apart from times there is also the method upto, for easily implementing a loop. ri offers a nice example for this, too:

```
$ ri -T Fixnum.upto
Fixnum.upto

(from ruby site)
Implementation from Integer
--------------------------------------------------
  int.upto(limit) {|i| block }  ->  self
  int.upto(limit)               ->  an_enumerator
--------------------------------------------------

Iterates block, passing in integer values from int up to and
including limit.

If no block is given, an enumerator is returned instead.

  5.upto(10) { |i| print i, " " }

produces:

  5 6 7 8 9 10
```

Arrays and Hashes

As in many programming languages, *arrays* and *hashes* are popular structures in Ruby for storing data.

Arrays

An array is a list of objects. Let's play around in irb:

```
$ irb
>> a = [1,2,3,4,5]
=> [1, 2, 3, 4, 5]
>> a.class
=> Array
>> exit
$
```

That is simple and easy to understand.

Let's see if it also works with strings in the array:

```
$ irb
>> a = ['Test', 'Banana', 'blue']
=> ["Test", "Banana", "blue"]
>> a.class
=> Array
>> a[1]
=> "Banana"
>> a[1].class
=> String
>> exit
$
```

That also works.

So all that's missing now is an array with a mixture of both. Obviously that will work, too, because the array stores objects and it does not matter which kind of objects they are (i.e. String, Fixnum, Float, ...). But a little test can't hurt:

```
$ irb
>> a = [1, 2.2, 'House', nil]
=> [1, 2.2, "House", nil]
>> a.class
=> Array
>> a[0]
=> 1
>> a[0].class
=> Fixnum
>> a[2]
=> "House"
>> a[2].class
=> String
>> exit
$
```

Arrays can also be created via the method new (like any class). Individual new elements can then be added at the end of an array via the method <<. Here is the corresponding example:

```
$ irb
>> a = Array.new
=> []
>> a << 'first item'
=> ["first item"]
>> a << 'second item'
=> ["first item", "second item"]
>> exit
$
```

Iterator each

You can work your way through an array piece by piece via the method each. Example:

```
$ irb
>> cart = ['eggs', 'butter']
=> ["eggs", "butter"]
>> cart.each do |item|
?>    puts item
>> end
eggs
butter
=> ["eggs", "butter"]
>> exit
$
```

Once more, ri provides help and an example in case you forget how to use each:

```
$ ri -T Array.each
Array.each

(from ruby site)

  ary.each {|item| block }   -> ary
  ary.each                   -> an_enumerator

Calls block once for each element in self, passing that element
as a parameter.

If no block is given, an enumerator is returned instead.

  a = [ "a", "b", "c" ]
  a.each {|x| print x, " -- " }

produces:

  a -- b -- c --
```

Hashes

A *Hash* is a list of *key/value pairs*. Here is an example with strings as keys:

```
$ irb
>> prices = { 'egg' => 0.1, 'butter' => 0.99 }
=> {"egg"=>0.1, "butter"=>0.99}
>> prices['egg']
=> 0.1
>> prices.count
=> 2
>> exit
$
```

Of course, hashes can store not just strings as objects in the values, but - as with arrays - also classes that you define yourself (see the section called "Arrays").

Symbols

Symbols are a strange concept and difficult to explain. But they are very useful and used frequently, amongst others with hashes. Normally, variables always create new objects:

```
$ irb
>> a = 'Example 1'
=> "Example 1"
>> a.object_id
=> 70124141350360
>> a = 'Example 2'
=> "Example 2"
>> a.object_id
=> 70124141316700
>> exit
$
```

In both cases, we have the variable a, but object ID is different. We could carry on in this way indefinitely. Each time, it would generate a different object ID and therefore a new object. In principle, this is no big deal and entirely logical in terms of object orientation. But it is also rather a waste of memory space.

A symbol is defined by a colon before the name and cannot store any values itself, but it always has the same object ID, so it is very well suited to be a *key*:

```
$ irb
>> :a.class
=> Symbol
>> :a.object_id
=> 702428
>> exit
$
```

Let's do another little experiment to make the difference clearer. We use a string object with the content "white" three times in a row and then the symbol :white three times in a row. For "white", a new object is created each time. For the symbol :white, only the first time:

```
$ irb
>> 'white'.object_id
=> 70342874305700
>> 'white'.object_id
=> 70342874300640
>> 'white'.object_id
=> 70342874271720
>> :white.object_id
=> 1088668
>> :white.object_id
=> 1088668
>> :white.object_id
=> 1088668
>> exit
$
```

Using symbols as key for hashes is much more memory efficient:

```
$ irb
>> colors = { black: '#000000', white: '#FFFFFF' }
=> {:black=>"#000000", :white=>"#FFFFFF"}
>> puts colors[:white]
#FFFFFF
=> nil
>> exit
$
```

You will frequently see symbols in Rails. If you want to find out more about symbols, go to the help page about the class Symbol via ri Symbol.

Iterator each

With the method each you can work your way through a Hash step by step. Example:

```
$ irb
>> colors = {black: '000000', white: '#FFFFFF' }
=> {:black=>"#000000", :white=>"#FFFFFF"}
>> colors.each do |key, value|
?>   puts "{key} #{value}"
>> end
black #000000
white #FFFFFF
=> {:black=>"#000000", :white=>"#FFFFFF"}
>> exit
$
```

Again, ri offers help and an example, in case you cannot remember one day how to use each:

```
$ ri -T Hash.each
Hash.each

(from ruby site)

    hsh.each       {| key, value | block } -> hsh
    hsh.each_pair {| key, value | block } -> hsh
    hsh.each                           -> an_enumerator
    hsh.each_pair                      -> an_enumerator

Calls block once for each key in hash, passing the key-value pair
as parameters.

If no block is given, an enumerator is returned instead.

    h = { "a" => 100, "b" => 200 }
    h.each {|key, value| puts "#{key} is #{value}" }

produces:

    a is 100
    b is 200
```

Range

The class Range represents an interval. The start and end points of the interval are defined enclosed in normal brackets and separated by two dots in between them. Here is an example in which we use a range like an iterator with each:

```
$ irb
>> (0..3)
=> 0..3
>> (0..3).class
=> Range
>> (0..3).each do |i|
?>   puts i
>> end
0
1
2
3
=> 0..3
>>
```

Via the method to_a you can generate an array from a Range:

```
>> (0..3).to_a
=> [0, 1, 2, 3]
>>
```

A range can be generated from objects of any type. Important is only that the objects can be compared via < ⇒ and use the method succ for counting on to the next value. So you can also use Range to represent letters:

```
>> ('a'..'h').to_a
=> ["a", "b", "c", "d", "e", "f", "g", "h"]
>>
```

As alternative notation, you may sometimes come across Range.new( ). In this case, the start and end points are not separated by two dots, but by a comma. This is what it looks like:

```
>> (0..3) == Range.new(0,3)
=> true
>> exit
$
```

First Steps with Rails

Now that you have painstakingly read your way through Ruby Basics we can move on to a more exciting bit. In this chapter, we will start our first Ruby on Rails project and find our way into the topic step by step.

 Once more, there will be minor chicken and egg problems.

Environment (Development)

By default a Rails project offers three different environments:

- Development
- Test
- Production

In this chapter, we are only working with the Development environment. Once you have gained a better feeling for Rails, we will start using tests and then we will need the corresponding environment (where, for example, the Test database is populated when you start a test and then cleared). Later, I will explain the various scenarios to show how you can roll out your Rails application from the Development environment to the Production environment.

The Development environment has everything you need for developing, apart from an editor and a web browser. So you do not need to install a special web server, but can use the integrated Rails web server. It does not exactly have extremely high performance, but you do not need that for developing. Later, you can switch to big web servers like Apache or Nginx. The same applies to the database.

In order to work in the Development environment, you do not need to make any changes to start with - all commands work by default.

SQLite-3 Database

In terms of the database, the main focus in this chapter is once more not on optimum performance, but on showing you a simple way of getting started. That's why we are using the SQLite-3 database. You already have everything you need fully installed and you don't need to worry about anything. Later I will explain how you can use other databases (for example MySQL).

Why Is It All in English?

If you are not a native English speaker, you should try to accept and even adopt Rails' love for the English language. Much of it will then be much easier and more logical. Most of the code then reads just like a normal English sentence. For example, many mechanisms automagically use plural or singular forms of normal English words. If you get used to naming database fields and tables with English terms (even if you are programming in a different language), then you can make use of the whole power of this magic. This mechanism is referred to as Inflector or *Inflections*.

If you are programming in a language other than English, it still makes sense to use English names for variables, classes and methods. You can write the comments in your own language, but if you take part in international projects, you should obviously write the comments in English as well. Yeah, sure ... well written code does not need any comments. ;-)

Static Content (HTML and Graphics Files)

If you are reading this text, you will already know that you can use Rails to somehow output web pages. The question is just how it's done. Let's first create a new Rails project.

Create Rails Project

Before we even get going, please check that you are using Ruby version 2.3:

```
$ ruby -v
ruby 2.3.0p0 (2015-12-25 revision 53290) [x86_64-darwin15]
$
```

Next, check if Rails 5.0 is also installed:

```
$ rails -v
Rails 5.0.0
$
```

That's looking good. If you have an older version of Ruby or Rails installed, please install the 5.0 version before you read any further.

Now we start by creating a new Rails project with the name testproject. Ruby on Rails is a framework, so we first need to set up the corresponding directory structure and basic configuration, including several scripts. Easy as pie, just use the command rails new testproject to create everything you need:

```
$ rails new testproject
    create
    create  README.rdoc
    create  Rakefile
    create  config.ru
    [...]
$
```

Next, we check if the new Rails application is working by launching the integrated web server.

 Depending on the operating system (for example, Mac OS X) and on   your firewall settings, you may see a popup window when first   starting a Rails application, asking you if the firewall should   permit the corresponding connection.

```
$ cd testproject
$ rails server
=> Booting Puma
=> Rails 5.0.0 application starting in development on http://localhost:3000
=> Run rails server -h for more startup options
=> Ctrl-C to shutdown server
I, [2016-01-20T12:55:48.556757 #22582]  INFO -- : Celluloid 0.17.3 is running in BACKPORTED
mode. [ http://git.io/vJf3J ]
Puma 2.15.3 starting...
* Min threads: 0, max threads: 16
* Environment: development
* Listening on tcp://localhost:3000
```

The start of the Rails application is looking good. It tells us:

```
Rails 5.0.0 application starting in development on http://localhost:3000
```

So let's go to the URL http://localhost:3000 in the web browser.

Looks good. Rails seems to be working fine.

 With a classic Ctrl+C you can stop the web server.

Static Pages

There are certain static pages, images and JavaScript files that are automatically output by Rails. Remember part of the output of the command rails new testproject:

```
[...]
create  public
create  public/404.html
create  public/422.html
create  public/500.html
create  public/favicon.ico
create  public/robots.txt
[...]
```

The directory name public and the files it contains already look very much like static pages. Let's have a go and create the file public/hello-world.html with the following content:

public/hello-world.html

```
<html>
<head>
  <title>Hello World!</title>
</head>
<body>
  <h1>Hello World!</h1>
  <p>An example page.</p>
</body>
</html>
```

Now start the Rails web server with `rails server`

```
$ rails server
=> Booting Puma
=> Rails 5.0.0 application starting in development on http://localhost:3000
=> Run rails server -h for more startup options
=> Ctrl-C to shutdown server
I, [2016-01-20T12:59:00.763428 #22606]  INFO -- : Celluloid 0.17.3 is running in BACKPORTED
mode. [ http://git.io/vJf3J ]
Puma 2.15.3 starting...
* Min threads: 0, max threads: 16
* Environment: development
* Listening on tcp://localhost:3000
```

We can have a look at this web page at the URL http://localhost:3000/hello-world:

No output in the log means: This page was not handled by the Rails framework. It was delivered directly from the webserver.

 We can of course also use the URL http://localhost:3000/hello-world.html. But Rails regards HTML and therefore the file ending .html as standard output format, so you can omit the .html here.

Now you know how you can integrate fully static pages in Rails. This is useful for pages that never change and that you want to work even if Rails is not currently working, for example because of an update. In a production environment, you would usually put a classic web server such as Apache or Nginx in front of the Rails server. Which is capable of autonomously delivering static files from the public directory. You'll learn how to set up a production webserver in "Web Server in Production Mode".

With Ctrl+C you can stop the Rails server.

Creating HTML Dynamically with erb

The content of an erb file will probably seem familiar to you. It is a mixture of HTML and Ruby code (erb stands for *e*mbedded *R*uby). erb pages are rendered as Views. This is the first time for us to get in touch with the MVC model. We need a controller to use a view. That can be created it via the generator rails generate controller. Let's have a look at the onboard help of this generator:

```
$ rails generate controller
Running via Spring preloader in process 23029
Usage:
  rails generate controller NAME [action action] [options]

[...]

Description:
    Stubs out a new controller and its views. Pass the controller name, either
    CamelCased or under_scored, and a list of views as arguments.

    To create a controller within a module, specify the controller name as a
    path like 'parent_module/controller_name'.

    This generates a controller class in app/controllers and invokes helper,
    template engine, assets, and test framework generators.

Example:
    rails generate controller CreditCards open debit credit close

    CreditCards controller with URLs like /credit_cards/debit.
        Controller: app/controllers/credit_cards_controller.rb
        Test:       test/controllers/credit_cards_controller_test.rb
        Views:      app/views/credit_cards/debit.html.erb [...]
        Helper:     app/helpers/credit_cards_helper.rb
```

Nice! We are kindly provided with an example further down:

```
rails generate controller CreditCard open debit credit close
```

Doesn't really fit the bill for our case but I am feeling brave and suggest that we simply try rails generate controller Example test

```
$ rails generate controller Example test
Running via Spring preloader in process 23045
      create  app/controllers/example_controller.rb
       route  get 'example/test'
      invoke  erb
      create    app/views/example
      create    app/views/example/test.html.erb
      invoke  test_unit
      create    test/controllers/example_controller_test.rb
      invoke  helper
      create    app/helpers/example_helper.rb
      invoke    test_unit
      invoke  assets
      invoke    coffee
      create      app/assets/javascripts/example.coffee
      invoke    css
      create      app/assets/stylesheets/example.css
$
```

Phew... that's a lot of stuff being created. Amongst others, the file app/views/example/test.html.erb. Let's have a closer look at it:

app/views/example/test.html.erb

```
<h1>Example#test</h1>
<p>Find me in app/views/example/test.html.erb</p>
```

It's HTML, but for it to be a valid HTML page, something is "missing" at the top and bottom (the missing HTML will be explained in the Layouts section). We launch the web server to test it:

```
$ rails server
```

and have a look at the web page in the browser at the URL http://localhost:3000/example/test:

In the log log/development.log we find the following lines:

```
Started GET "/example/test" for ::1 at 2016-01-20 13:10:01 +0100
Processing by ExampleController#test as HTML
  Rendered example/test.html.erb within layouts/application (0.8ms)
Completed 200 OK in 2226ms (Views: 2216.6ms | ActiveRecord: 0.0ms)
[...]
```

An HTTP GET request for the URI "/example/test". That was then apparently rendered as HTML by the controller ExampleController using the method test.

Now we just need to find the controller. Good thing you bought this book. ;-) All controllers are in the directory app/controllers, and there you go, we indeed find the corresponding file app/controllers/example_controller.rb.

```
$ tree app/controllers/
app/controllers/
├── application_controller.rb
├── concerns
└── example_controller.rb
```

Please open the file app/controllers/example_controller.rb with your favorite editor:

app/controllers/example_controller.rb

```
class ExampleController < ApplicationController
  def test
  end
end
```

That is very clear. The controller ExampleController is a descendant of the ApplicationController and contains currently just one method with the name test. This method contains currently no program logic.

You will probably ask yourself how Rails knows that for the URL path /example/test it should process the controller ExampleController and the method test. This is not determined by some magical logic, but by a *routing* configuration. The current routings can be listed with the command rails routes

```
$ rails routes
      Prefix Verb URI Pattern             Controller#Action
example_test GET  /example/test(.:format) example#test
```

These routes are configured in the file config/routes.rb which has been auto-filled by the controller generator with a route to example/test. The line which is important for us is the second one:

config/routes.rb

```
Rails.application.routes.draw do
  get 'example/test'

  # For details on the DSL available within this file, see
http://guides.rubyonrails.org/routing.html

  # Serve websocket cable requests in-process
  # mount ActionCable.server => '/cable'
end
```

In Routes we'll dive more into routes.

 A static file in the directory public always has higher priority than a route in the config/routes.rb! So if we were to save a static file public/example/test that file will be delivered.

Programming in an erb File

Erb pages can contain Ruby code. You can use it to program and give these page dynamic content.

Let's start with something very simple: adding 1 and 1. First we try out the code in irb:

```
$ irb
>> 1 + 1
=> 2
>> exit
$
```

That was easy.

If you want to output the result of Ruby code, enclose the code within a <%= ... %>.

We fill the erb file app/views/example/test.html.erb as follows:

app/views/example/test.html.erb

```
<h1>First experiment with erb</h1>
<p>Addition:
  <%= 1 + 1 %>
</p>
```

Then use rails server to launch the web server.

```
$ rails server
```

Visit that page with the URL http://localhost:3000/example/test

You may ask yourself: how can the result of adding two Fixnums be displayed as a String? Let's first look up in irb if it really is a Fixnum:

```
$ irb
>> 1.class
=> Fixnum
>> (1 + 1).class
=> Fixnum
```

Yes, both the number 1 and the result of 1 + 1 is a Fixnum. What happened? Rails is so intelligent that it automatically calls all objects in a view (that is the file test.html.erb) that are not already a string via the method .to_s, which always converts the content of the object to a string. Once more, a brief trip to irb:

```
>> (1 + 1).to_s
=> "2"
>> (1 + 1).to_s.class
=> String
>> exit
```

You are now going to learn the finer points of erb step by step. Don't worry, it's neither magic nor rocket science.

<% ... %> vs. <%= ... %>

In a `.html.erb` file, there are two kinds of Ruby code instructions in addition to the HTML elements:

- <% ... %>

  Executes the Ruby code it contains, but does not output anything (unless you explicitly use something like print or puts).

- <%= ... %>

  Executes the Ruby code it contains and outputs the result as a String. If it's not a String the method to_s will be called.

 The output of `<%= ⋯ %>` is automatically escaped. So you don't need to worry about "dangerous" HTML.

Let's use an example, to make sure it all makes sense. We use each to iterate through the Range (0..5). Edit the app/views/example/test.html.erb as follows:

app/views/example/test.html.erb

```
<p>Loop from 0 to 5:
<% (0..5).each do |i| %>
<%= "#{i}, " %>
<% end %>
</p>
```

Open this view in the browser:

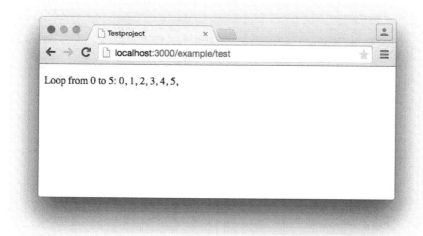

Let's now have a look at the HTML source code in the browser:

```html
<!DOCTYPE html>
<html>
  <head>
    <title>Testproject</title>
    [...]
  </head>

  <body>
    <p>Loop from 0 to 5:
0,
1,
2,
3,
4,
5,
</p>

  </body>
</html>
```

Now you have the important tools to use Ruby code in a view.

Q & A

I don't understand anything. I can't cope with the Ruby code. Could you please explain it again?

Is it possible that you have not completely worked your way through Ruby Basics? Please do take your time with it and have another thorough look. Otherwise, the rest won't make any sense here.

I can understand the Ruby code and the HTML output. But I don't get why some HTML code was rendered around it if I didn't even write that HTML code. Where does it come from, and can I influence it?

Excellent question! We will get to that in the next section.

Layouts

The erb file in the directory app/views/example/ only forms the core of the later HTML page. By default, an automatically generated `app/views/layouts/application.html.erb` is always rendered around it. Let's have a closer look at it:

app/views/layouts/application.html.erb

```
<!DOCTYPE html>
<html>
  <head>
    <title>Testproject</title>
    <%= csrf_meta_tags %>
    <%= action_cable_meta_tag %>

    <%= stylesheet_link_tag    'application', media: 'all', 'data-turbolinks-track' => true %>
    <%= javascript_include_tag 'application', 'data-turbolinks-track' => true %>
  </head>

  <body>
    <%= yield %>
  </body>
</html>
```

The interesting bit is the line

```
<%= yield %>
```

With `<%= yield %>` the view file is included here. The lines with the stylesheets, the JavaScript and the `csrf_meta_tags` can stay as they are for now. We'll have a look into that in Asset pipeline. No need to bother with that right now.

The file `app/views/layouts/application.html.erb` enables you to determine the basic layout for the entire Rails application. If you want to enter a <hr> for each page and above it a text, then you can do this between the `<%= yield %>` and the <body> tag:

app/views/layouts/application.html.erb

```
<!DOCTYPE html>
<html>
  <head>
    <title>Testproject</title>
    <%= csrf_meta_tags %>
    <%= action_cable_meta_tag %>

    <%= stylesheet_link_tag    'application', media: 'all', 'data-turbolinks-track' => true %>
    <%= javascript_include_tag 'application', 'data-turbolinks-track' => true %>
  </head>

  <body>
    <h1>My Header</h1>
    <hr>
    <%= yield %>
  </body>
</html>
```

You can also create other layouts in the directory `app/views/layouts/` and apply these layouts depending on the relevant situation. But let's leave it for now. The important thing is that you understand the basic concept.

Passing Instance Variables from a Controller to a View

One of the cardinal sins in the MVC model is to put too much program logic into the view. That's more or less what used to be done frequently in PHP programming in the past. I'm guilty of having done it myself. But one of the aims of MVC is that any HTML designer can create a view without having to worry about the programming. Yeah, yeah, ... if only it was always that easy. But let's just play it through in our minds: if I have a value in the controller that I want to display in the view, then I need a mechanism for this. This is referred to as *instance variable* and always starts with a @. If you are not 100 % sure any more which variable has which *scope*, then please have another quick look at "Scope of Variables".

In the following example, we insert an instance variable for the current time in the controller and then insert it in the view. We're taking programming intelligence from the view to the controller.

The controller file app/controllers/example_controller.rb looks like this:

app/controllers/example_controller.rb

```ruby
class ExampleController < ApplicationController
  def test
    @current_time = Time.now
  end
end
```

In the view file app/views/example/test.html.erb we can then access this instance variable:

app/views/example/test.html.erb

```erb
<p>
The current time is
<%= @current_time %>
</p>
```

With the controller and the view, we now have a clear separation of programming logic and presentation logic. Now we can automatically adjust the time in the controller in accordance with the user's time zone, without the designer of the page having to worry about it. As always, the method to_s is automatically applied in the view.

I am well aware that no-one will now jump up from their chair and shout: "Thank you for enlightening me! From now on, I will only program neatly in accordance with MVC." The above example is just the first small step in the right direction and shows how we can easily get values from the controller to the view with instance variables.

Partials

Even with small web projects, there are often elements that appear repeatedly, for example a *footer* on the page with contact info or a menu. Rails gives us the option of encapsulate this HTML code in form of *partials* and then integrating it within a view. A partial is also stored in the directory app/views/example/. But the file name must start with an underscore (_).

As an example, we now add a mini footer to our page in a separate partial. Copy the following content into the new file app/views/example/_footer.html.erb:

app/views/example/_footer.html.erb

```
<hr>
<p>
  Copyright 2009 - <%= Date.today.year %> the Easter Bunny.
</p>
```

 Yes, this is not the MVC way of doing it. Date.today.year should be defined in the Controller. I'm glad that you caught this mistake. I made this example to show the use of a partial.

We edit the file app/views/example/test.html.erb as follows and insert the partial via the command render:

app/views/example/test.html.erb

```
<p>Loop from 0 to 5:
<% (0..5).each do |i| %>
<%= "#{i}, " %>
<% end %>
</p>

<%= render "footer" %>
```

So now we have the following files in the directory app/views/example:

```
$ tree app/views/example/
app/views/example/
├────── _footer.html.erb
└────── test.html.erb
```

The new web page now looks like this:

 The name of a partial in the code is always specified *without* the preceding underscore (_) and *without* the file extension .erb and .html. But the actual file must have the underscore at the beginning of the file name and end with the file extension .erb and .html.

Partials can also be integrated from other areas of the subdirectory app/views. For example, you can create a directory app/views/shared for recurring and shared content and create a file _footer.html.erb in this directory. You would then integrate this file into the erb code via the line

```
<%= render "shared/footer" %>
```

Passing Variables to a Partial

Partials are great in the sense of the DRY (*D*on't *R*epeat *Y*ourself) concept. But what makes them really useful is the option of passing variables. Let's stick with the copyright example. If we want to pass the start year as value, we can integrate this by adding the following in the file app/views/example/_footer.html.erb:

app/views/example/_footer.html.erb

```
<hr>
<p>
Copyright <%= start_year %> - <%= Date.today.year %> the Easter Bunny.
</p>
```

So let's change the file app/views/example/test.html.erb as follows:

app/views/example/test.html.erb

```
<p>Loop from 0 to 5:
<% (0..5).each do |i| %>
<%= "#{i}, " %>
<% end %>
</p>

<%= render partial: "footer", locals: {start_year: '2000'} %>
```

If we now go to the URL http://localhost:3000/example/test, we see the 2000:

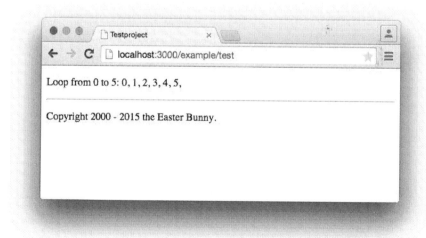

Sometimes you need a partial that partially uses a local variable and somewhere else you may need the same partial, but without the local variable. We can take care of this in the partial itself with an if statement:

```
<hr>
<p>
  Copyright
  <%= "#{start_year} - " if defined? start_year %>
  <%= Date.today.year %>
  the Easter Bunny.
</p>
```

 defined? can be used to check if an expression has been defined.

Now you can call this partial with `<%= render partial: "footer", locals: {start_year: '2000'} %>` and with `<%= render 'footer' %>`.

Further Documentation on Partials

We have really only barely scratched the surface here. Partials are very powerful tools. You can find the official Ruby on Rails documentation on partials at: http://guides.rubyonrails.org/layouts_and_rendering.html#using-partials.

The Rails Console

The *console* in Rails is nothing more than an irb (see section "irb") built around the Rails environment. The console is very useful both for developing and for administration purposes, because the whole Rails environment is represented and available.

I'll show you how to work with irb in this example application:

```
$ rails new pingpong
    [...]
$ cd pingpong
$ rails generate controller Game ping pong
    [...]
$
```

Start the Rails console with the command `rails console`:

```
$ rails console
Running via Spring preloader in process 23637
Loading development environment (Rails 5.0.0)
2.3.0 :001 >
```

And you can use exit to get back out:

```
2.3.0 :001 > exit
$
```

Many readers use this ebook on small mobile devises. For them I try to keep any code or terminal output width to a minimum. To save the real estate which is by default occupied by `2.3.0 :001 >` we can start `rails console` with the parameter -- --simple-prompt.

```
$ rails console -- --simple-prompt
Running via Spring preloader in process 23791
Loading development environment (Rails 5.0.0)
>> exit
$
```

Alternatively you can change the IRB configuration in the file .irbrc which is located in your home directory. If you want to have the simple prompt you have to add the following line in that file.

```
IRB.conf[:PROMPT_MODE] = :SIMPLE
```

In the console, you have access to all variables that are also available later in the proper application:

```
$ rails console
Running via Spring preloader in process 23817
Loading development environment (Rails 5.0.0)
>> Rails.env
=> "development"
>> Rails.root
=> #<Pathname:/Users/xyz/pingpong>
>> exit
$
```

In chapter "ActiveRecord" we are going to be working lots with the console and will soon begin to appreciate the possibilities the irb offers.

 One of my best buddies when developing Rails applications   is the Tab key. Whenever you are looking for a method for a   particular problem, recreate it in the Rails console and then   press the Tab key twice to list all available methods. The   names of the methods are usually self-exlanatory.

app

app is useful if you want to analyze things to do with routing:

```
$ rails console
Running via Spring preloader in process 23817
Loading development environment (Rails 5.0.0)
>> app.url_for(controller: 'game', action: 'ping')
=> "http://www.example.com/game/ping"
>> app.get '/game/ping'

Started GET "/game/ping" for 127.0.0.1 at 2016-01-20 15:37:03 +0100
Processing by GameController#ping as HTML
  Rendered game/ping.html.erb within layouts/application (1.3ms)
Completed 200 OK in 2136ms (Views: 2127.0ms | ActiveRecord: 0.0ms)
=> 200
>> exit
$
```

What is a Generator?

We have already used the command rails generate controller. It starts the generator with the name controller. There are other generators as well. You can use the command `rails generate` to display a list of available generators:

```
$ rails generate
Running via Spring preloader in process 23841
Usage: rails generate GENERATOR [args] [options]
[...]
Please choose a generator below.

Rails:
  assets
  channel
  controller
  generator
  helper
  integration_test
  jbuilder
  job
  mailer
  migration
  model
  resource
  scaffold
  scaffold_controller
  task

Coffee:
  coffee:assets

Js:
  js:assets

TestUnit:
  test_unit:generator
  test_unit:plugin
```

What does a generator do? A generator makes a programmer's job easier by doing some of the mindless tasks for you. It creates files and fills them with default content, depending on the parameters passed. You could do the same manually, without the generator. So you do not have to use a generator. It is primarily intended to save you work and avoid potential errors that can easily arise from mindless repetitive tasks.

 Someday you might want to create your own generator. Have a look at http://guides.rubyonrails.org/generators.html to find a description of how to do that.

Helper

A helper method takes care of recurring tasks in a view. For example, if you want to display stars (*) for rating a restaurant and not a number from 1 to 5, you can define the following helper in the file `app/helpers/application_helper.rb`:

```
module ApplicationHelper

  def render_stars(value)
    output = ''
    if (1..5).include?(value)
      value.times { output += '*'}
    end
    output
  end

end
```

With this helper, we can then apply the following code in a view:

```
<p>
  <b>Rating:</b> <%= render_stars(5) %>
</p>
```

You can also try out the helper in the console:

```
$ rails console
Running via Spring preloader in process 23849
Loading development environment (Rails 5.0.0)
>> helper.render_stars(5)
=> ""
>> helper.render_stars(3)
=> ""
>> exit**
$
```

There are lots of predefined helpers in Rails and we will use some of them in the next chapters. But you can also define your own custom helpers. Any of the helpers from the file app/helpers/application_helper.rb can be used in any view. Helpers that you want to be only available in certain views must be defined for each controller. When creating a controller, a file for helpers of that controller is automatically created in app/helpers. This gives you the option of defining helpers only for this controller or for the views of this controller.

All helpers are in the directory app/helpers/.

Debugging

Rails provides a couple of debug tools to make the developer's live easier.

debug

In any view you can use the debug helper to render an object with the YAML format within a <pre> tag. To display the value of @foo you can use the following line in your view:

```
<%= debug @foo %>
```

Web Console

The web-console gem provides a way to render a rails console views. So when you browser to a specific URL at the end of that page you'll get a console.

Let me show you this by example with this simple rails application:

```
$ rails new testapp
  [...]
$ cd testapp
$ rails generate controller page index
```

In the app/controllers/page_controller.rb we add the following code:

app/controllers/page_controller.rb

```
class PageController < ApplicationController
  def index
    @foo = 'bar'
  end
end
```

And in the view app/views/page/index.html.erb we'll add the console command:

app/views/page/index.html.erb

```
<h1>Page#index</h1>
<p>Find me in app/views/page/index.html.erb</p>

<%= console %>
```

After starting the rails application with rails server and browsing to the URL http://localhost:3000/page/index we get a web console at the bottom of the page. In it we have access to the instance variable @foo.

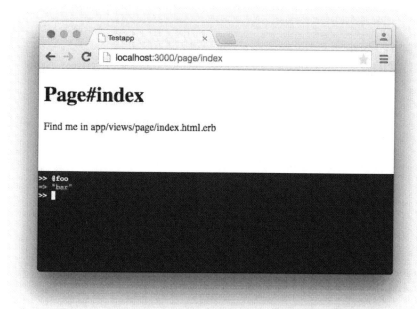

Other Debugging Tools

There are a couple of other build in debugging tools which are out of the scope of this introduction. Please have a look at http://guides.rubyonrails.org/debugging_rails_applications.html to get an overview.

Rails Lingo

Here you find a couple of words which you'll often find in the Ruby on Rails universe.

DRY - Don't repeat yourself

Many Rails programmers are big fans of DRY. DRY means purely and simply that you should try to place repeated programming logic into separate methods.

Refactoring

You often hear the word refactoring in the context of DRY. This involves functioning applications that are further improved. The application in itself remains unchanged in its interface. But its core is optimized, amongst others through DRY.

Convention Over Configuration

Convention over configuration (also known as coding by convention, see http://en.wikipedia.org/wiki/Convention_over_configuration) is an important pillar of a Rails application. It states that the programmer does not need to decide in favour of certain features when starting a project and set these via configuration parameters. It specifies an underlying basic consensus and this is set by default. But if you want to work outside of this conventional basic consensus, then you will need to change the corresponding parameters.

Model View Controller Architecture (MVC)

You have now already created a simple Rails application and in the next chapter you will dive deeply into the topic ActiveRecord. So now is a good time to very briefly introduce a few terms that often surface in the world of Rails.

According to Wikipedia http://en.wikipedia.org/wiki/Model-view-controller, MVC is a design pattern that separates the representation of information from the user's interaction with it.

MVC is a structure for software development. It was agreed that it makes sense to have one part of the software in one place and another part of the software in another place. Nothing more, nothing less.

This agreement has the enormous advantage that once you are used to this concept, you know exactly where you can find or need to integrate a certain functionaity in a Rails project.

Model

"Model" in this case means data model. By default, Rails applications are an ActiveRecord data model (see chapter "ActiveRecord").

All models can be found in the directory app/models/.

View

The "view" is responsible for the presentation of the application. It takes care of rendering the web page, an XML or JSON file. A view could also render a PDF or an ASCII text. It depends entirely on your application.

You will find all the views in the directory app/views/.

Controller

Once a web page call has ended up in a route (see chapter "Routes"), it goes from there to the controller. The route specifies a certain method (action) as target. This method can then fulfil the desired tasks (such as finding a specific set of data and saving it in an instance variable) and then renders the desired view.

All controllers can be found in the directory app/controllers/.

Abbreviations

There are a handful of abbreviations that make your life as a developer much easier. In the rest of this book, I have always used the full version of these commands, to make it clearer for beginners, but in practice, you will soon find that the abbreviations are easier to use.

- rails console

  Shorthand notation: rails c

- rails server

  Shorthand notation: rails s

- rails generate scaffold

  Shorthand notation: rails g scaffold

ActiveRecord

ActiveRecord is a level of abstraction that offers access to a SQL database. ActiveRecord implements the architectural pattern *Active Record*.

 This is referred to as object-relational-mapping or *ORM*.   I find it rather dry and boring, but in case you have trouble   going to sleep tonight, have a look at http://en.wikipedia.org/wiki/Object_relational_mapping.

One of the recipes for the success of Rails is surely the fact that is uses ActiveRecord. The programming and use "feels Ruby like" and it is much less susceptible to errors than pure SQL. When working with this chapter, it helps if you have some knowledge of SQL, but this is not required and also not essential for working with ActiveRecord.

This chapter is only about ActiveRecord. So I am not going to   integrate any tests to keep the examples as simple as possible.

Creating Database/"Model"

Model in this context refers to the data model of   Model-View-Controller (MVC).

As a first example, let's take a list of countries in Europe. First, we create a new Rails project:

```
$ rails new europe
  [...]
$ cd europe
$
```

Next, let's have a look at the help page for rails generate model:

```
$ rails generate model
Running via Spring preloader in process 24219
Usage:
  rails generate model NAME [field[:type][:index] field[:type][:index]] [options]

[...]
Description:
    Stubs out a new model. Pass the model name, either CamelCased or
    under_scored, and an optional list of attribute pairs as arguments.

    Attribute pairs are field:type arguments specifying the
    model's attributes. Timestamps are added by default, so you don't have to
    specify them by hand as 'created_at:datetime updated_at:datetime'.
[...]
```

The usage description rails generate model NAME [field[:type][:index] field[:type][:index]] [options] tells us that after rails generate model comes the name of the model and then the table fields. If you do not put :type after a table field name, it is assumed to be a string.

Let's create the *model* country:

```
$ rails generate model Country name population:integer
Running via Spring preloader in process 24227
      invoke  active_record
      create    db/migrate/20151215194714_create_countries.rb
      create    app/models/country.rb
      invoke    test_unit
      create      test/models/country_test.rb
      create      test/fixtures/countries.yml
$
```

The generator has created a database migration file with the name
db/migrate/20151215194714_create_countries.rb. It provides the following code:

db/migrate/20151215194714_create_countries.rb

```
class CreateCountries < ActiveRecord::Migration
  def change
    create_table :countries do |t|
      t.string :name
      t.integer :population

      t.timestamps null: false
    end
  end
end
```

A migration contains database changes. In this migration, a class CreateCountries is defined as a child of
ActiveRecord::Migration. The method change is used to define a migration and the associated roll-back.

With the command rails db:migrate we can apply the migrations, in other words, create the corresponding
database table:

```
$ rails db:migrate
== 20151215194714 CreateCountries: migrating
-- create_table(:countries)
   -> 0.0013s
== 20151215194714 CreateCountries: migrated (0.0014s)
$
```

 You will find more details on migrations in   the section "Migrations".

Let's have a look at the file app/models/country.rb:

app/models/country.rb

```
class Country < ApplicationRecord
end
```

Hmmm ... the class Country is a child of ApplicationRecord which inherits from ActiveRecord::Base. Makes
sense, as we are discussing ActiveRecord in this chapter. ;-)

The Attributes id, created_at **and** updated_at

Even if you cannot see it in the migration, we also get the attributes id, created_at und updated_at by default
for each ActiveRecord model. In the Rails console, we can output the attributes of the class Country by using

the class method `column_names`:

```
$ rails console
Running via Spring preloader in process 24257
Loading development environment (Rails 5.0.0)
>> Country.column_names
=> ["id", "name", "population", "created_at", "updated_at"]
>> exit
```

The attribute `created_at` stores the time when the record was initially created. `updated_at` stores the time of the last update for this record.

`id` is used a central identification of the record (primary key). The `id` is automatically incremented by 1 for each record.

Getters and Setters

To read and write values of a SQL table row you can use by ActiveRecord provided getters and setters. These `attr_accessors` are automatically created. The getter of the field `updated_at` for a given `Country` with the name germany would be `germany.updated_at`.

Possible Data Types in ActiveRecord

ActiveRecord is a *layer* between Ruby and various relational databases. Unfortunately, many SQL databases have different perspectives regarding the definition of columns and their content. But you do not need to worry about this, because ActiveRecord solves this problem transparently for you.

To generate a *model*, you can use the following field types:

Table 1. Field Types

Name	Description
binary	This is a BLOB (*Binary Large Object*) in the classical sense. Never heard of it? Then you probably won't need it. See also http://en.wikipedia.org/wiki/Binary_large_object
boolean	This is a BLOB (*Binary Large Object*) in the classical sense. Never heard of it? Then you probably won't need it. See also http://en.wikipedia.org/wiki/Binary_large_object
date	You can store a date here.
datetime	Here you can store a date including a time.
integer	For storing an integer. See also http://en.wikipedia.org/wiki/Integer_(computer_science)
decimal	For storing a decimal number.
primary_key	This is an integer that is automatically incremented by 1 by the database for each new entry. This field type is often used as key for linking different database tables or *models*. See also http://en.wikipedia.org/wiki/Unique_key

Name	Description
string	A string, in other words a sequence of any characters, up to a maximum of $2^8 - 1$ (= 255) characters. See also http://en.wikipedia.org/wiki/String_(computer_science)
text	Also a string - but considerably bigger. By default, up to 2^{16} (= 1. characters can be saved here.
time	A time.
timestamp	A time with date, filled in automatically by the database.

You can also define a decimal with the model generator. But you need to observe the special syntax (you have to use ' if you are using the Bash shell).

Example for creating a price with a decimal:

```
$ rails generate model product name 'price:decimal{7,2}'
[...]
$
```

That would generate this migration:

db/migrate/20121114110808_create_products.rb

```
class CreateProducts < ActiveRecord::Migration
  def change
    create_table :products do |t|
      t.string :name
      t.decimal :price, :precision => 7, :scale => 2

      t.timestamps
    end
  end
end
```

In xref:#migrations["Migrations"] we will provide more information on the individual data types and discuss available options.

Naming Conventions (Country vs. country vs. countries)

ActiveRecord automatically uses the English plural forms. So for the class Country, it's countries. If you are not sure about a term, you can also work with the class and method name.

```
>> Country.name.tableize
=> "countries"
>> Country.name.foreign_key
=> "country_id"
```

Database Configuration

Which database is used by default? Let's have a quick look at the configuration file for the database (config/database.yml):

```
# SQLite version 3.x
#   gem install sqlite3
#
#   Ensure the SQLite 3 gem is defined in your Gemfile
#   gem 'sqlite3'
#
default: &default
  adapter: sqlite3
  pool: 5
  timeout: 5000

development:
  <<: *default
  database: db/development.sqlite3

# Warning: The database defined as "test" will be erased and
# re-generated from your development database when you run "rake".
# Do not set this db to the same as development or production.
test:
  <<: *default
  database: db/test.sqlite3

production:
  <<: *default
  database: db/production.sqlite3
```

As we are working in development mode, Rails has created a new SQLite3 database db/development.sqlite3 as a result of rails db:migrate and will save all data there.

Fans of command line clients can use sqlite3 for viewing this database:

```
$ sqlite3 db/development.sqlite3
SQLite version 3.8.5 2014-08-15 22:37:57
Enter ".help" for usage hints.
sqlite> .tables
countries          schema_migrations
sqlite> .schema countries
CREATE TABLE "countries" ("id" INTEGER PRIMARY KEY AUTOINCREMENT NOT NULL,
"name" varchar, "population" integer, "created_at" datetime NOT NULL,
"updated_at" datetime NOT NULL);
sqlite> .exit
$
```

Adding Records

Actually, I would like to show you first how to view records, but to show records you have to create them first. So first, here is how you can create a new record with ActiveRecord.

create

The most frequently used method for creating a new record is create.

Let's try creating a country in the console with the command Country.create(name: 'Germany', population: 81831000)

```
$ rails console
Running via Spring preloader in process 24336
Loading development environment (Rails 5.0.0)
>> Country.create(name: 'Germany', population: 81831000)
   (0.3ms)  begin transaction SQL (1.3ms)  INSERT INTO "countries" ("name",
   "population", "created_at", "updated_at") VALUES (?, ?, ?, ?) [["name",
   "Germany"], ["population", 81831000], ["created_at", "2015-12-16
   13:32:37.748459"], ["updated_at", "2015-12-16 13:32:37.748459"]] (0.7ms)
   commit transaction
   => #<Country id: 1, name: "Germany", population:
   81831000, created_at: "2015-12-16 13:32:37", updated_at: "2015-12-16
   13:32:37">
>> exit
```

ActiveRecord saves the new record and outputs the executed SQL command in the development environment.
But to make absolutely sure it works, let's have a last look with the command line client sqlite3:

```
$ sqlite3 db/development.sqlite3
SQLite version 3.8.5 2014-08-15 22:37:57
Enter ".help" for usage hints.
sqlite> SELECT * FROM countries;
1|Germany|81831000|2015-12-16 13:32:37.748459|2015-12-16 13:32:37.748459
sqlite> .exit
$
```

Syntax

The method create can handle a number of different syntax constructs. If you want to create a single record,
you can do this with or without {}-brackets within the the ()-brackets:

- Country.create(name: 'Germany', population: 81831000)
- Country.create({name: 'Germany', population: 81831000})

Similarly, you can describe the attributes differently:

- Country.create(:name ⇒ 'Germany', :population ⇒ 81831000)
- Country.create('name' ⇒ 'Germany', 'population' ⇒ 81831000)
- Country.create(name: 'Germany', population: 81831000)

You can also pass an array of hashes to create and use this approach to create several records at once:

```
Country.create([{name: 'Germany'}, {name: 'France'}])
```

new

In addition to create there is also new. But you have to use the save method to save an object created with new
(which has both advantages and disadvantages):

```
$ rails console
Running via Spring preloader in process 24336
Loading development environment (Rails 5.0.0)
>> france = Country.new
=> #<Country id: nil, name: nil, population: nil, created_at: nil, updated_at:
nil>
>> france.name = 'France'
=> "France"
>> france.population = 65447374
=> 65447374
>> france.save
   (0.2ms)  begin transaction SQL (0.9ms)  INSERT INTO "countries" ("name",
   "population", "created_at", "updated_at") VALUES (?, ?, ?, ?) [["name",
   "France"], ["population", 65447374], ["created_at", "2015-12-16
   13:40:07.608858"], ["updated_at", "2015-12-16 13:40:07.608858"]] (9.4ms)
   commit transaction => true
>> france
=> #<Country id: 2, name: "France", population: 65447374, created_at:
"2015-12-16 13:40:07", updated_at: "2015-12-16 13:40:07">
```

You can also pass parameters for the new record directly to the method new, just as with create:

```
>> belgium = Country.new(name: 'Belgium', population: 10839905)
=> #<Country id: nil, name: "Belgium", population: 10839905, created_at: nil,
updated_at: nil>
>> belgium.save
   (0.2ms)  begin transaction SQL (0.4ms)  INSERT INTO "countries" ("name",
   "population", "created_at", "updated_at") VALUES (?, ?, ?, ?) [["name",
   "Belgium"], ["population", 10839905], ["created_at", "2015-12-16
   13:42:04.580377"], ["updated_at", "2015-12-16 13:42:04.580377"]] (9.3ms)
   commit transaction => true
>> exit
```

new_record?

With the method new_record? you can find out if a record has already been saved or not. If a new object has
been created with new and not yet been saved, then the result of new_record? is true. After a save it's false.

Example:

```
$ rails console
Running via Spring preloader in process 24336
Loading development environment (Rails 5.0.0)
>> netherlands = Country.new(name: 'Netherlands')
=> #<Country id: nil, name: "Netherlands", population: nil, created_at: nil,
updated_at: nil>
>> netherlands.new_record?
=> true
>> netherlands.save
   (0.2ms)  begin transaction SQL (0.5ms)  INSERT INTO "countries" ("name",
   "created_at", "updated_at") VALUES (?, ?, ?) [["name", "Netherlands"],
   ["created_at", "2015-12-16 13:48:03.114012"], ["updated_at", "2015-12-16
   13:48:03.114012"]] (0.8ms)  commit transaction => true
>> netherlands.new_record?
=> false
>> exit
```

For already existing records, you can also check for changes with the method `changed?` (see "changed?"). You can even use `netherland.population_changed?` to check if just the attribute `popluation` was changed.

first, last and all

In certain cases, you may need the first record, or the last one, or perhaps even all records. Conveniently, there is a ready-made method for each case. Let's start with the easiest ones: `first` and `last`.

```
$ rails console
Running via Spring preloader in process 24336
Loading development environment (Rails 5.0.0)
>> Country.first
  Country Load (0.8ms)  SELECT  "countries".* FROM "countries"  ORDER BY
  "countries"."id" ASC LIMIT 1 => #<Country id: 1, name: "Germany",
  population: 81831000, created_at: "2015-12-16 13:32:37", updated_at:
  "2015-12-16 13:32:37">
>> Country.last
  Country Load (0.4ms)  SELECT  "countries".* FROM "countries"  ORDER BY
  "countries"."id" DESC LIMIT 1 => #<Country id: 4, name: "Netherlands",
  population: nil, created_at: "2015-12-16 13:48:03", updated_at: "2015-12-16
  13:48:03">
```

And now all at once with `all`:

```
>> Country.all
  Country Load (0.3ms)  SELECT  "countries".* FROM "countries" =>
  <ActiveRecord::Relation [#<Country id: 1, name: "Germany", population:
  81831000, created_at: "2015-12-16 13:32:37", updated_at: "2015-12-16
  13:32:37">, #<Country id: 2, name: "France", population: 65447374,
  created_at: "2015-12-16 13:40:07", updated_at: "2015-12-16 13:40:07">,
  #<Country id: 3, name: "Belgium", population: 10839905, created_at:
  "2015-12-16 13:42:04", updated_at: "2015-12-16 13:42:04">, #<Country id: 4,
  name: "Netherlands", population: nil, created_at: "2015-12-16 13:48:03",
  updated_at: "2015-12-16 13:48:03">]>
```

But the objects created by `first`, `last` and `all` are different.

```
>> Country.first.class
  Country Load (0.2ms)  SELECT  "countries".* FROM "countries"  ORDER BY
  "countries"."id" ASC LIMIT 1 => Country(id: integer, name: string,
  population: integer, created_at: datetime, updated_at: datetime)
>> Country.all.class
=> Country::ActiveRecord_Relation
```

So `Country.first` is a `Country` which makes sense. But `Country.all` is something we haven't had yet. Let's use the console to get a better idea of it:

```
>> puts Country.all.to_yaml
  Country Load (0.4ms)  SELECT "countries".* FROM "countries"
---
- !ruby/object:Country
  attributes:
    id: 1
    name: Germany
    population: 81831000
    created_at: 2015-12-16 13:32:37.748459 Z
    updated_at: 2015-12-16 13:32:37.748459 Z
- !ruby/object:Country
  attributes:
    id: 2
    name: France
    population: 65447374
    created_at: 2015-12-16 13:40:07.608858 Z
    updated_at: 2015-12-16 13:40:07.608858 Z
[...]
=> nil
```

hmmm... by using the to_yaml method suddenly the database has work to do. The reason for this behavior is optimization. Let's assume that you want to chain a couple of methods. Than it might be better for ActiveRecord to wait till the very last second which it does. It only requests the data from the SQL database when it has to do it (it's called Lazy Loading). Until than it stores the request in a ActiveRecord::Relation.

The result of Country.all is actually an Array of Country.

If Country.all returns an array, then we should also be able to use iterators and each, right? Yes, of course! That is the beauty of it. Here is a little experiment with each:

```
>> Country.all.each do |country|
?>   puts country.name
>> end
  Country Load (0.3ms)  SELECT "countries".* FROM "countries"
Germany
France
Belgium
Netherlands
=> [#<Country id: 1, name: "Germany", [...]]
```

So can we also use .all.first as an alternative for .first? Yes, but it does not make much sense. Have a look for yourself:

```
>> Country.first
  Country Load (0.3ms)  SELECT  "countries".* FROM "countries"  ORDER BY
  "countries"."id" ASC LIMIT 1 => #<Country id: 1, name: "Germany",
  population: 81831000, created_at: "2015-12-16 13:32:37", updated_at:
  "2015-12-16 13:32:37">
>> Country.all.first
  Country Load (0.2ms)  SELECT  "countries".* FROM "countries"  ORDER BY
  "countries"."id" ASC LIMIT 1 => #<Country id: 1, name: "Germany",
  population: 81831000, created_at: "2015-12-16 13:32:37", updated_at:
  "2015-12-16 13:32:37">
```

Country.first and Country.all.first result in exact the same SQL query because ActiveRecord optimizes it.

Populating the Database with seeds.rb

With the file db/seeds.rb, the Rails gods have given us a way of feeding default values easily and quickly to a fresh installation. This is a normal Ruby program within the Rails environment. You have full access to all classes and methods of your application.

With that you don't need to enter everything manually with `rails console` to create all initial records in a new Rails application. You can use the file db/seeds.rb:

db/seeds.rb

```
Country.create(name: 'Germany', population: 81831000)
Country.create(name: 'France', population: 65447374)
Country.create(name: 'Belgium', population: 10839905)
Country.create(name: 'Netherlands', population: 16680000)
```

You then populate it with data via `rails db:seed`. To be on the safe side, you should always set up the database from scratch with `rails db:setup` in the context of this book and then automatically populate it with the file db/seeds.rb. Here is what is looks like:

```
$ rails db:setup
db/development.sqlite3 already exists
db/test.sqlite3 already exists
-- create_table("countries", {:force=>:cascade})
   -> 0.0148s
-- create_table("products", {:force=>:cascade})
   -> 0.0041s
-- initialize_schema_migrations_table()
   -> 0.0203s
-- create_table("countries", {:force=>:cascade})
   -> 0.0036s
-- create_table("products", {:force=>:cascade})
   -> 0.0036s
-- initialize_schema_migrations_table()
   -> 0.0008s
$
```

I use the file db/seeds.rb at this point because it offers a simple mechanism for filling an empty database with useful values. In the course of this book, this will make it easier for us to set up quick example scenarios.

It's all just Ruby code

The db/seeds.rb is a Ruby program. Correspondingly, we can also use the following approach as an alternative:

db/seeds.rb

```
country_list = [
  [ "Germany", 81831000 ],
  [ "France", 65447374 ],
  [ "Belgium", 10839905 ],
  [ "Netherlands", 16680000 ]
]

country_list.each do |name, population|
  Country.create( name: name, population: population )
end
```

The result is the same. I am showing you this example to make it clear that you can program normally within db/seeds.rb.

Generating seeds.rb **From Existing Data**

Sometimes it can be useful to export the current data pool of a Rails application into a db/seeds.rb. While writing this book, I encountered this problem in almost every chapter. Unfortunately, there is no standard approach for this. I am showing you what you can do in this case. There are other, more complex scenarios that can be derived from my approach.

We create our own little rake task for that. A rake task is a Ruby programm which is stored in the lib/tasks/ directory and which has full access to the Rails environment.

lib/tasks/export.rake

```
namespace :export do
  desc "Prints Country.all in a seeds.rb way."
  task :seeds_format => :environment do
    Country.order(:id).all.each do |country|
      bad_keys = ['created_at', 'updated_at', 'id']
      serialized = country.serializable_hash.
                   delete_if{|key,value| bad_keys.include?(key)}
      puts "Country.create(#{serialized})"
    end
  end
end
```

Then you can call the corresponding rake task with the command rails export:seeds_format:

```
$ rails export:seeds_format
Country.create({"name"=>"Germany", "population"=>81831000})
Country.create({"name"=>"France", "population"=>65447374})
Country.create({"name"=>"Belgium", "population"=>10839905})
Country.create({"name"=>"Netherlands", "population"=>16680000})
$
```

You can either expand this program so that the output is written directly into the db/seeds.rb or you can simply use the shell:

```
$ rails export:seeds_format > db/seeds.rb
```

Searching and Finding with Queries

The methods first and all are already quite nice, but usually you want to search for something more specific with a query.

For describing queries, we create a new Rails project:

```
$ rails new jukebox
  [...]
$ cd jukebox
$ rails generate model Album name release_year:integer
  [...]
$ rails db:migrate
  [...]
$
```

For the examples uses here, use a db/seeds.rb with the following content:

db/seeds.rb

```
Album.create(name: "Sgt. Pepper's Lonely Hearts Club Band", release_year: 1967)
Album.create(name: "Pet Sounds", release_year: 1966)
Album.create(name: "Revolver", release_year: 1966)
Album.create(name: "Highway 61 Revisited", release_year: 1965)
Album.create(name: "Rubber Soul", release_year: 1965)
Album.create(name: "What's Going On", release_year: 1971)
Album.create(name: "Exile on Main St.", release_year: 1972)
Album.create(name: "London Calling", release_year: 1979)
Album.create(name: "Blonde on Blonde", release_year: 1966)
Album.create(name: "The Beatles", release_year: 1968)
```

Then, set up the new database with rails db:setup:

```
$ rails db:setup
db/development.sqlite3 already exists
-- create_table("albums", {:force=>:cascade})
   -> 0.0135s
-- initialize_schema_migrations_table()
   -> 0.0226s
-- create_table("albums", {:force=>:cascade})
   -> 0.0022s
-- initialize_schema_migrations_table()
   -> 0.0037s
$
```

find

The simplest case is searching for a record via a primary key (by default, the id field in the database table). If I know the ID of an object, then I can search for the individual object or several objects at once via the ID:

```
$ rails console
Running via Spring preloader in process 24336
Loading development environment (Rails 5.0.0)
>> Album.find(2)
  Album Load (0.3ms)  SELECT "albums".* FROM "albums" WHERE "albums"."id" = ?
  LIMIT 1  [["id", 2]] => <Album id: 2, name: "Pet Sounds", release_year:
  1966, created_at: "2015-12-16 17:45:34", updated_at: "2015-12-16 17:45:34">
>> Album.find([1,3,7])
  Album Load (0.4ms)  SELECT "albums".* FROM "albums" WHERE "albums"."id" IN
  (1, 3, 7) => [<Album id: 1, [name: "Sgt. Pepper's Lonely Hearts Club Band",
  release_year: 1967, created_at: "2015-12-16 17:45:34", updated_at:
  "2015-12-16 17:45:34"]>, #<Album id: 3, name: "Revolver", release_year: 1966,
  created_at: "2015-12-16 17:45:34", updated_at: "2015-12-16 17:45:34">,
  #<Album id: 7, name: "Exile on Main St.", release_year: 1972, created_at:
  "2015-12-16 17:45:34", updated_at: "2015-12-16 17:45:34">]
```

If you always want to have an array as result, you also always have to pass an array as parameter:

```
>> Album.find(5).class
  Album Load (0.2ms)  SELECT "albums".* FROM "albums" WHERE "albums"."id" = ?
  LIMIT 1  [["id", 5]] => Album(id: integer, name: string, release_year:
  integer, created_at: datetime, updated_at: datetime)
>> Album.find([5]).class
  Album Load (0.2ms)  SELECT "albums".* FROM "albums" WHERE "albums"."id" = ?
  LIMIT 1  [["id", 5]] => Array
>> exit
```

 The method find generates an exception if the ID you are searching for does not have a record in the database. If in doubt, you should use the where method (see where).

where

With the method where, you can search for specific values in the database. Let's search for all albums from the year 1966:

```
$ rails console
Running via Spring preloader in process 24336
Loading development environment (Rails 5.0.0)
>> Album.where(release_year: 1966)
  Album Load (0.2ms)  SELECT "albums".* FROM "albums" WHERE "albums"."release_year" = ?
  [["release_year", 1966]]
=> <ActiveRecord::Relation [<Album id: 2, name: "Pet Sounds", release_year:
1966, created_at: "2015-12-16 17:45:34", updated_at: "2015-12-16 17:45:34">,
#<Album id: 3, name: "Revolver", release_year: 1966, created_at: "2015-12-16
17:45:34", updated_at: "2015-12-16 17:45:34">, #<Album id: 9, name: "Blonde on
Blonde", release_year: 1966, created_at: "2015-12-16 17:45:34", updated_at:
"2015-12-16 17:45:34">]>
>> Album.where(release_year: 1966).count
  (0.3ms)  SELECT COUNT(*) FROM "albums" WHERE "albums"."release_year" = ?
  [["release_year", 1966]] => 3
```

You can also use where to search for ranges:

```
>> Album.where(release_year: 1960..1966)
  Album Load (0.3ms)  SELECT "albums".* FROM "albums" WHERE ("albums"."release_year" BETWEEN
1960 AND 1966)
=> <ActiveRecord::Relation [<Album id: 2, name: "Pet Sounds", release_year:
1966, created_at: "2015-12-16 17:45:34", updated_at: "2015-12-16 17:45:34">,
#<Album id: 3, name: "Revolver", release_year: 1966, created_at: "2015-12-16
17:45:34", updated_at: "2015-12-16 17:45:34">, #<Album id: 4, name: "Highway
61 Revisited", release_year: 1965, created_at: "2015-12-16 17:45:34",
updated_at: "2015-12-16 17:45:34">, #<Album id: 5, name: "Rubber Soul",
release_year: 1965, created_at: "2015-12-16 17:45:34", updated_at: "2015-12-16
17:45:34">, #<Album id: 9, name: "Blonde on Blonde", release_year: 1966,
created_at: "2015-12-16 17:45:34", updated_at: "2015-12-16 17:45:34">]>
>> Album.where(release_year: 1960..1966).count
   (0.2ms)  SELECT COUNT(*) FROM "albums" WHERE ("albums"."release_year" BETWEEN 1960 AND 1966)
=> 5
```

And you can also specify several search factors simultaneously, separated by commas:

```
>> Album.where(release_year: 1960..1966, id: 1..5)
  Album Load (0.3ms)  SELECT "albums".* FROM "albums" WHERE ("albums"."release_year" BETWEEN
1960 AND 1966) AND ("albums"."id" BETWEEN 1 AND 5)
=> <ActiveRecord::Relation [<Album id: 2, name: "Pet Sounds", release_year:
1966, created_at: "2015-12-16 17:45:34", updated_at: "2015-12-16 17:45:34">,
#<Album id: 3, name: "Revolver", release_year: 1966, created_at: "2015-12-16
17:45:34", updated_at: "2015-12-16 17:45:34">, #<Album id: 4, name: "Highway
61 Revisited", release_year: 1965, created_at: "2015-12-16 17:45:34",
updated_at: "2015-12-16 17:45:34">, #<Album id: 5, name: "Rubber Soul",
release_year: 1965, created_at: "2015-12-16 17:45:34", updated_at: "2015-12-16
17:45:34">]>
```

Or an array of parameters:

```
>> Album.where(release_year: [1966, 1968])
  Album Load (0.4ms)  SELECT "albums".* FROM "albums" WHERE "albums"."release_year" IN (1966,
1968)
=> <ActiveRecord::Relation [<Album id: 2, name: "Pet Sounds", release_year:
1966, created_at: "2015-12-16 17:45:34", updated_at: "2015-12-16 17:45:34">,
#<Album id: 3, name: "Revolver", release_year: 1966, created_at: "2015-12-16
17:45:34", updated_at: "2015-12-16 17:45:34">, #<Album id: 9, name: "Blonde on
Blonde", release_year: 1966, created_at: "2015-12-16 17:45:34", updated_at:
"2015-12-16 17:45:34">, #<Album id: 10, name: "The Beatles", release_year:
1968, created_at: "2015-12-16 17:45:34", updated_at: "2015-12-16 17:45:34">]>
```

The result of where is always an array. Even if it only contains one hit or if no hit is returned (which will result
in an empty array). If you are looking for the first hit, you need to combine the method where with the method
first:

```
>> Album.where(release_year: [1966, 1968]).first
  Album Load (0.4ms)  SELECT  "albums".* FROM "albums" WHERE "albums"."release_year" IN (1966,
1968)  ORDER BY "albums"."id" ASC LIMIT 1
=> #<Album id: 2, name: "Pet Sounds", release_year: 1966, created_at: "2015-12-16 17:45:34",
updated_at: "2015-12-16 17:45:34">
>> Album.where(release_year: [1966, 1968]).first.class
  Album Load (0.4ms)  SELECT  "albums".* FROM "albums" WHERE "albums"."release_year" IN (1966,
1968)  ORDER BY "albums"."id" ASC LIMIT 1
=> Album(id: integer, name: string, release_year: integer, created_at: datetime, updated_at:
datetime)
>> exit
```

not

The method not provides a way to search for the exact oposite of a where query. Example:

```
$ rails console
Running via Spring preloader in process 24336
Loading development environment (Rails 5.0.0)
>> Album.where.not(release_year: 1968)
  Album Load (0.2ms)  SELECT  "albums".* FROM "albums" WHERE ("albums"."release_year" != ?)
[["release_year", 1968]]
=> <ActiveRecord::Relation [<Album id: 1, [...]]>
>> exit
```

or

The method or provides a way to combine queries with a logical or. Example:

```
>> Album.where(release_year: 1967).or(Album.where(name: 'The Beatles'))
  Album Load (0.1ms)  SELECT  "albums".* FROM "albums" WHERE ("albums"."release_year" = ? OR
"albums"."name" = ?)  [["release_year", 1967], ["name", "The Beatles"]]
=> <ActiveRecord::Relation [<Album id: 1, name: "Sgt. Pepper's Lonely Hearts Club Band",
release_year: 1967, created_at: "2016-01-21 10:15:51", updated_at: "2016-01-21 10:15:51">,
#<Album id: 10, name: "The Beatles", release_year: 1968, created_at: "2016-01-21 10:15:51",
updated_at: "2016-01-21 10:15:51">]>
```

SQL Queries with where

Sometimes there is no other way and you just have to define and execute your own SQL query. In
ActiveRecord, there are two different ways of doing this. One *sanitizes* each query before executing it and the
other passes the query on to the SQL database 1 to 1 as it is. Normally, you should always use the sanitized
version because otherwise you can easily fall victim to an *SQL injection* attack (see
http://en.wikipedia.org/wiki/Sql_injection).

 If you do not know much about SQL, you can safely skip this   section. The SQL
commands used here are not explained further.

Sanitized Queries

In this variant, all dynamic search parts are replaced by a question mark as placeholder and only listed as
parameters after the SQL string.

In this example, we are searching for all albums whose name contains the string "on":

```
$ rails console
Running via Spring preloader in process 24336
Loading development environment (Rails 5.0.0)
>> Album.where( 'name like ?', '%on%')
  Album Load (1.1ms)  SELECT "albums".* FROM "albums" WHERE (name like '%on%')
=> <ActiveRecord::Relation [<Album id: 1, [...]]>
```

Now the number of albums that were published from 1965 onwards:

```
>> Album.where( 'release_year > ?', 1964 ).count
  (0.2ms)  SELECT COUNT(*) FROM "albums" WHERE (release_year > 1964)
=> 10
```

The number of albums that are more recent than 1970 and whose name contains the string "on":

```
>> Album.where( 'name like ? AND release_year > ?', '%on%', 1970 ).count
  (0.3ms)  SELECT COUNT(*) FROM "albums" WHERE (name like '%on%' AND
  release_year > 1970)
=> 3
```

If the variable search_string contains the desired string, you can search for it as follows:

```
>> search_string = 'ing'
=> "ing"
>> Album.where( 'name like ?', "%#{search_string}%").count
  (0.2ms)  SELECT COUNT(*) FROM "albums" WHERE (name like '%ing%')
=> 2
>> exit
```

Dangerous SQL Queries

If you really know what you are doing, you can of course also define the SQL query completely and forego the *sanitizing* of the query.

Let's count all albums whose name contain the string "on":

```
$ rails console
Running via Spring preloader in process 24336
Loading development environment (Rails 5.0.0)
>> Album.where( "name like '%on%'" ).count
  (0.2ms)  SELECT COUNT(*) FROM "albums" WHERE (name like '%on%')
=> 5
>> exit
```

Please only use this variation if you know exactly what you are doing and once you have familiarized yourself with the topic SQL injections (see http://en.wikipedia.org/wiki/Sql_injection).

Lazy Loading

Lazy Loading is a mechanism that only carries out a database query if the program flow cannot be realised without the result of this query. Until then, the query is saved as ActiveRecord::Relation.

 Incidentally, the opposite of *lazy loading* is referred to as *eagerloading*.

Does it make sense in principle, but you aren't sure what the point of it all is? Then let's cobble together a query where we nest several methods. In the following example, a is defined more and more closely and only at the end (when calling the method all) the database query would really be executed in a production system. With the method ActiveRecord methods to_sql you can display the current SQL query.

```
$ rails console
Running via Spring preloader in process 24336
Loading development environment (Rails 5.0.0)
>> a = Album.where(release_year: 1965..1968)
  Album Load (0.2ms)  SELECT "albums".* FROM "albums" WHERE
  ("albums"."release_year" BETWEEN 1965 AND 1968)
=> <ActiveRecord::Relation [<Album id: 1, [...]]>
>> a.class
=> Album::ActiveRecord_Relation
>> a = a.order(:release_year)
  Album Load (0.3ms)  SELECT "albums".* FROM "albums" WHERE
  ("albums"."release_year" BETWEEN 1965 AND 1968)  ORDER BY
  "albums"."release_year" ASC
=> <ActiveRecord::Relation [<Album id: 4, [...]]>
>> a = a.limit(3)
  Album Load (0.4ms)  SELECT  "albums".* FROM "albums" WHERE
  ("albums"."release_year" BETWEEN 1965 AND 1968)  ORDER BY
  "albums"."release_year" ASC LIMIT 3
=> <ActiveRecord::Relation [<Album id: 4, [...]]>
>> exit
```

The console can be a bit tricky about this. It tries to help the developer by actually showing the result but in a non-console environment this would would only happen at the very last time.

Automatic Optimization

One of the great advantages of *lazy loading* is the automatic optimization of the SQL query through ActiveRecord.

Let's take the sum of all release years of the albums that came out in the 70s. Then we sort the albums alphabetically and then calculate the sum.

```
$ rails console
Running via Spring preloader in process 24336
Loading development environment (Rails 5.0.0)
>> Album.where(release_year: 1970..1979).sum(:release_year)
  (1.5ms)  SELECT SUM("albums"."release_year") FROM "albums" WHERE
  ("albums"."release_year" BETWEEN 1970 AND 1979)
=> 5922
>> Album.where(release_year: 1970..1979).order(:name).sum(:release_year)
  (0.3ms)  SELECT SUM("albums"."release_year") FROM "albums" WHERE
  ("albums"."release_year" BETWEEN 1970 AND 1979)
=> 5922
>> exit
```

Logically, the result is the same for both queries. But the interesting thing is that ActiveRecord uses the same SQL code for both queries. It has detected that order is completely irrelevant for sum and therefore took it out altogether.

 In case you are asking yourself why the first query took 1.5ms   and the second 0.3ms: ActiveRecord cached the results of the first SQL request.

order **and** reverse_order

To sort a database query, you can use the method order.

Example: all albums from the 60s, sorted by name:

```
$ rails console
Running via Spring preloader in process 24336
Loading development environment (Rails 5.0.0)
>> Album.where(release_year: 1960..1969).order(:name)
  Album Load (0.2ms)  SELECT "albums".* FROM "albums" WHERE
  ("albums"."release_year" BETWEEN 1960 AND 1969)  ORDER BY "albums"."name"
  ASC
=> <ActiveRecord::Relation [<Album id: 9, name: "Blonde on Blonde" [...]]>
```

With the method reverse_order you can reverse an order previously defined via order:

```
>> Album.where(release_year: 1960..1969).order(:name).reverse_order
  Album Load (0.3ms)  SELECT "albums".* FROM "albums" WHERE
  ("albums"."release_year" BETWEEN 1960 AND 1969)  ORDER BY "albums"."name"
  DESC
=> <ActiveRecord::Relation [<Album id: 10, name: "The Beatles" [...]]>
```

limit

The result of any search can be limited to a certain range via the method limit.

The first 5 albums from the 60s:

```
>> Album.where(release_year: 1960..1969).limit(5)
  Album Load (0.3ms)  SELECT  "albums".* FROM "albums" WHERE
  ("albums"."release_year" BETWEEN 1960 AND 1969) LIMIT 5
=> <ActiveRecord::Relation [<Album id: 1, [...]]>
```

All albums sorted by name, then the first 5 of those:

```
>> Album.order(:name).limit(5)
  Album Load (0.4ms)  SELECT  "albums".* FROM "albums"  ORDER BY
  "albums"."name" ASC LIMIT 5
=> <ActiveRecord::Relation [<Album id: 9, name: "Blonde [...]]>
```

offset

With the method offset, you can define the starting position of the method limit.

First, we return the first two records and then the first two records with an offset of 5:

```
>> Album.limit(2)
  Album Load (1.0ms)  SELECT  "albums".* FROM "albums" LIMIT 2
=> <ActiveRecord::Relation [<Album id: 1, [...]>, <Album id: 2, [...]]>
>> Album.limit(2).offset(5)
  Album Load (0.3ms)  SELECT  "albums".* FROM "albums" LIMIT 2 OFFSET 5
=> #<ActiveRecord::Relation [<Album id: 6, [...]>, #<Album id: 7, [...]>]>
```

group

With the method `group`, you can return the result of a query in grouped form.

Let's return all `albums`, grouped by their `release_year`:

```
$ rails console
Running via Spring preloader in process 24336
Loading development environment (Rails 5.0.0)
>> Album.group(:release_year)
  Album Load (0.3ms)  SELECT "albums".* FROM "albums" GROUP BY "albums"."release_year"
=> <ActiveRecord::Relation [<Album id: 5, name: "Rubber Soul", release_year:
1965, created_at: "2015-12-16 17:45:34", updated_at: "2015-12-16 17:45:34">,
#<Album id: 9, name: "Blonde on Blonde", release_year: 1966, created_at:
"2015-12-16 17:45:34", updated_at: "2015-12-16 17:45:34">, #<Album id: 1,
name: "Sgt. Pepper's Lonely Hearts Club Band", release_year: 1967, created_at:
"2015-12-16 17:45:34", updated_at: "2015-12-16 17:45:34">, #<Album id: 10,
name: "The Beatles", release_year: 1968, created_at: "2015-12-16 17:45:34",
updated_at: "2015-12-16 17:45:34">, #<Album id: 6, name: "What's Going On",
release_year: 1971, created_at: "2015-12-16 17:45:34", updated_at: "2015-12-16
17:45:34">, #<Album id: 7, name: "Exile on Main St.", release_year: 1972,
created_at: "2015-12-16 17:45:34", updated_at: "2015-12-16 17:45:34">, #<Album
id: 8, name: "London Calling", release_year: 1979, created_at: "2015-12-16
17:45:34", updated_at: "2015-12-16 17:45:34">]>
>> exit
$
```

pluck

Normally, ActiveRecord pulls all table columns from the database and leaves it up to the programmer to later pick out the components he is interested in. But in case of large amounts of data, it can be useful and above all much quicker to define a specific database field directly for the query. You can do this via the method `pluck`.

```
>> Album.where(release_year: 1960..1969).pluck(:name)
   (0.1ms)  SELECT "albums"."name" FROM "albums" WHERE
   ("albums"."release_year" BETWEEN 1960 AND 1969)
=> ["Sgt. Pepper's Lonely Hearts Club Band", "Pet Sounds", "Revolver",
"Highway 61 Revisited", "Rubber Soul", "Blonde on Blonde", "The Beatles"]
>> Album.where(release_year: 1960..1969).pluck(:name, :release_year)
   (0.3ms)  SELECT "albums"."name", "albums"."release_year" FROM "albums"
   WHERE ("albums"."release_year" BETWEEN 1960 AND 1969)
=> [["Sgt. Pepper's Lonely Hearts Club Band", 1967], ["Pet Sounds", 1966],
["Revolver", 1966], ["Highway 61 Revisited", 1965], ["Rubber Soul", 1965],
["Blonde on Blonde", 1966], ["The Beatles", 1968]]
```

As a result, `pluck` returns an array.

select

`select` works like `pluck` but returns an ActiveRecord::Relation.

```
>> Album.where(release_year: 1960..1969).select(:name)
  Album Load (0.2ms)  SELECT "albums"."name" FROM "albums" WHERE ("albums"."release_year"
BETWEEN 1960 AND 1969)
=> <ActiveRecord::Relation [<Album id: nil, name: "Sgt. Pepper's Lonely Hearts Club Band">,
#<Album id: nil, name: "Pet Sounds">, #<Album id: nil, name: "Revolver">, #<Album id: nil, name:
"Highway 61 Revisited">, #<Album id: nil, name: "Rubber Soul">, #<Album id: nil, name: "Blonde
on Blonde">, #<Album id: nil, name: "The Beatles">]>
```

first_or_create and first_or_initialize

The methods first_or_create and first_or_initialize are ways to search for a specific entry in your database
or create one if the entry doesn't exist already. Both have to be chained to a where search.

```
>> Album.where(name: 'Test')
  Album Load (0.2ms)  SELECT "albums".* FROM "albums" WHERE "albums"."name" =
? [["name", "Test"]]
=> #<ActiveRecord::Relation []>
>> test = Album.where(name: 'Test').first_or_create
  Album Load (0.3ms)  SELECT  "albums".* FROM "albums" WHERE "albums"."name" = ?  ORDER BY
"albums"."id" ASC LIMIT 1  [["name", "Test"]]
   (0.1ms)  begin transaction
  SQL (0.4ms)  INSERT INTO "albums" ("name", "created_at", "updated_at") VALUES (?, ?, ?)
[["name", "Test"], ["created_at", "2015-12-16 18:34:35.775645"], ["updated_at", "2015-12-16
18:34:35.775645"]]
   (9.2ms)  commit transaction
=> #<Album id: 11, name: "Test", release_year: nil, created_at: "2015-12-16 18:34:35",
updated_at: "2015-12-16 18:34:35">
```

Calculations

average

With the method average, you can calculate the average of the values in a particular column of the table. Our
data material is of course not really suited to this. But as an example, let's calculate the average release year of
all albums and then the same for albums from the 60s:

```
>> Album.average(:release_year)
   (0.3ms)  SELECT AVG("albums"."release_year") FROM "albums"
=> #<BigDecimal:7fd76fd027a0,'0.19685E4',18(36)>
>> Album.average(:release_year).to_s
   (0.2ms)  SELECT AVG("albums"."release_year") FROM "albums"
=> "1968.5"
>> Album.where( :release_year => 1960..1969 ).average(:release_year)
   (0.1ms)  SELECT AVG("albums"."release_year") FROM "albums" WHERE
   ("albums"."release_year" BETWEEN 1960 AND 1969)
=> #<BigDecimal:7fd76fc908d0,'0.1966142857 14286E4',27(36)>
>> Album.where( :release_year => 1960..1969 ).average(:release_year).to_s
   (0.3ms)  SELECT AVG("albums"."release_year") FROM "albums" WHERE
   ("albums"."release_year" BETWEEN 1960 AND 1969)
=> "1966.14285714286"
```

count

The name says it all: the method count counts the number of records.

First, we return the number of all albums in the database and then the number of albums from the 60s:

```
>> Album.count
   (0.1ms)  SELECT COUNT(*) FROM "albums"
=> 11
```

maximum

With the method maximum, you can output the item with the highest value within a query.

Let's look for the highest release year:

```
>> Album.maximum(:release_year)
   (0.2ms)  SELECT MAX("albums"."release_year") FROM "albums"
=> 1979
```

minimum

With the method minimum, you can output the item with the lowest value within a query.

Let's find the lowest release year:

```
>> Album.minimum(:release_year)
   (0.2ms)  SELECT MIN("albums"."release_year") FROM "albums"
=> 1965
```

sum

With the method sum, you can calculate the sum of all items in a specific column of the database query.

Let's find the sum of all release years:

```
>> Album.sum(:release_year)
   (0.2ms)  SELECT SUM("albums"."release_year") FROM "albums"
=> 19685
```

SQL EXPLAIN

Most SQL databases can provide detailed information on a SQL query with the command EXPLAIN. This does not make much sense for our mini application, but if you are working with a large database one day, then EXPLAIN is a good debugging method, for example to find out where to place an index. SQL EXPLAIN can be called with the method explain (it will be displayed in prettier form if you add a puts):

```
>> Album.where(release_year: 1960..1969)
  Album Load (0.2ms)  SELECT "albums".* FROM "albums" WHERE
  ("albums"."release_year" BETWEEN 1960 AND 1969)
=> <ActiveRecord::Relation [<Album id: 1, [...]>]>
>> Album.where(release_year: 1960..1969).explain
  Album Load (0.3ms)  SELECT "albums".* FROM "albums" WHERE
  ("albums"."release_year" BETWEEN 1960 AND 1969)
=> EXPLAIN for: SELECT "albums".* FROM "albums" WHERE ("albums"."release_year"
BETWEEN 1960 AND 1969)
0|0|0|SCAN TABLE albums
```

Batches

ActiveRecord stores the results of a query in Memory. With very large tables and results that can become a performance issue. To address this you can use the find_each method which splits up the query into batches with the default size of 1,000 (can be configured with the :batch_size option). Our example Album table is too small to show the effect but the method would be used like this:

```
>> Album.where(release_year: 1960..1969).find_each do |album|
?>   puts album.name.upcase
>> end
  Album Load (0.2ms)  SELECT  "albums".* FROM "albums" WHERE
  ("albums"."release_year" BETWEEN 1960 AND 1969)  ORDER BY "albums"."id" ASC
  LIMIT 1000
SGT. PEPPER'S LONELY HEARTS CLUB BAND
PET SOUNDS
REVOLVER
HIGHWAY 61 REVISITED
RUBBER SOUL
BLONDE ON BLONDE
THE BEATLES
=> nil
```

Editing a Record

Adding and searching data is quite nice, but often you want to edit a record. To show how that's done I use the album database from the section "Searching and Finding with Queries".

Simple Editing

Simple editing of a record takes place with the following steps:

- Finding the record and creating a corresponding instance
- Changing the attribute
- Saving the record via the method ActiveRecord methods save

We are now searching for the album "The Beatles" and changing its name to "A Test":

```
$ rails console
Running via Spring preloader in process 24336
Loading development environment (Rails 5.0.0)
>> beatles_album = Album.where(name: 'The Beatles').first
  Album Load (0.2ms)  SELECT  "albums".* FROM "albums" WHERE "albums"."name" = ?  ORDER BY
"albums"."id" ASC LIMIT 1  [["name", "The Beatles"]]
=> #<Album id: 10, name: "The Beatles", release_year: 1968, created_at: "2015-12-16 17:45:34",
updated_at: "2015-12-16 17:45:34">
>> beatles_album.name
=> "The Beatles"
>> beatles_album.name = 'A Test'
=> "A Test"
>> beatles_album.save
   (0.1ms)  begin transaction
  SQL (0.6ms)  UPDATE "albums" SET "name" = ?, "updated_at" = ? WHERE "albums"."id" = ?
[["name", "A Test"], ["updated_at", "2015-12-16 18:46:03.851575"], ["id", 10]]
   (9.2ms)  commit transaction
=> true
>> exit
```

Active Model Dirty

ActiveModel::Dirty provides simple mechanisms to track changes of an ActiveRecord Model.

changed?

If you are not sure if a record has been changed and not yet saved, you can check via the method changed?:

```
>> beatles_album = Album.where(id: 10).first
  Album Load (0.4ms)  SELECT  "albums".* FROM "albums" WHERE "albums"."id" = ?
  ORDER BY "albums"."id" ASC LIMIT 1  [["id", 10]]
=> #<Album id: 10, name: "A Test", release_year: 1968, created_at: "2015-12-16
17:45:34", updated_at: "2015-12-16 18:46:03">
>> beatles_album.changed?
=> false
>> beatles_album.name = 'The Beatles'
=> "The Beatles"
>> beatles_album.changed?
=> true
>> beatles_album.save
   (0.1ms)  begin transaction SQL (0.6ms)  UPDATE "albums" SET "name" = ?,
   "updated_at" = ? WHERE "albums"."id" = ?  [["name", "The Beatles"],
   ["updated_at", "2015-12-16 18:47:26.794527"], ["id", 10]] (9.2ms)  commit
   transaction
=> true
>> beatles_album.changed?
=> false
```

_changed?

An attribute name followed by _changed? tracks changes to a specific attribute.

```
>> beatles_album = Album.where(id: 10).first
  Album Load (0.5ms)  SELECT  "albums".* FROM "albums" WHERE "albums"."id" = ? ORDER BY
"albums"."id" ASC LIMIT ?  [["id", 10], ["LIMIT", 1]]
=> #<Album id: 10, name: "The Beatles", release_year: 1968, created_at: "2016-01-21 10:15:51",
updated_at: "2016-01-21 10:15:51">
>> beatles_album.release_year_changed?
=> false
>> beatles_album.release_year = 1900
=> 1900
>> beatles_album.release_year_changed?
=> true
```

update

With the method update you can change several attributes of an object in one go and then immediately save
them automatically.

Let's use this method within the example used in the section "Simple Editing":

```
>> first_album = Album.first
  Album Load (0.1ms)  SELECT  "albums".* FROM "albums" ORDER BY "albums"."id" ASC LIMIT ?
[["LIMIT", 1]]
=> #<Album id: 1, name: "Sgt. Pepper's Lonely Hearts Club Band", release_year: 1967, created_at:
"2016-01-21 10:15:51", updated_at: "2016-01-21 10:15:51">
>> first_album.changed?
=> false
>> first_album.update(name: 'Another Test')
   (0.1ms)  begin transaction
  SQL (0.4ms)  UPDATE "albums" SET "name" = ?, "updated_at" = ? WHERE "albums"."id" = ?
[["name", "Another Test"], ["updated_at", 2016-01-21 12:11:27 UTC], ["id", 1]]
   (0.9ms)  commit transaction
=> true
>> first_album.changed?
=> false
>> first_album
=> #<Album id: 1, name: "Another Test", release_year: 1967, created_at: "2016-01-21 10:15:51",
updated_at: "2016-01-21 12:11:27">
```

Locking

There are many ways of locking a database. By default, Rails uses "optimistic locking" of records. To activate
locking a model needs to have an attribute with the name lock_version which has to be an integer. To show
how it works I'll create a new Rails project with a Product model. Then I'll try to change the price of the first
Product on two different instances. The second change will raise an ActiveRecord::StaleObjectError.

Example setup:

```
$ rails new shop
  [...]
$ cd shop
$ rails generate model Product name 'price:decimal{8,2}' lock_version:integer
  [...]
$ rails db:migrate
  [...]
$
```

Raising an `ActiveRecord::StaleObjectError`:

```
$ rails console
Running via Spring preloader in process 24336
Loading development environment (Rails 5.0.0)
>> Product.create(name: 'Orange', price: 0.5)
   (0.1ms)  begin transaction SQL (0.7ms)  INSERT INTO "products" ("name",
   "price", "created_at", "updated_at", "lock_version") VALUES (?, ?, ?, ?, ?)
   [["name", "Orange"], ["price", 0.5], ["created_at", "2015-12-16
   19:02:17.338531"], ["updated_at", "2015-12-16 19:02:17.338531"],
   ["lock_version", 0]]
   (1.0ms)  commit transaction
=> #<Product id: 1, name: "Orange", price:
#<BigDecimal:7feb59231198,'0.5E0',9(27)>, lock_version: 0, created_at:
"2015-12-16 19:02:17", updated_at: "2015-12-16 19:02:17">
>> a = Product.first
  Product Load (0.4ms)  SELECT  "products".* FROM "products"  ORDER BY
  "products"."id" ASC LIMIT 1
=> #<Product id: 1, name: "Orange", price:
#<BigDecimal:7feb5918a870,'0.5E0',9(27)>, lock_version: 0, created_at:
"2015-12-16 19:02:17", updated_at: "2015-12-16 19:02:17">
>> b = Product.first
  Product Load (0.3ms)  SELECT  "products".* FROM "products"  ORDER BY
  "products"."id" ASC LIMIT 1 => #<Product id: 1, name: "Orange", price:
#<BigDecimal:7feb59172d60,'0.5E0',9(27)>, lock_version: 0, created_at:
  "2015-12-16 19:02:17", updated_at: "2015-12-16 19:02:17">
>> a.price = 0.6
=> 0.6
>> a.save
   (0.1ms)  begin transaction
  SQL (0.4ms)  UPDATE "products" SET "price" = 0.6, "updated_at" = '2015-12-16
  19:02:59.514736', "lock_version" = 1 WHERE "products"."id" = ? AND
  "products"."lock_version" = ?  [["id", 1], ["lock_version", 0]]
   (9.1ms)  commit transaction
=> true
>> b.price = 0.7
=> 0.7
>> b.save
   (0.1ms)  begin transaction
  SQL (0.3ms)  UPDATE "products" SET "price" = 0.7, "updated_at" = '2015-12-16
  19:03:08.408511', "lock_version" = 1 WHERE "products"."id" = ? AND
  "products"."lock_version" = ?  [["id", 1], ["lock_version", 0]]
   (0.1ms)  rollback transaction
ActiveRecord::StaleObjectError: Attempted to update a stale object: Product
[...]
>> exit
```

You have to deal with the conflict by rescuing the exception and fix the conflict depending on your business logic.

 Please make sure to add a `lock_version` hidden field in your forms when using this mechanism with a WebGUI.

has_many – 1:n Association

In order to explain `has_many`, let's create a bookshelf application. In this database, there is a model with `books` and a model with `authors`. As a `book` can have multiple `authors`, we need a 1:n association (*one-to-many association*) to represent it.

 Associations are also sometimes referred to as *relations* or *relationships.*

First, we create a Rails application:

```
$ rails new bookshelf
  [...]
$ cd bookshelf
$
```

Now we create the model for the books:

```
$ rails generate model book title
  [...]
$
```

And finally, we create the database table for the authors. In this, we need an assignment field to the books table. This *foreign key* is always set by default as name of the referenced object (here: book) with an attached _id:

```
$ rails generate model author book_id:integer first_name last_name
  [...]
$
```

Then execute a rails db:migrate so that the database tables are actually created:

```
$ rails db:migrate
  [...]
$
```

Let's have a look at this on the *console*:

```
$ rails console
Running via Spring preloader in process 24336
Loading development environment (Rails 5.0.0)
>> Book.column_names
=> ["id", "title", "created_at", "updated_at"]
>> Author.column_names
=> ["id", "book_id", "first_name", "last_name", "created_at", "updated_at"]
>> exit
```

The two database tables are set up and can be used with ActiveRecord. But ActiveRecord does not yet know anything of the 1:n relation between them. But this can be done in two small steps.

First we add the line has_many :authors in the app/models/book.rb file to set the 1:n relationship:

app/models/book.rb

```
class Book < ApplicationRecord
  has_many :authors
end
```

Than we add `belongs_to :book` in the `app/models/author.rb` file to get the other way around configured (this is not always needed but often comes in handy):

app/models/author.rb

```ruby
class Author < ApplicationRecord
  belongs_to :book
end
```

These two simple definitions form the basis for a good deal of ActiveRecord magic. It will generate a bunch of cool new methods for us to link both models.

references modifier

Instead of creating a `book_id` attribute you can also use the `references` modifier with the model generator. By that you'll save a little bit of time because it will not only create a `book_id` attribute but add the `belongs_to :book` code in the `app/models/author.rb` file too. It even adds an index in the migration.

 It does not add the `has_many` code.

The above example could be done with this code:

```
$ rails new bookshelf
  [...]
$ cd bookshelf
$ rails generate model book title
[...]
$ rails generate model author book:references first_name last_name
[...]
$ rails db:migrate
[...]
$
```

Creating Records

In this example, we want to save a record for the book "Homo faber" by Max Frisch.

Manually

We drop the database with `rails db:reset`

```
$ rails db:reset
  [...]
$
```

Before using the magic we'll insert a book with an author manually. For that we have to use the book's id in the `book_id` attribute to create the author.

```
$ rails console
Running via Spring preloader in process 24336
Loading development environment (Rails 5.0.0)
>> book = Book.create(title: 'Homo faber')
[...]
>> author = Author.create(book_id: book.id, first_name: 'Max', last_name:
   'Frisch')
[...]
>> exit
```

Entering the book_id manually in this way is of course not very practical and prone to errors. The next section describes a better way.

create

We can use the method create of authors to add new authors to each Book object. These automatically get the correct book_id:

```
$ rails db:reset
  [...]
$ rails console
Running via Spring preloader in process 24336
Loading development environment (Rails 5.0.0)
>> book = Book.create(title: 'Homo faber')
[...]
>> author = book.authors.create(first_name: 'Max', last_name: 'Frisch')
[...]
>> exit
```

You could also place the authors.create() directly behind the Book.create():

```
$ rails db:reset
  [...]
$ rails console
Running via Spring preloader in process 24336
Loading development environment (Rails 5.0.0)
>> Book.create(title: 'Homo faber').authors.create(first_name: 'Max', last_name: 'Frisch')
[...]
>> exit
```

As create also accepts an array of hashes as an alternative to a single hash, you can also create multiple authors for a book in one go:

```
$ rails db:reset
  [...]
$ rails console
Running via Spring preloader in process 24336
Loading development environment (Rails 5.0.0)
>> Book.create(title: 'Example').authors.create([{last_name: 'A'}, {last_name: 'B'}])
[...]
>> exit
```

build

The method build resembles create. But the record is not saved. This only happens after a save:

```
$ rails db:reset
  [...]
$ rails console
Running via Spring preloader in process 24336
Loading development environment (Rails 5.0.0)
>> book = Book.create(title: 'Homo faber')
[...]
>> author = book.authors.build(first_name: 'Max', last_name: 'Frisch')
[...]
>> author.new_record?
=> true
>> author.save
[...]
>> author.new_record?
=> false
>> exit
```

When using create and build, you of course have to observe logical dependencies, otherwise there will be an error. For example, you cannot chain two build methods. Example:

```
$ rails console
Running via Spring preloader in process 24336
Loading development environment (Rails 5.0.0)
>> Book.build(title: 'Example').authors.build(last_name: 'A')
NoMethodError: undefined method `build' for #<Class:0x007f9e10059050>
[...]
>> exit
```

Accessing Records

First we need example data. Please populate the file db/seeds.rb with the following content:

```
Book.create(title: 'Homo faber').authors.create(first_name: 'Max', last_name:
'Frisch')
Book.create(title: 'Der Besuch der alten Dame').authors.create(first_name:
'Friedrich', last_name: 'Dürrenmatt')
Book.create(title: 'Julius Shulman: The Last Decade').authors.create([
  {first_name: 'Thomas', last_name: 'Schirmbock'},
  {first_name: 'Julius', last_name: 'Shulman'},
  {first_name: 'Jürgen', last_name: 'Nogai'}
  ])
Book.create(title: 'Julius Shulman: Palm Springs').authors.create([
  {first_name: 'Michael', last_name: 'Stern'},
  {first_name: 'Alan', last_name: 'Hess'}
  ])
Book.create(title: 'Photographing Architecture and Interiors').authors.create([
  {first_name: 'Julius', last_name: 'Shulman'},
  {first_name: 'Richard', last_name: 'Neutra'}
  ])
Book.create(title: 'Der Zauberberg').authors.create(first_name: 'Thomas',
last_name: 'Mann')
Book.create(title: 'In einer Familie').authors.create(first_name: 'Heinrich',
last_name: 'Mann')
```

Now drop the database and refill it with the db/seeds.rb:

```
$ rails db:reset
```

The convenient feature of the 1:n assignment in ActiveRecord is the particularly easy access to the n instances. Let's look at the first book and it's authors:

```
$ rails console
Running via Spring preloader in process 24336
Loading development environment (Rails 5.0.0)
>> Book.first
[...]
>> Book.first.authors
  Book Load (0.3ms)  SELECT  "books".* FROM "books"  ORDER BY "books"."id" ASC
  LIMIT 1
  Author Load (0.3ms)  SELECT "authors".* FROM "authors" WHERE
  "authors"."book_id" = ?  [["book_id", 1]]
=> <ActiveRecord::Associations::CollectionProxy [<Author id: 1, book_id: 1,
first_name: "Max", last_name: "Frisch", created_at: "2015-12-17 09:08:49",
updated_at: "2015-12-17 09:08:49">]>
```

Isn't that cool?! You can access the records simply via the plural form of the n model. The result is returned as array. Hm, maybe it also works the other way round?

```
>> Author.first.book
   Author Load (0.3ms)  SELECT  "authors".* FROM "authors"  ORDER BY
   "authors"."id" ASC LIMIT 1
   Book Load (0.2ms)  SELECT  "books".* FROM "books" WHERE "books"."id" = ?
   LIMIT 1  [["id", 1]]
=> #<Book id: 1, title: "Homo faber", created_at: "2015-12-17 09:08:49",
updated_at: "2015-12-17 09:08:49">
>> exit
```

Bingo! Accessing the associated Book class is also very easy. And as it's only a single record (belongs_to), the singular form is used in this case.

 If there was no author for this book, the result would be an empty array. If no book is associated with an author, then ActiveRecord outputs the value nil as Book.

Searching For Records

Before we can start searching, we again need defined example data. Please fill the file db/seeds.rb with the following content:

db/seeds.rb

```
Book.create(title: 'Homo faber').authors.create(first_name: 'Max', last_name: 'Frisch')
Book.create(title: 'Der Besuch der alten Dame').authors.create(first_name: 'Friedrich',
last_name: 'Dürrenmatt')
Book.create(title: 'Julius Shulman: The Last Decade').authors.create([
  {first_name: 'Thomas', last_name: 'Schirmbock'},
  {first_name: 'Julius', last_name: 'Shulman'},
  {first_name: 'Jürgen', last_name: 'Nogai'}
  ])
Book.create(title: 'Julius Shulman: Palm Springs').authors.create([
  {first_name: 'Michael', last_name: 'Stern'},
  {first_name: 'Alan', last_name: 'Hess'}
  ])
Book.create(title: 'Photographing Architecture and Interiors').authors.create([
  {first_name: 'Julius', last_name: 'Shulman'},
  {first_name: 'Richard', last_name: 'Neutra'}
  ])
Book.create(title: 'Der Zauberberg').authors.create(first_name: 'Thomas', last_name: 'Mann')
Book.create(title: 'In einer Familie').authors.create(first_name: 'Heinrich', last_name: 'Mann')
```

Now drop the database and refill it with the db/seeds.rb:

```
$ rails db:reset
```

And off we go. First we check how many books are in the database:

```
$ rails console
Running via Spring preloader in process 24336
Loading development environment (Rails 5.0.0)
>> Book.count
   (0.1ms)  SELECT COUNT(*) FROM "books"
=> 7
```

And how many authors?

```
>> Author.count
   (0.2ms)  SELECT COUNT(*) FROM "authors"
=> 11
>> exit
```

joins

To find all books that have at least one author with the surname 'Mann' we use a *join*.

```
$ rails console
Running via Spring preloader in process 24336
Loading development environment (Rails 5.0.0)
>> Book.joins(:authors).where(:authors => {last_name: 'Mann'})
   Book Load (0.2ms)  SELECT "books".* FROM "books" INNER JOIN "authors" ON
   "authors"."book_id" = "books"."id" WHERE "authors"."last_name" = ?
   [["last_name", "Mann"]]
=> <ActiveRecord::Relation [<Book id: 6, title: "Der Zauberberg",
created_at: "2015-12-17 09:13:31", updated_at: "2015-12-17 09:13:31">, #<Book
id: 7, title: "In einer Familie", created_at: "2015-12-17 09:13:31",
updated_at: "2015-12-17 09:13:31">]>
```

The database contains two books with the author 'Mann'. In the SQL, you can see that the method joins
executes an INNER JOIN.

Of course, we can also do it the other way round. We could search for the author of the book 'Homo faber':

```
>> Author.joins(:book).where(:books => {title: 'Homo faber'})
   Author Load (0.3ms)  SELECT "authors".* FROM "authors" INNER JOIN "books" ON
   "books"."id" = "authors"."book_id" WHERE "books"."title" = ? [["title",
   "Homo faber"]]
=> <ActiveRecord::Relation [<Author id: 1, book_id: 1, first_name: "Max",
last_name: "Frisch", created_at: "2015-12-17 09:13:31", updated_at:
"2015-12-17 09:13:31">]>
```

includes

includes is very similar to the method joins (see joins). Again, you can use it to search within a 1:n association.
Let's once more search for all books with an author whose surname is 'Mann':

```
$ rails console
Running via Spring preloader in process 24336
Loading development environment (Rails 5.0.0)
>> Book.includes(:authors).where(:authors => {last_name: 'Mann'})
   SQL (1.1ms)  SELECT "books"."id" AS t0_r0, "books"."title" AS t0_r1,
   "books"."created_at" AS t0_r2, "books"."updated_at" AS t0_r3, "authors"."id"
   AS t1_r0, "authors"."book_id" AS t1_r1, "authors"."first_name" AS t1_r2,
   "authors"."last_name" AS t1_r3, "authors"."created_at" AS t1_r4,
   "authors"."updated_at" AS t1_r5 FROM "books" LEFT OUTER JOIN "authors" ON
   "authors"."book_id" = "books"."id" WHERE "authors"."last_name" = ?
   [["last_name", "Mann"]]
=> <ActiveRecord::Relation [<Book id: 6, title: "Der Zauberberg",
created_at: "2015-12-17 09:13:31", updated_at: "2015-12-17 09:13:31">, #<Book
id: 7, title: "In einer Familie", created_at: "2015-12-17 09:13:31",
updated_at: "2015-12-17 09:13:31">]>
```

In the console output, you can see that the SQL code is different from the joins query.

joins only reads in the Book records and includes also reads the associated Authors. As you can see even in our little example, this obviously takes longer (0.2 ms vs. 1.1 ms).

joins vs. includes

Why would you want to use includes at all? Well, if you already know before the query that you will later need all author data, then it makes sense to use includes, because then you only need one database query. That is a lot faster than starting a seperate query for each n.

In that case, would it not be better to always work with includes? No, it depends on the specific case. When you are using includes, a lot more data is transported initially. This has to be cached and processed by ActiveRecord, which takes longer and requires more resources.

delete and destroy

With the methods destroy, destroy_all, delete and delete_all you can delete records, as described in "Delete/Destroy a Record". In the context of has_many, this means that you can delete the Author records associated with a Book in one go:

```
$ rails console
Running via Spring preloader in process 24336
Loading development environment (Rails 5.0.0)
>> book = Book.where(title: 'Julius Shulman: The Last Decade').first
  Book Load (0.2ms)  SELECT  "books".* FROM "books" WHERE "books"."title" = ?
  ORDER BY "books"."id" ASC LIMIT 1  [["title", "Julius Shulman: The Last
  Decade"]]
=> <Book id: 3, title: "Julius Shulman: The Last Decade", created_at:
"2015-12-17 09:13:31", updated_at: "2015-12-17 09:13:31">
>> book.authors.count
   (0.3ms)  SELECT COUNT() FROM "authors" WHERE "authors"."book_id" = ?
   [["book_id", 3]]
=> 3
>> book.authors.destroy_all
  Author Load (0.3ms)  SELECT "authors". FROM "authors" WHERE
  "authors"."book_id" = ?  [["book_id", 3]]
   (0.1ms)  begin transaction
  SQL (0.5ms)  DELETE FROM "authors" WHERE "authors"."id" = ?  [["id", 3]]
  SQL (0.1ms)  DELETE FROM "authors" WHERE "authors"."id" = ?  [["id", 4]]
  SQL (0.1ms)  DELETE FROM "authors" WHERE "authors"."id" = ?  [["id", 5]]
   (9.3ms)  commit transaction
=> [<Author id: 3, book_id: 3, first_name: "Thomas", last_name: "Schirmbock",
created_at: "2015-12-17 09:13:31", updated_at: "2015-12-17 09:13:31">,
#<Author id: 4, book_id: 3, first_name: "Julius", last_name: "Shulman",
created_at: "2015-12-17 09:13:31", updated_at: "2015-12-17 09:13:31">,
#<Author id: 5, book_id: 3, first_name: "Jürgen", last_name: "Nogai",
created_at: "2015-12-17 09:13:31", updated_at: "2015-12-17 09:13:31">]
>> book.authors.count
   (0.2ms)  SELECT COUNT(*) FROM "authors" WHERE "authors"."book_id" = ?
   [["book_id", 3]]
=> 0
```

Options

I can't comment on all possible options at this point. But I'd like to show you the most often used ones. For all others, please refer to the Ruby on Rails documentation that you can find on the Internet at http://rails.rubyonrails.org/classes/ActiveRecord/Associations/ClassMethods.html.

belongs_to

The most important option for `belongs_to` is.

touch: true

It automatically sets the field `updated_at` of the entry in the table `Book` to the current time when an `Author` is edited. In the `app/models/author.rb`, it would look like this:

app/models/author.rb

```
class Author < ApplicationRecord
  belongs_to :book, touch: true
end
```

has_many

The most important options for `has_many` are.

dependent: :destroy

If a book is removed, then it usually makes sense to also automatically remove all authors dependent on this book. This can be done via `:dependent ⇒ :destroy` in the `app/models/book.rb`:

app/models/book.rb

```
class Book < ApplicationRecord
  has_many :authors, dependent: :destroy
end
```

In the following example, we destroy the first book in the database table. All authors of this book are also automatically destroyed:

```
$ rails console
Running via Spring preloader in process 24336
Loading development environment (Rails 5.0.0)
>> Book.first
  Book Load (0.2ms)  SELECT  "books".* FROM "books"  ORDER BY "books"."id" ASC
  LIMIT 1
=> <Book id: 1, title: "Homo faber", created_at: "2015-12-17 09:13:31",
updated_at: "2015-12-17 09:13:31">
>> Book.first.authors
  Book Load (0.2ms)  SELECT  "books".* FROM "books"  ORDER BY "books"."id" ASC
  LIMIT 1
  Author Load (0.2ms)  SELECT "authors".* FROM "authors" WHERE
  "authors"."book_id" = ?  [["book_id", 1]]
=> #<ActiveRecord::Associations::CollectionProxy [<Author id: 1, book_id: 1,
first_name: "Max", last_name: "Frisch", created_at: "2015-12-17 09:13:31",
updated_at: "2015-12-17 09:13:31">]>
>> Book.first.destroy
  Book Load (0.3ms)  SELECT  "books".* FROM "books"  ORDER BY "books"."id" ASC
  LIMIT 1
  (0.1ms)  begin transaction
  Author Load (0.1ms)  SELECT "authors".* FROM "authors" WHERE
  "authors"."book_id" = ?  [["book_id", 1]]
  SQL (1.6ms)  DELETE FROM "authors" WHERE "authors"."id" = ?  [["id", 1]]
  SQL (0.1ms)  DELETE FROM "books" WHERE "books"."id" = ?  [["id", 1]]
  (9.1ms)  commit transaction
=> #<Book id: 1, title: "Homo faber", created_at: "2015-12-17 09:13:31",
updated_at: "2015-12-17 09:13:31">
>> Author.exists?(1)
>> exit**
```

 Please always remember the difference between the methods   destroy (see "destroy")
and delete (see the "delete"). This association only works with the method destroy.

has_many .., through: ...

Here I need to elaborate a bit: you will probably have noticed that in our book-author example we have sometimes been entering authors several times in the authors table. Normally, you would of course not do this. It would be better to enter each author only once in the authors table and take care of the association with the books via an intermediary table. For this purpose, there is has_many ⋯, through: :⋯.

This kind of association is called Many-to-Many (n:n) and we'll discuss it in detail in the section "Many-to-Many - n:n Association".

Many-to-Many – n:n Association

Up to now, we have always associated a database table directly with another table. For many-to-many, we will associate two tables via a third table. As example for this kind of relation, we use an order in a very basic online shop. In this type of shop system, a Product can appear in several orders (Order) and at the same time an order can contain several products. This is referred to as many-to-many. Let's recreate this scenario with code.

Preparation

Create the shop application:

```
$ rails new shop
  [...]
$ cd shop
```

A model for products:

```
$ rails generate model product name 'price:decimal{7,2}'
  [...]
$
```

A model for an order:

```
$ rails generate model order delivery_address
  [...]
$
```

And a model for individual items of an order:

```
$ rails generate model line_item order:references product:references
quantity:integer
  [...]
$
```

Then, create the database:

```
$ rails db:migrate
  [...]
$
```

The Association

An order (Order) consists of one or several items (LineItem). This LineItem consists of the order_id, a product_id and the number of items ordered (quantity). The individual product is defined in the product database (Product).

Associating the models happens as always in the directory app/models. First, in the file app/models/order.rb:

app/models/order.rb

```
class Order < ApplicationRecord
  has_many :line_items
  has_many :products, through: :line_items
end
```

Then in the counterpart in the file app/models/product.rb:

app/models/product.rb

```
class Product < ApplicationRecord
  has_many :line_items
  has_many :orders, through: :line_items
end
```

The file app/models/line_item.rb: has been filled by the generator:

app/models/line_item.rb

```ruby
class LineItem < ApplicationRecord
  belongs_to :order
  belongs_to :product
end
```

The Association Works Transparent

As we implement the associations via has_many, most things will already be familiar to you from the section "has_many - 1:n Association". I am going to discuss a few examples. For more details, see the section "has_many - 1:n Association".

First we populate our product database with the following values:

```
$ rails console
Running via Spring preloader in process 24336
Loading development environment (Rails 5.0.0)
>> milk = Product.create(name: 'Milk (1 liter)', price: 0.45)
   (0.4ms)  begin transaction
  SQL (0.7ms)  INSERT INTO "products" ("name", "price", "created_at",
  "updated_at") VALUES (?, ?, ?, ?) [["name", "Milk (1 liter)"], ["price",
  0.45], ["created_at", "2015-12-17 11:46:22.832375"], ["updated_at",
  "2015-12-17 11:46:22.832375"]]
   (0.9ms)  commit transaction
=> #<Product id: 1, name: "Milk (1 liter)", price:
#<BigDecimal:7fa8249f0aa0,'0.45E0',9(27)>, created_at: "2015-12-17 11:46:22",
updated_at: "2015-12-17 11:46:22">
>> butter = Product.create(name: 'Butter (250 gr)', price: 0.75)
   (0.1ms)  begin transaction
  SQL (1.3ms)  INSERT INTO "products" ("name", "price", "created_at",
  "updated_at") VALUES (?, ?, ?, ?) [["name", "Butter (250 gr)"], ["price",
  0.75], ["created_at", "2015-12-17 11:46:34.798486"], ["updated_at",
  "2015-12-17 11:46:34.798486"]]
   (9.1ms)  commit transaction
=> #<Product id: 2, name: "Butter (250 gr)", price:
#<BigDecimal:7fa823d42fb0,'0.75E0',9(27)>, created_at: "2015-12-17 11:46:34",
updated_at: "2015-12-17 11:46:34">
>> flour = Product.create(name: 'Flour (1 kg)', price: 0.45)
   (0.1ms)  begin transaction
  SQL (0.5ms)  INSERT INTO "products" ("name", "price", "created_at",
  "updated_at") VALUES (?, ?, ?, ?) [["name", "Flour (1 kg)"], ["price",
  0.45], ["created_at", "2015-12-17 11:46:42.711399"], ["updated_at",
  "2015-12-17 11:46:42.711399"]]
   (9.1ms)  commit transaction
=> #<Product id: 3, name: "Flour (1 kg)", price:
#<BigDecimal:7fa823d200c8,'0.45E0',9(27)>, created_at: "2015-12-17 11:46:42",
updated_at: "2015-12-17 11:46:42">
```

Now we create a new Order object with the name order:

```
>> order = Order.new(delivery_address: '123 Acme Street, ACME STATE 12345')
=> #<Order id: nil, delivery_address: "123 Acme Street, ACME STATE 12345",
created_at: nil, updated_at: nil>
```

Logically, this new order does not yet contain any products:

```
>> order.products.count
=> 0
```

As often, there are several ways of adding products to the order. The simplest way: as the products are integrated as array, you can simply insert them as elements of an array:

```
>> order.products << milk
=> <ActiveRecord::Associations::CollectionProxy [<Product id: 1, name: "Milk
(1 liter)", price: #<BigDecimal:7fa8249f0aa0,'0.45E0',9(27)>, created_at:
"2015-12-17 11:46:22", updated_at: "2015-12-17 11:46:22">]>
```

But if the customer wants to buy three liters of milk instead of one liter, we need to enter it in the LineItem (in the linking element) table. ActiveRecord already build an object for us:

```
>> order.line_items
=> <ActiveRecord::Associations::CollectionProxy [<LineItem id: nil,
order_id: nil, product_id: 1, quantity: nil, created_at: nil, updated_at:
nil>]>
```

But the object is not yet saved in the database. After we do this via save, we can change the quantity in the LineItem object:

```
>> order.save
   (0.1ms)  begin transaction
  SQL (0.6ms)  INSERT INTO "orders" ("delivery_address", "created_at",
  "updated_at") VALUES (?, ?, ?)  [["delivery_address", "123 Acme Street, ACME
  STATE 12345"], ["created_at", "2015-12-17 11:49:43.968385"], ["updated_at",
  "2015-12-17 11:49:43.968385"]]
  SQL (0.3ms)  INSERT INTO "line_items" ("product_id", "order_id",
  "created_at", "updated_at") VALUES (?, ?, ?, ?)  [["product_id", 1],
  ["order_id", 1], ["created_at", "2015-12-17 11:49:43.971970"],
  ["updated_at", "2015-12-17 11:49:43.971970"]]
   (9.2ms)  commit transaction
=> true
>> order.line_items.first.update_attributes(quantity: 3)
   (0.1ms)  begin transaction
  SQL (0.4ms)  UPDATE "line_items" SET "quantity" = ?, "updated_at" = ? WHERE
  "line_items"."id" = ?  [["quantity", 3], ["updated_at", "2015-12-17
  11:49:53.529842"], ["id", 1]]
   (9.2ms)  commit transaction
=> true
```

Alternatively, we can also buy butter twice directly by adding a LineItem:

```
>> order.line_items.create(product_id: butter.id, quantity: 2)
   (0.1ms)  begin transaction
  SQL (0.5ms)  INSERT INTO "line_items" ("product_id", "quantity", "order_id",
  "created_at", "updated_at") VALUES (?, ?, ?, ?, ?)  [["product_id", 2],
  ["quantity", 2], ["order_id", 1], ["created_at", "2015-12-17
  11:50:26.181117"], ["updated_at", "2015-12-17 11:50:26.181117"]]
   (8.3ms)  commit transaction
=> #<LineItem id: 2, order_id: 1, product_id: 2, quantity: 2, created_at:
"2015-12-17 11:50:26", updated_at: "2015-12-17 11:50:26">
```

When creating a line_item we bypass the has_many: ⋯ :through ⋯ logic. The database
table contains all the correct information but order hasn't been updated:

```
>> order.products
=> <ActiveRecord::Associations::CollectionProxy [<Product id: 1, name:
"Milk (1 liter)", price: #<BigDecimal:7fa8249f0aa0,'0.45E0',9(27)>,
created_at: "2015-12-17 11:46:22", updated_at: "2015-12-17 11:46:22">]>
```

But in the database table, it is of course correct:

```
>> Order.first.products
   Order Load (0.4ms)  SELECT  "orders".* FROM "orders"  ORDER BY
   "orders"."id" ASC LIMIT 1
   Product Load (0.3ms)  SELECT "products".* FROM "products" INNER JOIN
   "line_items" ON "products"."id" = "line_items"."product_id" WHERE
   "line_items"."order_id" = ?  [["order_id", 1]]
=> <ActiveRecord::Associations::CollectionProxy [<Product id: 1, name:
"Milk (1 liter)", price: #<BigDecimal:7fa82824a630,'0.45E0',9(27)>,
created_at: "2015-12-17 11:46:22", updated_at: "2015-12-17 11:46:22">,
#<Product id: 2, name: "Butter (250 gr)", price:
#<BigDecimal:7fa8282496e0,'0.75E0',9(27)>, created_at: "2015-12-17
11:46:34", updated_at: "2015-12-17 11:46:34">]>
```

In this specific case, you would need to reload the object from the database via the method
reload:

```
>> order.reload
   Order Load (0.4ms)  SELECT  "orders".* FROM "orders"  WHERE
   "orders"."id" = ? LIMIT 1  [["id", 1]]
=> <Order id: 1, delivery_address: "123 Acme Street, ACME STATE 12345",
created_at: "2015-12-17 11:49:43", updated_at: "2015-12-17 11:49:43">
>> order.products
   Product Load (0.2ms)  SELECT "products".* FROM "products" INNER JOIN
   "line_items" ON "products"."id" = "line_items"."product_id" WHERE
   "line_items"."order_id" = ?  [["order_id", 1]]
=> #<ActiveRecord::Associations::CollectionProxy [<Product id: 1, name:
"Milk (1 liter)", price: #<BigDecimal:7fa828229ef8,'0.45E0',9(27)>,
created_at: "2015-12-17 11:46:22", updated_at: "2015-12-17 11:46:22">,
#<Product id: 2, name: "Butter (250 gr)", price:
#<BigDecimal:7fa8282289e0,'0.75E0',9(27)>, created_at: "2015-12-17
11:46:34", updated_at: "2015-12-17 11:46:34">]>
```

Let's enter a second order with all available products into the system:

```
>> order2 = Order.create(delivery_address: '2, Test Road')
   (0.2ms)  begin transaction
  SQL (0.4ms)  INSERT INTO "orders" ("delivery_address", "created_at",
  "updated_at") VALUES (?, ?, ?)  [["delivery_address", "2, Test Road"],
  ["created_at", "2015-12-17 11:55:08.141811"], ["updated_at", "2015-12-17
  11:55:08.141811"]]
   (9.0ms)  commit transaction
=> <Order id: 2, delivery_address: "2, Test Road", created_at: "2015-12-17
11:55:08", updated_at: "2015-12-17 11:55:08">
>> order2.products << Product.all
  Product Load (0.3ms)  SELECT "products".* FROM "products"
   (0.1ms)  begin transaction
  SQL (0.4ms)  INSERT INTO "line_items" ("order_id", "product_id", "created_at",
  [...]
  SQL (0.1ms)  INSERT INTO "line_items" ("order_id", "product_id", "created_at",
  [...]
  SQL (0.1ms)  INSERT INTO "line_items" ("order_id", "product_id", "created_at",
  [...]
   (8.4ms)  commit transaction
  Product Load (0.2ms)  SELECT "products".* FROM "products" INNER JOIN
  "line_items" ON "products"."id" = "line_items"."product_id" WHERE
  "line_items"."order_id" = ?  [["order_id", 2]]
=> #<ActiveRecord::Associations::CollectionProxy [<Product id: 1, name: "Milk
(1 liter)", price: #<BigDecimal:7fa8289189d0,'0.45E0',9(27)>, created_at:
"2015-12-17 11:46:22", updated_at: "2015-12-17 11:46:22">, #<Product id: 2,
name: "Butter (250 gr)", price: #<BigDecimal:7fa828912030,'0.75E0',9(27)>,
created_at: "2015-12-17 11:46:34", updated_at: "2015-12-17 11:46:34">,
#<Product id: 3, name: "Flour (1 kg)", price:
#<BigDecimal:7fa82890ba78,'0.45E0',9(27)>, created_at: "2015-12-17 11:46:42",
updated_at: "2015-12-17 11:46:42">]>
>> order.save
   (0.1ms)  begin transaction
   (0.1ms)  commit transaction
=> true
```

Now we can try out the opposite direction of this many-to-many association. Let's search for all orders that contain the first product:

```
>> Product.first.orders
  Product Load (0.1ms)  SELECT  "products".* FROM "products"  ORDER BY
  "products"."id" ASC LIMIT 1
  Order Load (0.2ms)  SELECT "orders".* FROM "orders" INNER JOIN "line_items"
  ON "orders"."id" = "line_items"."order_id" WHERE "line_items"."product_id" =
  ?  [["product_id", 1]]
=> <ActiveRecord::Associations::CollectionProxy [<Order id: 1,
delivery_address: "123 Acme Street, ACME STATE 12345", created_at: "2015-12-17
11:49:43", updated_at: "2015-12-17 11:49:43">, #<Order id: 2,
delivery_address: "2, Test Road", created_at: "2015-12-17 11:55:08",
updated_at: "2015-12-17 11:55:08">]>
```

Of course, we can also work with a joins (see "joins") and search for all orders that contain the product "Milk (1 liter)":

```
>> Order.joins(:products).where(:products => {name: 'Milk (1 liter)'})
  Order Load (0.4ms)  SELECT "orders".* FROM "orders" INNER JOIN "line_items"
  ON "line_items"."order_id" = "orders"."id" INNER JOIN "products" ON
  "products"."id" = "line_items"."product_id" WHERE "products"."name" = ?
  [["name", "Milk (1 liter)"]]
=> <ActiveRecord::Relation [<Order id: 1, delivery_address: "123 Acme
Street, ACME STATE 12345", created_at: "2015-12-17 11:49:43", updated_at:
"2015-12-17 11:49:43">, #<Order id: 2, delivery_address: "2, Test Road",
created_at: "2015-12-17 11:55:08", updated_at: "2015-12-17 11:55:08">]>
```

has_one – 1:1 Association

Similar to has_many (see xref:#has95many-1n-association["has_many - 1:n Association"]), the method has_one also creates a logical relation between two models. But in contrast to has_many, one record is only ever associated with exactly one other record in has_one. In most practical cases of application, it logically makes sense to put both into the same model and therefore the same database table, but for the sake of completeness I also want to discuss `has_one here.

 You can probably safely skip has_one without losing any sleep.

In the examples, I assume that you have already read and understood the section "has_many - 1:n Association". I am not going to explain methods like build (see "build") again but assume that you already know the basics.

Preparation

We use the example from the Rails documentation (see http://api.rubyonrails.org/classes/ActiveRecord/Associations/ClassMethods.html) and create an application containing employees and offices. Each employee has an office. First the application:

```
$ rails new office-space
  [...]
$ cd office-space
$
```

And now the two models:

```
$ rails generate model employee last_name
  [...]
$ rails generate model office location employee_id:integer
  [...]
$ rails db:migrate
  [...]
$
```

Association

The association in the file app/models/employee.rb:

app/models/employee.rb

```ruby
class Employee < ApplicationRecord
  has_one :office
end
```

And its counterpart in the file app/models/office.rb:

app/models/office.rb

```ruby
class Office < ApplicationRecord
  belongs_to :employee
end
```

Options

The options of has_one are similar to those of has_many. So for details, please refer to "Options" or
http://api.rubyonrails.org/classes/ActiveRecord/Associations/ClassMethods.html#method-i-has_one.

Console Examples

Let's start the console and create two employees:

```
$ rails console
Running via Spring preloader in process 24336
Loading development environment (Rails 5.0.0)
>> Employee.create(last_name: 'Udelhoven')
   (0.1ms)  begin transaction
  SQL (0.5ms)  INSERT INTO "employees" ("last_name", "created_at",
  "updated_at") VALUES (?, ?, ?) [["last_name", "Udelhoven"], ["created_at",
  "2015-12-17 12:23:35.499672"], ["updated_at", "2015-12-17 12:23:35.499672"]]
   (0.9ms)  commit transaction
=> #<Employee id: 1, last_name: "Udelhoven", created_at: "2015-12-17
12:23:35", updated_at: "2015-12-17 12:23:35">
>> Employee.create(last_name: 'Meier')
   (0.1ms)  begin transaction
  SQL (0.5ms)  INSERT INTO "employees" ("last_name", "created_at",
  "updated_at") VALUES (?, ?, ?) [["last_name", "Meier"], ["created_at",
  "2015-12-17 12:23:49.983219"], ["updated_at", "2015-12-17 12:23:49.983219"]]
   (9.5ms)  commit transaction
=> #<Employee id: 2, last_name: "Meier", created_at: "2015-12-17 12:23:49",
updated_at: "2015-12-17 12:23:49">
```

Now the first employee gets his own office:

```
>> Office.create(location: '2nd floor', employee_id: Employee.first.id)
  Employee Load (0.3ms)  SELECT  "employees".* FROM "employees"  ORDER BY
  "employees"."id" ASC LIMIT 1
   (0.1ms)  begin transaction
  SQL (0.5ms)  INSERT INTO "offices" ("location", "employee_id", "created_at",
  "updated_at") VALUES (?, ?, ?, ?) [["location", "2nd floor"],
  ["employee_id", 1], ["created_at", "2015-12-17 12:24:30.575972"],
  ["updated_at", "2015-12-17 12:24:30.575972"]]
   (0.8ms)  commit transaction
=> #<Office id: 1, location: "2nd floor", employee_id: 1, created_at:
"2015-12-17 12:24:30", updated_at: "2015-12-17 12:24:30">
```

Both directions can be accessed the normal way:

```
>> Employee.first.office
  Employee Load (0.4ms)  SELECT  "employees".* FROM "employees"  ORDER BY
  "employees"."id" ASC LIMIT 1
  Office Load (0.3ms)  SELECT  "offices".* FROM "offices" WHERE
  "offices"."employee_id" = ? LIMIT 1  [["employee_id", 1]]
=> #<Office id: 1, location: "2nd floor", employee_id: 1, created_at:
"2015-12-17 12:24:30", updated_at: "2015-12-17 12:24:30">
>> Office.first.employee
  Office Load (0.3ms)  SELECT  "offices".* FROM "offices"  ORDER BY
  "offices"."id" ASC LIMIT 1
  Employee Load (0.2ms)  SELECT  "employees".* FROM "employees" WHERE
  "employees"."id" = ? LIMIT 1  [["id", 1]]
=> #<Employee id: 1, last_name: "Udelhoven", created_at: "2015-12-17
12:23:35", updated_at: "2015-12-17 12:23:35">
```

For the second employee, we use the automatically generated method create_office (with has_many, we would use offices.create here):

```
>> Employee.last.create_office(location: '1st floor')
  Employee Load (0.3ms)  SELECT  "employees".* FROM "employees"  ORDER BY
  "employees"."id" DESC LIMIT 1
   (0.1ms)  begin transaction
  SQL (0.4ms)  INSERT INTO "offices" ("location", "employee_id", "created_at",
  "updated_at") VALUES (?, ?, ?, ?)  [["location", "1st floor"],
  ["employee_id", 2], ["created_at", "2015-12-17 12:26:11.291450"],
  ["updated_at", "2015-12-17 12:26:11.291450"]]
   (8.2ms)  commit transaction
  Office Load (0.2ms)  SELECT  "offices".* FROM "offices" WHERE
  "offices"."employee_id" = ? LIMIT 1  [["employee_id", 2]]
=> #<Office id: 2, location: "1st floor", employee_id: 2, created_at:
"2015-12-17 12:26:11", updated_at: "2015-12-17 12:26:11">
```

Removing is intuitively done via destroy:

```
>> Employee.first.office.destroy
  Employee Load (0.3ms)  SELECT  "employees".* FROM "employees"  ORDER BY
  "employees"."id" ASC LIMIT 1
  Office Load (0.1ms)  SELECT  "offices".* FROM "offices" WHERE
  "offices"."employee_id" = ? LIMIT 1  [["employee_id", 1]]
   (0.1ms)  begin transaction
  SQL (0.4ms)  DELETE FROM "offices" WHERE "offices"."id" = ?  [["id", 1]]
   (9.1ms)  commit transaction
=> #<Office id: 1, location: "2nd floor", employee_id: 1, created_at:
"2015-12-17 12:24:30", updated_at: "2015-12-17 12:24:30">
>> Employee.first.office
  Employee Load (0.3ms)  SELECT  "employees".* FROM "employees"  ORDER BY
  "employees"."id" ASC LIMIT 1
  Office Load (0.2ms)  SELECT  "offices".* FROM "offices" WHERE
  "offices"."employee_id" = ? LIMIT 1  [["employee_id", 1]]
=> nil
```

If you create a new `Office` for an `Employee` with an existing `Office` then you will not get an error message:

```
>> Employee.last.create_office(location: 'Basement')
  Employee Load (0.2ms)  SELECT  "employees".* FROM "employees"  ORDER
  BY "employees"."id" DESC LIMIT 1
   (0.1ms)  begin transaction
  SQL (0.4ms)  INSERT INTO "offices" ("location", "employee_id",
  "created_at", "updated_at") VALUES (?, ?, ?, ?)  [["location",
  "Basement"], ["employee_id", 2], ["created_at", "2015-12-17
  12:27:56.518229"], ["updated_at", "2015-12-17 12:27:56.518229"]]
   (9.2ms)  commit transaction
  Office Load (0.2ms)  SELECT  "offices".* FROM "offices" WHERE
  "offices"."employee_id" = ? LIMIT 1  [["employee_id", 2]]
   (0.1ms)  begin transaction
  SQL (0.4ms)  UPDATE "offices" SET "employee_id" = ?, "updated_at" = ?
  WHERE "offices"."id" = ?  [["employee_id", nil], ["updated_at",
  "2015-12-17 12:27:56.531948"], ["id", 2]]
   (0.9ms)  commit transaction
=> #<Office id: 3, location: "Basement", employee_id: 2, created_at:
"2015-12-17 12:27:56", updated_at: "2015-12-17 12:27:56">
>> Employee.last.office
  Employee Load (0.3ms)  SELECT  "employees".* FROM "employees"  ORDER
  BY "employees"."id" DESC LIMIT 1
  Office Load (0.1ms)  SELECT  "offices".* FROM "offices" WHERE
  "offices"."employee_id" = ? LIMIT 1  [["employee_id", 2]]
=> #<Office id: 3, location: "Basement", employee_id: 2, created_at:
"2015-12-17 12:27:56", updated_at: "2015-12-17 12:27:56">
```

The old `Office` is even still in the database (the `employee_id` was automatically set to `nil`):

```
>> Office.all
  Office Load (0.2ms)  SELECT "offices".* FROM "offices"
=> <ActiveRecord::Relation [<Office id: 2, location: "1st floor",
employee_id: nil, created_at: "2015-12-17 12:26:11", updated_at:
"2015-12-17 12:27:56">, #<Office id: 3, location: "Basement",
employee_id: 2, created_at: "2015-12-17 12:27:56", updated_at:
"2015-12-17 12:27:56">]>
>> exit
```

has_one vs. belongs_to

Both has_one and belongs_to offer the option of representing a 1:1 relationship. The difference in practice is in the programmer's personal preference and the location of the foreign key. In general, has_one tends to be used very rarely and depends on the degree of normalization of the data schema.

Polymorphic Associations

Already the word "polymorphic" will probably make you tense up. What can it mean? Here is what the website http://api.rubyonrails.org/classes/ActiveRecord/Associations/ClassMethods.html tells us: "Polymorphic associations on models are not restricted on what types of models they can be associated with." Well, there you go - as clear as mud! ;-)

I am showing you an example in which we create a model for cars (Car) and a model for bicycles (Bike). To describe a car or bike, we use a model to tag it (Tag). A car and a bike can have any number of tags. The application:

```
$ rails new example
  [...]
$ cd example
$
```

Now the three required models:

```
$ rails generate model Car name
  [...]
$ rails generate model Bike name
  [...]
$ rails generate model Tag name taggable:references{polymorphic}
  [...]
$ rails db:migrate
  [...]
$
```

Car and Bike are clear. For Tag we use the migration shortcut taggable:references{polymorphic} to generate the fields taggable_type and taggable_id, to give ActiveRecord an opportunity to save the assignment for the polymorphic association. We have to enter it accordingly in the model.

The model generator already filed the app/models/tag.rb file with the configuration for the polymorphic association:

app/models/tag.rb

```
class Tag < ApplicationRecord
  belongs_to :taggable, polymorphic: true
end
```

For the other models we have to add the polymorphic association manually:

app/models/car.rb

```
class Car < ApplicationRecord
  has_many :tags, as: :taggable
end
```

app/models/bike.rb

```
class Bike < ApplicationRecord
  has_many :tags, as: :taggable
end
```

For Car and Bike we use an additional :as: :taggable when defining has_many. For Tag we use belongs_to :taggable, polymorphic: true to indicate the polymorphic association to ActiveRecord.

 The suffix *"able"* in the name *"taggable"* is commonly used in Rails, but not obligatory. For creating the association we now not only need the ID of the entry, but also need to know which *model* it actually is. So the term *"taggable_type"* makes sense.

Let's go into the *console* and create a car and a bike:

```
$ rails console
Running via Spring preloader in process 24336
Loading development environment (Rails 5.0.0)
>> beetle = Car.create(name: 'Beetle')
   (0.1ms)  begin transaction
  SQL (0.8ms)  INSERT INTO "cars" ("name", "created_at", "updated_at") VALUES
  (?, ?, ?)  [["name", "Beetle"], ["created_at", "2015-12-17
  13:39:54.793336"], ["updated_at", "2015-12-17 13:39:54.793336"]]
   (0.8ms)  commit transaction
=> #<Car id: 1, name: "Beetle", created_at: "2015-12-17 13:39:54", updated_at:
"2015-12-17 13:39:54">
>> mountainbike = Bike.create(name: 'Mountainbike')
   (0.1ms)  begin transaction
  SQL (0.3ms)  INSERT INTO "bikes" ("name", "created_at", "updated_at") VALUES
  (?, ?, ?)  [["name", "Mountainbike"], ["created_at", "2015-12-17
  13:39:55.896512"], ["updated_at", "2015-12-17 13:39:55.896512"]]
   (9.0ms)  commit transaction
=> #<Bike id: 1, name: "Mountainbike", created_at: "2015-12-17 13:39:55",
updated_at: "2015-12-17 13:39:55">
```

Now we define for each a tag with the color of the corresponding object:

```
>> beetle.tags.create(name: 'blue')
   (0.1ms)  begin transaction
  SQL (1.0ms)  INSERT INTO "tags" ("name", "taggable_id", "taggable_type",
  "created_at", "updated_at") VALUES (?, ?, ?, ?, ?)  [["name", "blue"],
  ["taggable_id", 1], ["taggable_type", "Car"], ["created_at", "2015-12-17
  13:41:04.984444"], ["updated_at", "2015-12-17 13:41:04.984444"]]
   (0.9ms)  commit transaction
=> #<Tag id: 1, name: "blue", taggable_id: 1, taggable_type: "Car",
created_at: "2015-12-17 13:41:04", updated_at: "2015-12-17 13:41:04">
>> mountainbike.tags.create(name: 'black')
   (0.1ms)  begin transaction
  SQL (0.7ms)  INSERT INTO "tags" ("name", "taggable_id", "taggable_type",
  "created_at", "updated_at") VALUES (?, ?, ?, ?, ?)  [["name", "black"],
  ["taggable_id", 1], ["taggable_type", "Bike"], ["created_at", "2015-12-17
  13:41:17.315318"], ["updated_at", "2015-12-17 13:41:17.315318"]]
   (8.2ms)  commit transaction
=> #<Tag id: 2, name: "black", taggable_id: 1, taggable_type: "Bike",
created_at: "2015-12-17 13:41:17", updated_at: "2015-12-17 13:41:17">
```

For the beetle, we add another Tag:

```
>> beetle.tags.create(name: 'Automatic')
   (0.1ms)  begin transaction
  SQL (0.4ms)  INSERT INTO "tags" ("name", "taggable_id", "taggable_type",
  "created_at", "updated_at") VALUES (?, ?, ?, ?, ?)  [["name", "Automatic"],
  ["taggable_id", 1], ["taggable_type", "Car"], ["created_at", "2015-12-17
  13:41:51.042746"], ["updated_at", "2015-12-17 13:41:51.042746"]]
   (9.2ms)  commit transaction
=> #<Tag id: 3, name: "Automatic", taggable_id: 1, taggable_type: "Car",
created_at: "2015-12-17 13:41:51", updated_at: "2015-12-17 13:41:51">
```

Let's have a look at all Tag items:

```
>> Tag.all
  Tag Load (0.3ms)  SELECT "tags".* FROM "tags"
=> <ActiveRecord::Relation [<Tag id: 1, name: "blue", taggable_id: 1,
taggable_type: "Car", created_at: "2015-12-17 13:41:04", updated_at:
"2015-12-17 13:41:04">, #<Tag id: 2, name: "black", taggable_id: 1,
taggable_type: "Bike", created_at: "2015-12-17 13:41:17", updated_at:
"2015-12-17 13:41:17">, #<Tag id: 3, name: "Automatic", taggable_id: 1,
taggable_type: "Car", created_at: "2015-12-17 13:41:51", updated_at:
"2015-12-17 13:41:51">]>
```

And now all tags of the beetle:

```
>> beetle.tags
  Tag Load (0.3ms)  SELECT "tags".* FROM "tags" WHERE "tags"."taggable_id" = ?
  AND "tags"."taggable_type" = ?  [["taggable_id", 1], ["taggable_type",
  "Car"]]
=> <ActiveRecord::Associations::CollectionProxy [<Tag id: 1, name: "blue",
taggable_id: 1, taggable_type: "Car", created_at: "2015-12-17 13:41:04",
updated_at: "2015-12-17 13:41:04">, #<Tag id: 3, name: "Automatic",
taggable_id: 1, taggable_type: "Car", created_at: "2015-12-17 13:41:51",
updated_at: "2015-12-17 13:41:51">]>
```

Of course you can also check which object the last Tag belongs to:

```
>> Tag.last.taggable
  Tag Load (0.3ms)  SELECT  "tags".* FROM "tags"  ORDER BY "tags"."id" DESC
  LIMIT 1
  Car Load (0.4ms)  SELECT  "cars".* FROM "cars" WHERE "cars"."id" = ? LIMIT 1
  [["id", 1]]
=> #<Car id: 1, name: "Beetle", created_at: "2015-12-17 13:39:54", updated_at:
"2015-12-17 13:39:54">
>> exit
```

Polymorphic associations are always useful if you want to normalize the database structure. In this example, we could also have defined a model CarTag and BikeTag, but as Tag is the same for both, a polymorphic association makes more sense in this case.

Options

Polymorphic associations can be configured with the same options as a normal xref:#has95many-1n-association[has_many association].

Delete/Destroy a Record

To remove a database record, you can use the methods destroy and delete. It's quite easy to confuse these two terms, but they are different and after a while you get used to it.

As an example, we use the following Rails application:

```
$ rails new bookshelf
  [...]
$ cd bookshelf
$ rails generate model book title
  [...]
$ rails generate model author book:references first_name last_name
  [...]
$ rails db:migrate
  [...]
$
```

app/models/book.rb

```
class Book < ApplicationRecord
  has_many :authors, dependent: :destroy
end
```

app/models/author.rb

```
class Author < ApplicationRecord
  belongs_to :book
end
```

destroy

With destroy you can remove a record and any existing dependencies are also taken into account (see for example :dependent ⇒ :destroy in the section "options"). Simply put: to be on the safe side, it's better to use destroy because then the Rails system does more for you.

Let's create a record and then destroy it again:

```
$ rails console
Running via Spring preloader in process 24336
Loading development environment (Rails 5.0.0)
>> book = Book.create(title: 'Homo faber')
   (0.1ms)  begin transaction
  SQL (0.7ms)  INSERT INTO "books" ("title", "created_at", "updated_at")
  VALUES (?, ?, ?)  [["title", "Homo faber"], ["created_at", "2015-12-17
  13:49:58.092997"], ["updated_at", "2015-12-17 13:49:58.092997"]]
   (9.0ms)  commit transaction
=> #<Book id: 1, title: "Homo faber", created_at: "2015-12-17 13:49:58",
updated_at: "2015-12-17 13:49:58">
>> Book.count
   (0.3ms)  SELECT COUNT() FROM "books"
=> 1
>> book.destroy
   (0.1ms)  begin transaction
  Author Load (0.1ms)  SELECT "authors". FROM "authors" WHERE
  "authors"."book_id" = ?  [["book_id", 1]]
  SQL (0.3ms)  DELETE FROM "books" WHERE "books"."id" = ?  [["id", 1]]
   (9.0ms)  commit transaction
=> #<Book id: 1, title: "Homo faber", created_at: "2015-12-17 13:49:58",
updated_at: "2015-12-17 13:49:58">
>> Book.count
   (0.5ms)  SELECT COUNT(*) FROM "books"
=> 0
```

As we are using the option dependent: :destroy in the Book model, we can also automatically remove all authors:

```
>> Book.create(title: 'Homo faber').authors.create(first_name: 'Max',
   last_name: 'Frisch')
   (0.1ms)  begin transaction
  SQL (0.4ms)  INSERT INTO "books" ("title", "created_at", "updated_at")
  VALUES (?, ?, ?)  [["title", "Homo faber"], ["created_at", "2015-12-17
  13:50:43.062148"], ["updated_at", "2015-12-17 13:50:43.062148"]]
   (9.1ms)  commit transaction
   (0.1ms)  begin transaction
  SQL (0.3ms)  INSERT INTO "authors" ("first_name", "last_name", "book_id",
  "created_at", "updated_at") VALUES (?, ?, ?, ?, ?)  [["first_name", "Max"],
  ["last_name", "Frisch"], ["book_id", 2], ["created_at", "2015-12-17
  13:50:43.083211"], ["updated_at", "2015-12-17 13:50:43.083211"]]
   (0.9ms)  commit transaction
=> #<Author id: 1, book_id: 2, first_name: "Max", last_name: "Frisch",
created_at: "2015-12-17 13:50:43", updated_at: "2015-12-17 13:50:43">
>> Author.count
   (0.2ms)  SELECT COUNT() FROM "authors"
=> 1
>> Book.first.destroy
  Book Load (0.3ms)  SELECT  "books". FROM "books"  ORDER BY "books"."id" ASC
  LIMIT 1
   (0.1ms)  begin transaction
  Author Load (0.1ms)  SELECT "authors".* FROM "authors" WHERE
  "authors"."book_id" = ?  [["book_id", 2]]
  SQL (0.3ms)  DELETE FROM "authors" WHERE "authors"."id" = ?  [["id", 1]]
  SQL (0.1ms)  DELETE FROM "books" WHERE "books"."id" = ?  [["id", 2]]
   (9.1ms)  commit transaction
=> #<Book id: 2, title: "Homo faber", created_at: "2015-12-17 13:50:43",
updated_at: "2015-12-17 13:50:43">
>> Author.count
   (0.2ms)  SELECT COUNT(*) FROM "authors"
=> 0
```

When removing records, please always consider the difference between the content of the database table and the value of the currently removed object. The instance is *frozen* after removing the database field. So it is no longer in the database, but still present in the program, yet it can no longer be modified there. It is read-only. To check, you can use the method frozen?:

```
>> book = Book.create(title: 'Homo faber')
   (0.2ms)  begin transaction
  SQL (0.5ms)  INSERT INTO "books" ("title", "created_at", "updated_at")
  VALUES (?, ?, ?)  [["title", "Homo faber"], ["created_at", "2015-12-17
  13:51:41.460050"], ["updated_at", "2015-12-17 13:51:41.460050"]]
   (8.9ms)  commit transaction
=> #<Book id: 3, title: "Homo faber", created_at: "2015-12-17 13:51:41",
updated_at: "2015-12-17 13:51:41">
>> book.destroy
   (0.1ms)  begin transaction
  Author Load (0.2ms)  SELECT "authors".* FROM "authors" WHERE
  "authors"."book_id" = ?  [["book_id", 3]]
  SQL (0.5ms)  DELETE FROM "books" WHERE "books"."id" = ?  [["id", 3]]
   (9.2ms)  commit transaction
=> #<Book id: 3, title: "Homo faber", created_at: "2015-12-17 13:51:41",
updated_at: "2015-12-17 13:51:41">
>> Book.count
   (0.2ms)  SELECT COUNT(*) FROM "books"
=> 0
>> book
=> #<Book id: 3, title: "Homo faber", created_at: "2015-12-17 13:51:41",
updated_at: "2015-12-17 13:51:41">
>> book.frozen?
=> true
```

The record has been removed from the database, but the object with all its data is still present in the running Ruby program. So could we then revive the entire record? The answer is yes, but it will then be a new record:

```
>> Book.create(title: book.title)
   (0.1ms)  begin transaction
  SQL (0.3ms)  INSERT INTO "books" ("title", "created_at", "updated_at")
  VALUES (?, ?, ?)  [["title", "Homo faber"], ["created_at", "2015-12-17
  13:52:51.438501"], ["updated_at", "2015-12-17 13:52:51.438501"]]
   (8.7ms)  commit transaction
=> #<Book id: 4, title: "Homo faber", created_at: "2015-12-17 13:52:51",
updated_at: "2015-12-17 13:52:51">
>> exit
```

delete

With delete you can remove a record directly from the database. Any dependencies to other records in the *model* are not taken into account. The method delete only deletes that one row in the database and nothing else.

Let's create a book with one author and then remove the book with delete:

```
$ rails db:reset
  [...]
$ rails console
Running via Spring preloader in process 24336
Loading development environment (Rails 5.0.0)
>> Book.create(title: 'Homo faber').authors.create(first_name: 'Max',
   last_name: 'Frisch')
   (0.5ms)  begin transaction
   [...]
   (0.8ms)  commit transaction
=> #<Author id: 1, book_id: 1, first_name: "Max", last_name: "Frisch",
created_at: "2015-12-17 13:54:46", updated_at: "2015-12-17 13:54:46">
>> Author.count
   (0.2ms)  SELECT COUNT() FROM "authors"
=> 1
>> Book.last.delete
   Book Load (0.2ms)  SELECT  "books". FROM "books"  ORDER BY "books"."id"
   DESC LIMIT 1
   SQL (1.5ms)  DELETE FROM "books" WHERE "books"."id" = ?  [["id", 1]]
=> #<Book id: 1, title: "Homo faber", created_at: "2015-12-17 13:54:46",
updated_at: "2015-12-17 13:54:46">
>> Author.count
   (0.2ms)  SELECT COUNT() FROM "authors"
=> 1
>> Book.count
   (0.2ms)  SELECT COUNT() FROM "books"
=> 0
>> exit
```

The record of the book 'Homo faber' is deleted, but the author is still in the database.

As with destroy, an object also gets frozen when you use delete (see "destroy"). The record is already removed from the database, but the object itself is still there.

Transactions

In the world of databases, the term transaction refers to a block of SQL statements that must be executed together and without interruption. If an error should occur within the transaction, the database is reset to the state before the start of the transaction.

Now and again, there are areas of application where you need to carry out a database transaction. The classic example is transferring money from one account to another. That only makes sense if both actions (debiting one account and crediting the recipient's account) are executed.

A transaction follows this pattern:

```
ApplicationRecord.transaction do
  Book.create(:title => 'A')
  Book.create(:title => 'B')
  Book.create(:title => 'C').authors.create(:last_name => 'Z')
end
```

Transactions are a complex topic. If you want to find out more, you can consult the ri help on the shell via ri ActiveRecord::Transactions::ClassMethods.

The methods `save` and `destroy` are automatically executed within the transaction *wrapper*. That way, Rails ensures that no undefined state can arise for these two methods.

 Transactions are not natively supported by all databases. In that case, the code will still work, but you no longer have the security of the transaction.

Scopes

When programming Rails applications, it is sometimes clearer and simpler to define frequent searches as separate methods. In Rails speak, these are referred to as *NamedScope*. These NamedScopes can be chained, just like other methods.

Preparation

We build a little online shop:

```
$ rails new shop
  [...]
$ cd shop
$ rails generate model product name 'price:decimal{7,2}' weight:integer
  in_stock:boolean expiration_date:date
  [...]
$ rails db:migrate
  [...]
$
```

Please populate the file db/seeds.rb with the following content:

db/seeds.rb

```
Product.create(name: 'Milk (1 liter)', weight: 1000, in_stock: true, price:
0.45, expiration_date: Date.today + 14.days)
Product.create(name: 'Butter (250 g)', weight: 250, in_stock: true, price:
0.75, expiration_date: Date.today + 14.days)
Product.create(name: 'Flour (1 kg)', weight: 1000, in_stock: false, price:
0.45, expiration_date: Date.today + 100.days)
Product.create(name: 'Jelly Babies (6 x 300 g)', weight: 1500, in_stock: true,
price: 4.96, expiration_date: Date.today + 1.year)
Product.create(name: 'Super-Duper Cake Mix', in_stock: true, price: 11.12,
expiration_date: Date.today + 1.year)
Product.create(name: 'Eggs (12)', in_stock: true, price: 2, expiration_date:
Date.today + 7.days)
Product.create(name: 'Peanuts (8 x 200 g bag)', in_stock: false, weight: 1600,
price: 17.49, expiration_date: Date.today + 1.year)
```

Now drop the database and repopulate it with the db/seeds.rb:

```
$ rails db:reset
  [...]
$
```

Defining a Scope

If we want to count products that are in stock in our online shop, then we can use the following query each time:

```
$ rails console
Running via Spring preloader in process 24336
Loading development environment (Rails 5.0.0)
>> Product.where(in_stock: true).count
   (0.1ms)  SELECT COUNT(*) FROM "products" WHERE "products"."in_stock" = 't'
=> 5
>> exit
```

But we could also define a NamedScope available in the app/models/product.rb:

app/models/product.rb

```
class Product < ApplicationRecord
  scope :available, -> { where(in_stock: true) }
end
```

And then use it:

```
$ rails console
Running via Spring preloader in process 24336
Loading development environment (Rails 5.0.0)
>> Product.available.count
   (0.1ms)  SELECT COUNT(*) FROM "products" WHERE "products"."in_stock" = 't'
=> 5
>> exit
```

Let's define a second NamedScope for this example in the app/models/product.rb:

app/models/product.rb

```
class Product < ApplicationRecord
  scope :available, -> { where(in_stock: true) }
  scope :cheap, -> { where(price: 0..1) }
end
```

Now we can chain both named scopes to output all cheap products that are in stock:

```
$ rails console
Running via Spring preloader in process 24336
Loading development environment (Rails 5.0.0)
>> Product.cheap.count
   (0.3ms)  SELECT COUNT() FROM "products" WHERE ("products"."price" BETWEEN
   0 AND 1)
=> 3
>> Product.cheap.available.count
   (0.3ms)  SELECT COUNT() FROM "products" WHERE ("products"."price" BETWEEN
   0 AND 1) AND "products"."in_stock" = 't'
=> 2
>> exit
```

Passing in Arguments

If you need a NamedScope that can also process parameters, then that is no problem either. The following example outputs products that are cheaper than the specified value. The app/models/product.rb looks like this:

app/models/product.rb

```
class Product < ApplicationRecord
  scope :cheaper_than, ->(price) { where("price < ?", price) }
end
```

Now we can count all products that cost less than 50 cent:

```
$ rails console
Running via Spring preloader in process 24336
Loading development environment (Rails 5.0.0)
>> Product.cheaper_than(0.5).count
   (0.2ms)  SELECT COUNT(*) FROM "products" WHERE (price < 0.5)
=> 2
>> exit
```

Creating New Records with Scopes

Let's use the following app/models/product.rb:

app/models/product.rb

```
class Product < ApplicationRecord
  scope :available, -> { where(in_stock: true) }
end
```

With this NamedScope we can not only find all products that are in stock, but also create new products that contain the value true in the field in_stock:

```
$ rails console
Running via Spring preloader in process 24336
Loading development environment (Rails 5.0.0)
>> product = Product.available.build
=> #<Product id: nil, name: nil, price: nil, weight: nil, in_stock: true,
expiration_date: nil, created_at: nil, updated_at: nil>
>> product.in_stock
=> true
>> exit
```

This works with the method build (see "build") and create (see "create").

Validation

Non-valid records are frequently a source of errors in programs. With validates, Rails offers a quick and easy way of validating them. That way you can be sure that only meaningful records will find their way into your database.

Preparation

Let's create a new application for this chapter:

```
$ rails new shop
  [...]
$ cd shop
$ rails generate model product name 'price:decimal{7,2}' weight:integer
  in_stock:boolean expiration_date:date
  [...]
$ rails db:migrate
  [...]
$
```

The Basic Idea

For each model, there is a matching model file in the directory app/models/. In this Ruby code, we can not only define database dependencies, but also implement all validations. The advantage: Every programmer knows where to find it.

Without any validation, we can create an empty record in a model without a problem:

```
$ rails console
Running via Spring preloader in process 24336
Loading development environment (Rails 5.0.0)
>> product = Product.create
[...]
=> #<Product id: 1, name: nil, price: nil, weight: nil, in_stock: nil, expiration_date: nil,
created_at: "2016-01-21 13:18:31", updated_at: "2016-01-21 13:18:31">
>> exit
```

But in practice, this record with no content doesn't make any sense. A Product needs to have a name and a price. That's why we can define validations in ActiveRecord. Then you can ensure as programmer that only records that are valid for you are saved in your database.

To make the mechanism easier to understand, I am going to jump ahead a bit and use the presence helper. Please fill your app/models/product.rb with the following content:

app/models/product.rb

```ruby
class Product < ApplicationRecord
  validates :name,
            presence: true

  validates :price,
            presence: true
end
```

Now we try again to create an empty record in the console:

```
$ rails console
Running via Spring preloader in process 24336
Loading development environment (Rails 5.0.0)
>> product = Product.create
   (0.1ms)  begin transaction
   (0.1ms)  rollback transaction
=> #<Product id: nil, name: nil, price: nil, weight: nil, in_stock: nil,
expiration_date: nil, created_at: nil, updated_at: nil>
```

Watch out for the `rollback transaction` part and the missing id of the `Product` object! Rails began the transaction of creating a new record but for some reason it couldn't do it. So it had to rollback the transaction. The validation method intervened before the record was saved. So validating happens before saving.

Can we access the errors? Yes, via the method `errors` or with `errors.messages` we can look at the errors that occurred:

```
>> product.errors
=> <ActiveModel::Errors:0x007ff515a71680 @base=<Product id: nil, name: nil,
price: nil, weight: nil, in_stock: nil, expiration_date: nil, created_at: nil,
updated_at: nil>, @messages={:name=>["can't be blank"], :price=>["can't be
blank"]}>
>> product.errors.messages
=> {:name=>["can't be blank"], :price=>["can't be blank"]}
```

This error message was defined for a human and English-speaking user.

Only once we assign a value to the attributes `name` and `price`, we can save the object:

```
>> product.name = 'Milk (1 liter)'
=> "Milk (1 liter)"
>> product.price = 0.45
=> 0.45
>> product.save
   (0.1ms)  begin transaction
  SQL (0.5ms)  INSERT INTO "products" ("name", "price", "created_at",
  "updated_at") VALUES (?, ?, ?, ?)  [["name", "Milk (1 liter)"], ["price",
  0.45], ["created_at", "2015-12-17 17:59:09.293831"], ["updated_at",
  "2015-12-17 17:59:09.293831"]]
   (9.0ms)  commit transaction
=> true
```

valid?

The method `valid?` indicates in boolean form if an object is valid. So you can check the validity already before you save:

```
>> product = Product.new
=> #<Product id: nil, name: nil, price: nil, weight: nil, in_stock: nil,
expiration_date: nil, created_at: nil, updated_at: nil>
>> product.valid?
=> false
```

save(validate: false)

As so often in life, you can find a way around everything. If you pass the parameter `:validate ⇒ false` to the method `save`, the data of `Validation` is saved:

```
>> product = Product.new
=> #<Product id: nil, name: nil, price: nil, weight: nil, in_stock: nil,
expiration_date: nil, created_at: nil, updated_at: nil>
>> product.valid?
=> false
>> product.save
   (0.1ms)  begin transaction
   (0.1ms)  rollback transaction
=> false
>> product.save(validate: false)
   (0.1ms)  begin transaction
  SQL (0.5ms)  INSERT INTO "products" ("created_at", "updated_at") VALUES (?,
  ?)  [["created_at", "2015-12-17 18:01:46.173590"], ["updated_at",
  "2015-12-17 18:01:46.173590"]]
   (9.1ms)  commit transaction
=> true
>> exit
```

 I assume that you understand the problems involved here.   Please only use this option
if there is a really good reason   to do so.

presence

In our model product there are a few fields that must be filled in in any case. We can achieve this via presence.

app/models/product.rb

```
class Product < ApplicationRecord
  validates :name,
            presence: true

  validates :price,
            presence: true
end
```

If we try to create an empty user record with this, we get lots of validation errors:

```
$ rails console
Running via Spring preloader in process 24336
Loading development environment (Rails 5.0.0)
>> product = Product.create
   (0.1ms)  begin transaction
   (0.1ms)  rollback transaction
=> #<Product id: nil, name: nil, price: nil, weight: nil, in_stock: nil,
expiration_date: nil, created_at: nil, updated_at: nil>
>> product.errors.messages
=> {:name=>["can't be blank"], :price=>["can't be blank"]}
```

Only once we have entered all the data, the record can be saved:

```
>> product.name = 'Milk (1 liter)'
=> "Milk (1 liter)"
>> product.price = 0.45
=> 0.45
>> product.save
   (0.1ms)  begin transaction
  SQL (0.6ms)  INSERT INTO "products" ("name", "price", "created_at",
  "updated_at") VALUES (?, ?, ?, ?) [["name", "Milk (1 liter)"], ["price",
  0.45], ["created_at", "2015-12-17 18:04:26.587946"], ["updated_at",
  "2015-12-17 18:04:26.587946"]]
   (9.2ms)  commit transaction
=> true
>> exit
```

length

With length you can limit the length of a specific attribute. It's easiest to explain using an example. Let us limit the maximum length of the name to 20 and the minimum to 2.

app/models/product.rb

```ruby
class Product < ApplicationRecord
  validates :name,
            presence: true,
            length: { in: 2..20 }

  validates :price,
            :presence => true
end
```

If we now try to save a Product with a name that consists in one letter, we get an error message:

```
$ rails console
Running via Spring preloader in process 24336
Loading development environment (Rails 5.0.0)
>> product = Product.create(:name => 'M', :price => 0.45)
   (0.1ms)  begin transaction
   (0.1ms)  rollback transaction
=> #<Product id: nil, name: "M", price:
#<BigDecimal:7ff735513400,'0.45E0',9(27)>, weight: nil, in_stock: nil,
expiration_date: nil, created_at: nil, updated_at: nil>
>> product.errors.messages
=> {:name=>["is too short (minimum is 2 characters)"]}
```

Options

length can be called with the following options.

minimum

The minimum length of an attribute. Example:

```ruby
validates :name,
          presence: true,
          length: { minimum: 2 }
```

116

too_short

Defines the error message of :minimum. Default: "is too short (min is %d characters)". Example:

```
validates :name,
          presence: true,
          length: { minimum: 5 ,
          too_short: "must have at least %{count} characters"}
```

maximum

The maximum length of an attribute. Example:

```
validates :name,
          presence: true,
          length: { maximum: 20 }
```

too_long

Defines the error message of :maximum. Default: "is too long (maximum is %d characters)". Example:

```
validates :name,
          presence: true,
          length: { maximum: 20 ,
          too_long: "must have at most %{count} characters" }
```

 For all error messages, please note the chapter Internationalization.

is

Is exactly the specified number of characters long. Example:

```
validates :name,
          presence: true,
          length: { is: 8 }
```

:in or :within

Defines a length interval. The first number specifies the minimum number of the range and the second the maximum. Example:

```
validates :name,
          presence: true,
          length: { in: 2..20 }
```

tokenizer

You can use this to define how the attribute should be split for counting. Default: lambda{ |value| value.split(//) } (individual characters are counted). Example (for counting words):

```
validates :content,
          presence: true,
          length: { in: 2..20 },
          tokenizer: lambda {|str| str.scan(/\w+/)}
```

numericality

With numericality you can check if an attribute is a number. It's easier to explain if we use an example.

app/models/product.rb

```
class Product < ApplicationRecord
  validates :name,
            presence: true,
            length: { in: 2..20 }

  validates :price,
            presence: true

  validates :weight,
            numericality: true
end
```

If we now use a weight that consists of letters or contains letters instead of numbers, we will get an error message:

```
$ rails console
Running via Spring preloader in process 24336
Loading development environment (Rails 5.0.0)
>> product = Product.create(name: 'Milk (1 liter)',
   price: 0.45, weight: 'abc')
   (0.1ms)  begin transaction
   (0.1ms)  rollback transaction
=> #<Product id: nQil, name: "Milk (1 liter)", price: #<BigDecimal:7fca1ec90ed8,'0.45E0',9(27)>,
weight: 0, in_stock: nil, expiration_date: nil, created_at: nil, updated_at: nil>
>> product.errors.messages
=> {:weight=>["is not a number"]}
>> exit
```

 You can use numericality to define the content as number even   if an attribute is saved as string in the database.

Options

numericality can be called with the following options.

only_integer

The attribute can only contain an integer. Default: false. Example:

```
validates :weight,
          numericality: { only_integer: true }
```

greater_than

The number saved in the attribute must be greater than the specified value. Example:

```
validates :weight,
          numericality: { greater_than: 100 }
```

greater_than_or_equal_to

The number saved in the attribute must be greater than or equal to the specified value. Example:

```
validates :weight,
          numericality: { greater_than_or_equal_to: 100 }
```

equal_to

Defines a specific value that the attribute must have. Example:

```
validates :weight,
          numericality: { equal_to: 100 }
```

less_than

The number saved in the attribute must be less than the specified value. Example:

```
validates :weight,
          numericality: { less_than: 100 }
```

less_than_or_equal_to

The number saved in the attribute must be less than or equal to the specified value. Example:

```
validates :weight,
          numericality: { less_than_or_equal_to: 100 }
```

odd

The number saved in the attribute must be an odd number. Example:

```
validates :weight,
          numericality: { odd: true }
```

even

The number saved in the attribute must be an even number. Example:

```
validates :weight,
          numericality: { even: true }
```

uniqueness

With uniqueness you can define that the value of this attribute must be unique in the database. If you want a product in the database to have a unique name that appears nowhere else, then you can use this validation:

app/models/product.rb

```
class Product < ApplicationRecord
  validates :name,
            presence: true,
            uniqueness: true
end
```

If we now try to create a new `Product` with a `name` that already exists, then we get an error message:

```
$ rails console
Running via Spring preloader in process 24336
Loading development environment (Rails 5.0.0)
>> Product.last
  Product Load (0.2ms)  SELECT  "products".* FROM "products"  ORDER BY
  "products"."id" DESC LIMIT 1
=> #<Product id: 4, name: "Milk (1 liter)", price:
#<BigDecimal:7fdccb1960b8,'0.45E0',9(27)>, weight: nil, in_stock: nil,
expiration_date: nil, created_at: "2015-12-17 18:04:26", updated_at:
"2015-12-17 18:04:26">
>> product = Product.create(name: 'Milk (1 liter)')
   (0.1ms)  begin transaction
  Product Exists (0.2ms)  SELECT  1 AS one FROM "products" WHERE
  "products"."name" = 'Milk (1 liter)' LIMIT 1
   (0.1ms)  rollback transaction
=> #<Product id: nil, name: "Milk (1 liter)", price: nil, weight: nil,
in_stock: nil, expiration_date: nil, created_at: nil, updated_at: nil>
>> product.errors.messages
=> {:name=>["has already been taken"]}
>> exit
```

 The validation via `uniqueness` is no absolute guarantee that the attribute is unique in the database. A race condition could occur (see http://en.wikipedia.org/wiki/Race_condition). A detailed discussion of this effect would go beyond the scope of book aimed at beginners (this phenomenon is extremely rare).

Options

`uniqueness` can be called with the following options.

scope

Defines a scope for the uniqueness. If we had a differently structured phone number database (with just one field for the phone number), then we could use this option to specify that a phone number must only be saved once per user. Here is what it would look like:

```
validates :name,
          presence: true,
          uniqueness: { scope: :user_id }
```

case_sensitive

Checks for uniqueness of upper and lower case as well. Default: false. Example:

```
validates :name,
          presence: true,
          uniqueness: { case_sensitive: true }
```

inclusion

With inclusion you can define from which values the content of this attribute can be created. For our example, we can demonstrate it using the attribute in_stock.

app/models/product.rb

```
class Product < ApplicationRecord
  validates :name,
            presence: true

  validates :in_stock,
            inclusion: { in: [true, false] }
end
```

In our data model, a Product must be either true or false for in_stock (there must not be a nil). If we enter a different value than true or false, a validation error is returned:

```
$ rails console
Running via Spring preloader in process 24336
Loading development environment (Rails 5.0.0)
>> product = Product.create(name: 'Milk low-fat (1 liter)')
   (0.1ms)  begin transaction
   (0.1ms)  rollback transaction
=> #<Product id: nil, name: "Milk low-fat (1 liter)", price: nil, weight: nil,
in_stock: nil, expiration_date: nil, created_at: nil, updated_at: nil>
>> product.errors.messages
=> {:in_stock=>["is not included in the list"]}
>> exit
```

 Always remember the power of Ruby! For example, you can generate the   enumerable object always live from another database. In other words,   the validation is not defined statically.

Options

inclusion can be called with the following option.

message

For outputting custom error messages. Default: "is not included in the list". Example:

```
validates :in_stock,
          inclusion: { in: [true, false],
                       message: 'this one is not allowed' }
```

 For all error messages, please note the chapter   Internationalization.

exclusion

exclusion is the inversion of inclusion. You can define from which values the content of this attribute must not be created.

app/models/product.rb

```ruby
class Product < ApplicationRecord
  validates :name,
            presence: true

  validates :in_stock,
            exclusion: { in: [nil] }
end
```

 Always remember the power of Ruby! For example, you can generate the enumerable object always live from another database. In other words, the validation does not have to be defined statically.

Options

exclusion can be called with the following option.

message

For outputting custom error messages. Example:

```ruby
validates :in_stock,
          inclusion: { in: [nil],
                       message: 'this one is not allowed' }
```

 For all error messages, please note the chapter Internationalization.

format

With format you can define via a regular expression (see http://en.wikipedia.org/wiki/Regular_expression) how the content of an attribute can be structured.

With format you can for example carry out a simple validation of the syntax of an e-mail address:

```ruby
validates :email,
          format: { with: /\A([^@\s]+)@((?:[-a-z0-9]+\.)+[a-z]{2,})\Z/i }
```

 It should be obvious that the e-mail address validation shown here is not complete. It is just meant to be an example. You can only use it to check the syntactic correctness of an e-mail address.

Options

validates_format_of can be called with the following options:

- :message

  For outputting a custom error message. Default: "is invalid". Example:

```
validates :email,
          format: { with: /\A([^@\s]+)@((?:[-a-z0-9]+\.)+[a-z]{2,})\Z/i,
                    message: 'is not a valid email address' }
```

 For all error messages, please note the chapter Internationalization.

General Validation Options

There are some options that can be used for all validations.

allow_nil

Allows the value nil. Example:

```
validates :email,
          format: { with: /\A([^@\s]+)@((?:[-a-z0-9]+\.)+[a-z]{2,})\Z/i },
          allow_nil: true
```

allow_blank

As allow_nil, but additionally with an empty string. Example:

```
validates :email,
          format: { with: /\A([^@\s]+)@((?:[-a-z0-9]+\.)+[a-z]{2,})\Z/i },
          allow_blank: true
```

on

With on, a validation can be limited to the events create, update or safe. In the following example, the validation only takes effect when the record is initially created (during the create):

```
validates :email,
          format: { with: /\A([^@\s]+)@((?:[-a-z0-9]+\.)+[a-z]{2,})\Z/i },
          on: :create
```

if and unless

if or unless call the specified method and only execute the validation if the result of the method is true:

```
validates :name,
          presence: true,
          if: :today_is_monday?

def today_is_monday?
  Date.today.monday?
end
```

proc

:proc calls a Proc object. The functionality of a Proc object is beyond the scope of this book. I give you an example how to use it without describing the magic behind.

```
validates :name,
          presence: true,
          if: Proc.new { |a| a.email == 'test@test.com' }
```

Writing Custom Validations

Now and then, you want to do a validation where you need custom program logic. For such cases, you can define custom validations.

Defining Validations with Your Own Methods

Let's assume you are a big shot hotel mogul and need a reservation system.

```
$ rails new my_hotel
  [...]
$ cd my_hotel
$ rails generate model reservation start_date:date end_date:date room_type
  [...]
$ rails db:migrate
  [...]
$
```

Then we specify in the app/models/reservation.rb that the attributes start_date and end_date must be present in any case, plus we use the method reservation_dates_must_make_sense to make sure that the start_date is before the end_date:

app/models/reservation.rb

```
class Reservation < ApplicationRecord
  validates :start_date,
            presence: true

  validates :end_date,
            presence: true

  validate :reservation_dates_must_make_sense

  private
  def reservation_dates_must_make_sense
    if end_date <= start_date
      errors.add(:start_date, 'has to be before the end date')
    end
  end
end
```

With errors.add we can add error messages for individual attributes. With errors.add_to_base you can add error messages for the whole object.

Let's test the validation in the console:

```
$ rails console
Running via Spring preloader in process 24336
Loading development environment (Rails 5.0.0)
>> reservation = Reservation.new(start_date: Date.today, end_date: Date.today)
=> #<Reservation id: nil, start_date: "2015-12-17", end_date: "2015-12-17",
room_type: nil, created_at: nil, updated_at: nil>
>> reservation.valid?
=> false
>> reservation.errors.messages
=> {:start_date=>["has to be before the end date"]}
>> reservation.end_date = Date.today + 1.day
=> Sat, 18 Apr 2015
>> reservation.valid?
=> true
>> reservation.save
[...]
=> true
>> exit
```

Further Documentation

The topic validations is described very well in the official Rails documentation at
http://guides.rubyonrails.org/active_record_validations.html.

Migrations

SQL database tables are generated in Rails with *migrations* and they should also be changed with *migrations*.
If you create a model with `rails generate model`, a corresponding migration file is automatically created in the
directory db/migrate/. I am going to show you the principle using the example of a shop application. Let's
create one first:

```
$ rails new shop
  [...]
$ cd shop
$
```

Then we generate a Product model:

```
$ rails generate model product name 'price:decimal{7,2}' weight:integer
  in_stock:boolean expiration_date:date
      invoke  active_record
      create    db/migrate/20151217184823_create_products.rb
      create    app/models/product.rb
      invoke    test_unit
      create      test/models/product_test.rb
      create      test/fixtures/products.yml
$
```

The migrations file db/migrate/20151217184823_create_products.rb was created. Let's have a closer look at it:

db/migrate/20151217184823_create_products.rb

```
class CreateProducts < ActiveRecord::Migration
  def change
    create_table :products do |t|
      t.string :name
      t.decimal :price, precision: 7, scale: 2
      t.integer :weight
      t.boolean :in_stock
      t.date :expiration_date

      t.timestamps null: false
    end
  end
end
```

The method change creates and deletes the database table in case of a rollback. The migration files have embedded the current time in the file name and are processed in chronological order during a migration (in other words, when you call rails db:migrate).

```
$ rails db:migrate
== 20151217184823 CreateProducts: migrating ===================================
-- create_table(:products)
   -> 0.0015s
== 20151217184823 CreateProducts: migrated (0.0016s) ==========================
$
```

Only those migrations that have not been executed yet are processed. If we call rails db:migrate again, nothing happens, because the corresponding migration has already been executed:

```
$ rails db:migrate
$
```

But if we manually delete the database with rm and then call rails db:migrate again, the migration is repeated:

```
$ rm db/development.sqlite3
$ rails db:migrate
== 20151217184823 CreateProducts: migrating ===================================
-- create_table(:products)
   -> 0.0017s
== 20151217184823 CreateProducts: migrated (0.0018s) ==========================
$
```

After a while we realise that we want to save not just the weight for some products, but also the height. So we need another database field. There is an easy to remember syntax for this, rails generate migration add_*:

```
$ rails generate migration addHeightToProduct height:integer
      invoke  active_record
      create    db/migrate/20151217185307_add_height_to_product.rb
$
```

In the migration file db/migrate/20151217185307_add_height_to_product.rb we once again find a change method:

```
class AddHeightToProduct < ActiveRecord::Migration
  def change
    add_column :products, :height, :integer
  end
end
```

With `rails db:migrate` we can start in the new migration:

```
$ rails db:migrate
== 20151217185307 AddHeightToProduct: migrating ===============================
-- add_column(:products, :height, :integer)
   -> 0.0086s
== 20151217185307 AddHeightToProduct: migrated (0.0089s) ======================
$
```

In the *console* we can look at the new field. It was added after the field `updated_at`:

```
$ rails console
Running via Spring preloader in process 24336
Loading development environment (Rails 5.0.0)
>> Product.column_names
=> ["id", "name", "price", "weight", "in_stock", "expiration_date",
"created_at", "updated_at", "height"]
>> exit
```

> ❗ Please note that you need to add the new field   in attr_accessible in
> app/models/product.rb, otherwise   you will not have access to the height attribute.

What if you want to look at the previous state of things? No problem. You can easily go back to the previous version with `rails db:rollback`:

```
$ rails db:rollback
== 20151217185307 AddHeightToProduct: reverting ===============================
-- remove_column(:products, :height, :integer)
   -> 0.0076s
== 20151217185307 AddHeightToProduct: reverted (0.0192s) ======================
$
```

Each migration has its own version number. You can find out the version number of the current status via `rails db:version`:

```
$ rails db:version
Current version: 20151217184823
$
```

> ❗ Please note that all version numbers and timestamps only apply   to the example
> printed here. If you recreate the example, you   will of course get a different
> timestamp for your own example.

You will find the corresponding version in the directory db/migrate:

```
$ ls db/migrate/
20151217184823_create_products.rb
20151217185307_add_height_to_product.rb
$
```

You can go to a specific migration via `rails db:migrate VERSION=` and add the appropriate version number after the equals sign. The number zero represents the version zero, in other words the start.

Let's try it out:

```
$ rails db:migrate VERSION=0
== 20151217184823 CreateProducts: reverting =====================================
-- drop_table(:products)
   -> 0.0007s
== 20151217184823 CreateProducts: reverted (0.0032s) ============================

$
```

The table was deleted with all data. We are back to square one.

Which Database is Used?

The database table is created through the migration. As you can see, the table names automatically get the plural of the _model_s (Person vs. people). But in which database are the tables created? This is defined in the configuration file `config/database.yml`:

config/database.yml

```
# SQLite version 3.x
#   gem install sqlite3
#
#   Ensure the SQLite 3 gem is defined in your Gemfile
#   gem 'sqlite3'
#
default: &default
  adapter: sqlite3
  pool: 5
  timeout: 5000

development:
  <<: *default
  database: db/development.sqlite3

# Warning: The database defined as "test" will be erased and
# re-generated from your development database when you run "rake".
# Do not set this db to the same as development or production.
test:
  <<: *default
  database: db/test.sqlite3

production:
  <<: *default
  database: db/production.sqlite3
```

Three different databases are defined there in YAML format (see http://www.yaml.org/ or http://en.wikipedia.org/wiki/YAML). For us, only the development database is relevant for now (first item). By

128

default, Rails usesSQLite3 there. SQLite3 may not be the correct choice for the analysis of the weather data collected worldwide, but for a quick and straightforward development of Rails applications you will quickly learn to appreciate it. In the production environment, you can later still switch to "big" databases such as MySQL or PostgreSQL.

To satisfy your curiosity, we have a quick look at the database with the command line tool sqlite3:

```
$ sqlite3 db/development.sqlite3
SQLite version 3.8.5 2014-08-15 22:37:57
Enter ".help" for usage hints.
sqlite> .tables
schema_migrations
sqlite> .quit
$
```

Nothing in it. Of course not, as we have not yet run the migration:

```
$ rails db:migrate
== 20151217184823 CreateProducts: migrating ===================================
-- create_table(:products)
   -> 0.0019s
== 20151217184823 CreateProducts: migrated (0.0020s) ==========================

== 20151217185307 AddHeightToProduct: migrating ===============================
-- add_column(:products, :height, :integer)
   -> 0.0007s
== 20151217185307 AddHeightToProduct: migrated (0.0008s) ======================

$ sqlite3 db/development.sqlite3
SQLite version 3.8.5 2014-08-15 22:37:57
Enter ".help" for usage hints.
sqlite> .tables
products            schema_migrations
sqlite> .schema products
CREATE TABLE "products" ("id" INTEGER PRIMARY KEY AUTOINCREMENT NOT NULL,
"name" varchar, "price" decimal(7,2), "weight" integer, "in_stock" boolean,
"expiration_date" date, "created_at" datetime NOT NULL, "updated_at" datetime
NOT NULL, "height" integer);
sqlite> .quit
```

The table schema_migrations is used for the versioning of the migrations. This table is created during the first migration carried out by Rails, if it does not yet exist.

Creating Index

I assume that you know what a database index is. If not, you will find a brief introduction at http://en.wikipedia.org/wiki/Database_index. In brief: you can use it to quickly search for a specific table column.

In our production database, we should index the field name in the products table. We create a new migration for that purpose:

```
$ rails generate migration create_index
     invoke  active_record
     create    db/migrate/20151217190442_create_index.rb
$
```

In the file db/migrate/20121120142002_create_index.rb we create the index with add_index in the method self.up, and in the method self.down we delete it again with remove_index:

db/migrate/20121120142002_create_index.rb

```ruby
class CreateIndex < ActiveRecord::Migration
  def up
    add_index :products, :name
  end

  def down
    remove_index :products, :name
  end
end
```

With rails db:migrate we create the index:

```
$ rails db:migrate
== CreateIndex: migrating ================================================
-- add_index(:products, :name)
   -> 0.0010s
== CreateIndex: migrated (0.0011s) =======================================

$
```

Of course we don't have to use the up and down method. We can use change too. The migration for the new index would look like this:

```ruby
class CreateIndex < ActiveRecord::Migration
  def change
    add_index :products, :name
  end
end
```

You can also create an index directly when you generate the model. In our case (an index for the attribute name) the command would look like this:

```
$ rails generate model product name:string:index
$ cat db/migrate/20151217191435_create_products.rb
class CreateProducts < ActiveRecord::Migration
  def change
    create_table :products do |t|
      t.string :name

      t.timestamps null: false
    end
    add_index :products, :name
  end
end
$
```

Automatically Added Fields (id, created_at **and** updated_at)

Rails kindly adds the following fields automatically in the default migration:

- id:integer

  This is the unique ID of the record. The field is automatically incremented by the database. For all SQL fans: NOT NULL AUTO_INCREMENT

- created_at:datetime

  The field is filled automatically by ActiveRecord when a record is created.

- updated_at:datetime

  The field is automatically updated to the current time whenever the record is edited.

So you don't have to enter these fields yourself when generating the model.

At first you may ask yourself: "Is that really necessary? Does it make sense?". But after a while you will learn to appreciate these automatic fields. Omitting them would usually be false economy.

Further Documentation

The following webpages provide excellent further information on the topic migration:

- http://api.rubyonrails.org/classes/ActiveRecord/Migration.html
  http://api.rubyonrails.org/classes/ActiveRecord/ConnectionAdapters/TableDefinition.html

- http://railscasts.com/episodes/107-migrations-in-rails-2-1

  This screencast is a bit dated (Rails version 2.1), but still good if you are trying to understand the basics.

- http://www.dizzy.co.uk/ruby_on_rails/cheatsheets/rails-migrations

Callbacks

Callbacks are defined programming hooks in the life of an ActiveRecord object. You can find a list of all callbacks at http://api.rubyonrails.org/classes/ActiveRecord/Callbacks.html. Here are the most frequently used callbacks:

- before_validation

  Executed before the validation.

- after_validation

  Executed after the validation.

- before_save

  Executed before each save.

- before_create

  Executed before the first save.

- after_save

  Executed after every save.

- after_create

  Executed after the first save.

A callback is always executed in the model. Let's assume you always want to save an e-mail address in a `User` model in lower case, but also give the user of the web interface the option to enter upper case letters. You could use a `before_save` callback to convert the attribute `email` to lower case via the method `downcase`.

The Rails application:

```
$ rails new shop
  [...]
$ cd shop
$ rails generate model user email login
  [...]
$ rails db:migrate
  [...]
$
```

Here is what the model `app/models/user.rb` would look like. The interesting stuff is the `before_save` part:

app/models/user.rb

```ruby
class User < ApplicationRecord
  validates :login,
            presence: true

  validates :email,
            presence: true,
            format: { :with => /\A([^@\s]+)@((?:[-a-z0-9]+\.)+[a-z]{2,})\Z/i }

  before_save :downcase_email

  private

  def downcase_email
    self.email = self.email.downcase
  end

end
```

Let's see in the console if it really works as we want it to:

```
$ rails console
Running via Spring preloader in process 24336
Loading development environment (Rails 5.0.0)
>> User.create(login: 'smith', email: 'SMITH@example.com')
  (0.1ms)  begin transaction
  SQL (0.5ms)  INSERT INTO "users" ("login", "email", "created_at",
"updated_at") VALUES (?, ?, ?, ?) [["login", "smith"], ["email",
"smith@example.com"], ["created_at", "2015-12-17 19:22:20.928994"],
["updated_at", "2015-12-17 19:22:20.928994"]]
  (9.0ms)  commit transaction
=> #<User id: 1, email: "smith@example.com", login: "smith", created_at:
"2015-12-17 19:22:20", updated_at: "2015-12-17 19:22:20">
>> exit
```

Even though the e-mail address was entered partly with a capital letters, ActiveRecord has indeed converted all letters automatically to lower case via the `before_save` callback.

In the chapter "Action Mailer" you will find an example for the same model where we use an `after_create` callback to automatically send an e-mail to a newly created user. In the section "Default Values" you will find an example for defining a default value for a new object via an after_initialize callback.

Default Values

If you need specific default values for an ActiveRecord object, you can easily implement this with the after_initialize callback. This method is called by ActiveRecord when a new object is created. Let's assume we have a model Order and the minimum order quantity is always 1, so we can enter 1 directly as default value when creating a new record.

Let's set up a quick example:

```
$ rails new shop
  [...]
$ cd shop
$ rails generate model order product_id:integer quantity:integer
  [...]
$ rails db:migrate
  [...]
$
```

We write an after_initialize callback into the file app/models/order.rb:

app/models/order.rb

```
class Order < ApplicationRecord
  after_initialize :set_defaults

  private
  def set_defaults
    self.quantity ||= 1
  end
end
```

And now we check in the console if a new order object automatically contains the quantity 1:

```
$ rails console
Running via Spring preloader in process 24336
Loading development environment (Rails 5.0.0)
>> order = Order.new
=> #<Order id: nil, product_id: nil, quantity: 1, created_at: nil, updated_at:
nil>
>> order.quantity
=> 1
>> exit
```

That's working fine.

Scaffolding and REST

Introduction

Scaffolding means purely and simply that a basic *scaffold* for an application is created with a generator. This scaffold not only contains the *model* but also a simple Web GUI (*views*) and of course a *controller*. The programming paradigm used for this is REST (Representational State Transfer).

You can find a definition of REST at wikipedia.org/wiki/Representational_state_transfer. My super short version: the inventor Roy Fielding described in 2000 how you can access data with a simple set of rules within the concept of CRUD and the specification of the Hypertext Transfer Protocol (HTTP). CRUD is the abbreviation for Create (SQL: INSERT), Read (SQL: SELECT), Update (SQL: UPDATE) and Delete (SQL: Delete). This created URLs that are easy to read for humans and have a certain logic. In this chapter, you will see examples showing the individual paths for the different CRUD functions.

I think the greatest frustration with Rails arises regularly from the fact that many beginners use scaffolding to get quick results without having proper basic knowledge of Ruby and without knowing what ActiveRecord is. They don't know what to do next. Fortunately, you have worked your way through the chapters "Ruby Basics", "First Steps with Rails" and "ActiveRecord", so you will be able to understand and use scaffolding straight away.

Redirects and Flash Messages

Scaffolding uses redirects and flash messages. So we have to make a little detour first to understand scaffolding.

Redirects

The name says it all, really: *redirects* are commands that you can use within the controller to "skip", i.e. redirect, to other web pages.

 A redirect returns to the browser the response 302 Moved   with the new target. So each redirect does a roundtrip to   the browser and back.

Let's create a new Rails project for a suitable example:

```
$ rails new redirect_example
[...]
$ cd redirect_example
```

Before we can redirect, we need a controller with at least two different methods. Off we go with a ping pong example:

```
$ rails generate controller Game ping pong
      create  app/controllers/game_controller.rb
       route  get 'game/pong'
       route  get 'game/ping'
      invoke  erb
      create    app/views/game
      create    app/views/game/ping.html.erb
      create    app/views/game/pong.html.erb
      invoke  test_unit
      create    test/controllers/game_controller_test.rb
      invoke  helper
      create    app/helpers/game_helper.rb
      invoke    test_unit
      invoke  assets
      invoke    coffee
      create      app/assets/javascripts/game.coffee
      invoke    scss
      create      app/assets/stylesheets/game.scss
```

The controller app/controllers/game_controller.rb has the following content:

app/controllers/game_controller.rb

```
class GameController < ApplicationController
  def ping
  end

  def pong
  end
end
```

Now for the redirect: how can we achieve that we get immediately redirected to the method pong when we go to http://localhost:3000/game/ping? Easy, you will say, we just change the route in config/routes.rb. And you are right. So we don't necessarily need a redirect. But if we want to process something else in the method ping before redirecting, then this is only possible by using a redirect_to in the controller app/controllers/game_controller.rb:

app/controllers/game_controller.rb

```
class GameController < ApplicationController
  def ping
    logger.info '+++ Example +++'
    redirect_to game_pong_path
  end

  def pong
  end
end
```

But what is game_pong_path? Let's have a look a the routes generated for this Rails application:

```
$ rails routes
   Prefix Verb URI Pattern          Controller#Action
game_ping GET  /game/ping(.:format) game#ping
game_pong GET  /game/pong(.:format) game#pong
```

As you can see, the route to the *action* ping of the controller GameController now gets the name game_ping (see beginning of the line). We could also write the redirect like this:

```
redirect_to :action => 'pong'
```

I will explain the details and the individual options of the redirect later in the context of each specific case. For now, you just need to know that you can redirect not just to another method, but also to another controller or an entirely different web page.

When we try to go to http://localhost:3000/game/ping we are automatically redirected to http://localhost:3000/game/pong and in the log output we see this:

```
Started GET "/game/ping" for 127.0.0.1 at 2015-04-15 17:50:04 +0200
Processing by GameController#ping as HTML
+++ Example +++
Redirected to http://localhost:3000/game/pong
Completed 302 Found in 14ms (ActiveRecord: 0.0ms)


Started GET "/game/pong" for 127.0.0.1 at 2015-04-15 17:50:04 +0200
Processing by GameController#pong as HTML
  Rendered game/pong.html.erb within layouts/application (2.1ms)
Completed 200 OK in 2128ms (Views: 2127.4ms | ActiveRecord: 0.0ms)
```

redirect_to :back

If you want to redirect the user of your web application to the page he has just been you can use redirect_to :back. This is very useful in a scenario where your user first has to login to get access to a specific page.

Flash Messages

In my eyes, the term *"flash messages"* is somewhat misleading. Almost anyone would associate the term "*Flash*" with more or less colorful web pages that were implemented with the Adobe Shockwave Flash Plug-in. But in Ruby on Rails, flash messages are something completely different. They are messages that are displayed, for example on the new page after a redirect (see section Redirects).

Flash messages are good friends with redirects. The two often work together in a team to give the user feedback on an action he just carried out. A typical example of a flash message is the system feedback when a user has logged in. Often the user is redirected back to the original page and gets the message "You are now logged in."

As an example, we are once more constructing the ping pong scenario from section "Redirects":

```
$ rails new pingpong
  [...]
$ cd pingpong
$ rails generate controller Game ping pong
  [...]
```

We fill the app/controllers/game_controller.rb with the following content:

app/controllers/game_controller.rb

```
class GameController < ApplicationController
  def ping
    redirect_to game_pong_path, notice: 'Ping-Pong!'
  end

  def pong
  end
end
```

Now we start the Rails web server with `rails server` and use the browser to go to http://localhost:3000/game/ping. We are redirected from ping to pong. But the flash message "Ping-Pong!" is nowhere to be seen. We first need to expand `app/views/layouts/application.html.erb`:

app/views/layouts/application.html.erb

```
<!DOCTYPE html>
<html>
<head>
  <title>Pingpong</title>
  <%= stylesheet_link_tag    'application', media: 'all', 'data-turbolinks-track' => true %>
  <%= javascript_include_tag 'application', 'data-turbolinks-track' => true %>
  <%= csrf_meta_tags %>
</head>
<body>
  <% flash.each do |name, message| %>
    <p>
      <i><%= "#{name}: #{message}" %></i>
    </p>
  <% end %>

  <%= yield %>
</body>
</html>
```

Now we see the flash message at the top of the page when we go to http://localhost:3000/game/ping in the browser:

137

If we go to http://localhost:3000/game/pong we still see the normal Pong page. But if we go to http://localhost:3000/game/ping we are redirected to the Pong page and then the flash message is displayed at the top.

 If you do not see a flash message that you were expecting, first check in the view to see if the flash message is output there.

Different Types of Flash Message

Flash messages are automagically passed to the view in a hash. By default, there are three different types: error, warning and notice. You can also invent your own category and then get it in the view later.

You can set a flash message by writing the hash directly too:

```
flash[:notice] = 'Ping-Pong!'
```

Please have a look at the official documentation at http://guides.rubyonrails.org/action_controller_overview.html#the-flash for more information.

Why Are There Flash Messages At All?

You may wonder why there are flash messages in the first place. Couldn't you just build them yourself if you need them? Yes, indeed. But flash messages have the advantage that they offer a defined approach that is the same for any programmer. So you don't need to start from scratch every single time you need one.

Generating a Scaffold

Let's first use scaffolding to create a list of products for an online shop. First, we need to create a new Rails application:

```
$ rails new shop
  [...]
$ cd shop
```

Let's look at the scaffolding options:

```
$ rails generate scaffold
Usage:
  rails generate scaffold NAME [field[:type][:index] field[:type][:index]]
  [options]

[...]

Examples:
    rails generate scaffold post
    rails generate scaffold post title body:text published:boolean
    rails generate scaffold purchase amount:decimal tracking_id:integer:uniq
    rails generate scaffold user email:uniq password:digest
```

I'll keep it short: for our current state of knowledge, we can use rails generate scaffold just like rails generate model. Let's create the scaffold for the products:

```
$ rails generate scaffold product name 'price:decimal{7,2}'
      invoke  active_record
      create    db/migrate/20151218150127_create_products.rb
      create    app/models/product.rb
      invoke    test_unit
      create      test/models/product_test.rb
      create      test/fixtures/products.yml
      invoke  resource_route
       route    resources :products
      invoke  scaffold_controller
      create    app/controllers/products_controller.rb
      invoke    erb
      create      app/views/products
      create      app/views/products/index.html.erb
      create      app/views/products/edit.html.erb
      create      app/views/products/show.html.erb
      create      app/views/products/new.html.erb
      create      app/views/products/_form.html.erb
      invoke    test_unit
      create      test/controllers/products_controller_test.rb
      invoke    helper
      create      app/helpers/products_helper.rb
      invoke      test_unit
      invoke    jbuilder
      create      app/views/products/index.json.jbuilder
      create      app/views/products/show.json.jbuilder
      invoke  assets
      invoke    coffee
      create      app/assets/javascripts/products.coffee
      invoke    css
      create      app/assets/stylesheets/products.css
      invoke  css
      create    app/assets/stylesheets/scaffold.css
```

As you can see, rails generate scaffold has already created the model. So we can directly call rails db:migrate:

```
$ rails db:migrate
== 20151218150127 CreateProducts: migrating ====================================
-- create_table(:products)
   -> 0.0023s
== 20151218150127 CreateProducts: migrated (0.0024s) ===========================
```

Let's create the first six products in the db/seeds.rb. I am not quite sure about Walter Scheel, but after all, this book is all about Rails, not German post-war history.

```
Product.create(name: 'Apple', price: 1)
Product.create(name: 'Orange', price: 1)
Product.create(name: 'Pineapple', price: 2.4)
Product.create(name: 'Marble cake', price: 3)
```

Populate with the example data:

```
$ rails db:seed
```

The Routes

`rails generate scaffold` has created a route (more on this later in the chapter "Routes"), a controller and several views for us.

We could also have done all of this manually. Scaffolding is merely an automatism that does the work for us for some basic things. This is assuming that you always want to view, create and delete records.

Without diving too deeply into the topic routes, let's just have a quick look at the available routes for our example. You need to run `rails routes`:

```
$ rails routes
       Prefix Verb   URI Pattern                  Controller#Action
     products GET    /products(.:format)          products#index
              POST   /products(.:format)          products#create
  new_product GET    /products/new(.:format)      products#new
 edit_product GET    /products/:id/edit(.:format) products#edit
      product GET    /products/:id(.:format)      products#show
              PATCH  /products/:id(.:format)      products#update
              PUT    /products/:id(.:format)      products#update
              DELETE /products/:id(.:format)      products#destroy
```

These are all the routes and consequently URLs available in this Rails application. All routes invoke actions (in other words, methods) in the `ProductsController`.

The Controller

Now it's about time we had a look at the file `app/controllers/products_controller.rb`. Scaffold automatically creates the methods index, show, new, create, update and destroy. These methods or actions are called by the routes.

Here is the content of `app/controllers/products_controller.rb`

app/controllers/products_controller.rb

```ruby
class ProductsController < ApplicationController
  before_action :set_product, only: [:show, :edit, :update, :destroy]

  # GET /products
  # GET /products.json
  def index
    @products = Product.all
  end

  # GET /products/1
  # GET /products/1.json
  def show
  end

  # GET /products/new
  def new
    @product = Product.new
  end

  # GET /products/1/edit
  def edit
  end

  # POST /products
```

```ruby
  # POST /products.json
  def create
    @product = Product.new(product_params)

    respond_to do |format|
      if @product.save
        format.html { redirect_to @product, notice: 'Product was successfully created.' }
        format.json { render :show, status: :created, location: @product }
      else
        format.html { render :new }
        format.json { render json: @product.errors, status: :unprocessable_entity }
      end
    end
  end

  # PATCH/PUT /products/1
  # PATCH/PUT /products/1.json
  def update
    respond_to do |format|
      if @product.update(product_params)
        format.html { redirect_to @product, notice: 'Product was successfully updated.' }
        format.json { render :show, status: :ok, location: @product }
      else
        format.html { render :edit }
        format.json { render json: @product.errors, status: :unprocessable_entity }
      end
    end
  end

  # DELETE /products/1
  # DELETE /products/1.json
  def destroy
    @product.destroy
    respond_to do |format|
      format.html { redirect_to products_url, notice: 'Product was successfully destroyed.' }
      format.json { head :no_content }
    end
  end

  private
    # Use callbacks to share common setup or constraints between actions.
    def set_product
      @product = Product.find(params[:id])
    end

    # Never trust parameters from the scary internet, only allow the white list through.
    def product_params
      params.require(:product).permit(:name, :price)
    end
end
```

Let us take a moment and go through this controller.

set_product

A before_action calls a private method to set an instance variable @product for the actions :show, :edit, :update and :destroy. That DRYs it up nicely:

```
before_action :set_product, only: [:show, :edit, :update, :destroy]

[...]

private
  # Use callbacks to share common setup or constraints between actions.
  def set_product
    @product = Product.find(params[:id])
  end
[...]
```

index

The index method sets the instance variable @products. It contains the result of Product.all.

```
# GET /products
# GET /products.json
def index
  @products = Product.all
end
```

show

The show method doesn't do anything. set_product before_action already set the instance variable @product. So there is not more to do.

```
# GET /products/1
# GET /products/1.json
def show
end
```

new

The new method creates a new instance of Product and saves it in the instance variable @product.

```
# GET /products/new
def new
  @product = Product.new
end
```

edit

The edit method doesn't do anything. the set_product before_action already set the instance variable @product. So there is not more to do.

```
# GET /products/1/edit
def edit
end
```

create

The create method uses Product.new to create a new instance of Product and stores it in @product. The private method product_params is used to filter the trusted parameters with a white list. When @product was

```
```

successfully saved a `redirect` to the `show` action is initiated for html requests. If a validation error occurred the `new` action will be rendered.

```ruby
# POST /products
# POST /products.json
def create
  @product = Product.new(product_params)

  respond_to do |format|
    if @product.save
      format.html { redirect_to @product, notice: 'Product was successfully
      created.' }
      format.json { render :show, status: :created, location: @product }
    else
      format.html { render :new }
      format.json { render json: @product.errors, status:
      :unprocessable_entity }
    end
  end
end

[...]

# Never trust parameters from the scary internet, only allow the white list
# through.
def product_params
  params.require(:product).permit(:name, :price)
end
```

update

The `update` method tries to update @product with the `product_params`. The private method `product_params` is used to filter the trusted parameters with a white list. When @product was successfully updated a `redirect` to the `show` action is initiated for html requests. If a validation error occured the `edit` action will be rendered.

```
# PATCH/PUT /products/1
# PATCH/PUT /products/1.json
def update
  respond_to do |format|
    if @product.update(product_params)
      format.html { redirect_to @product, notice: 'Product was successfully
      updated.' }
      format.json { render :show, status: :ok, location: @product }
    else
      format.html { render :edit }
      format.json { render json: @product.errors, status:
      :unprocessable_entity }
    end
  end
end

[...]

# Never trust parameters from the scary internet, only allow the white list
# through.
def product_params
  params.require(:product).permit(:name, :price)
end
```

destroy

The destroy method destroys @product and redirects an html request to the index action.

```
# DELETE /products/1
# DELETE /products/1.json
def destroy
  @product.destroy
  respond_to do |format|
    format.html { redirect_to products_url, notice: 'Product was successfully
    destroyed.' }
    format.json { head :no_content }
  end
end
```

The Views

Now we start the Rails web server:

```
$ rails server
=> Booting Puma
=> Rails 5.0.0 application starting in development on http://localhost:3000
=> Run rails server -h for more startup options
=> Ctrl-C to shutdown server
I, [2016-01-21T14:55:01.110254 #46894]  INFO -- : Celluloid 0.17.3 is running in BACKPORTED
mode. [ http://git.io/vJf3J ]
Puma 2.15.3 starting...
* Min threads: 0, max threads: 16
* Environment: development
* Listening on tcp://localhost:3000
```

Now a little drum roll ... dramatic suspense ... launch the web browser and go to the URL http://localhost:3000/products. You can see the list of products as simple web page.

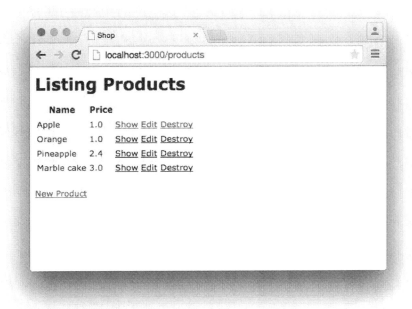

Figure 1. Products index

If you now click the link *New Product*, you will see an input form for a new record:

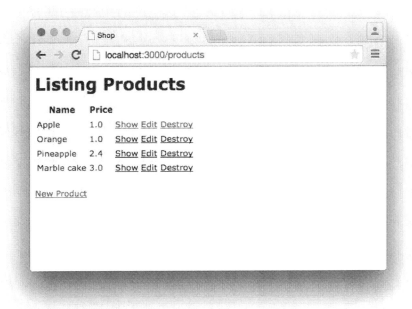

Figure 2. Products new

Use your browser's Back button to go back and click on the *Show* link in the first line. You will then see the following page:

Figure 3. Products show

If you now click *Edit*, you will see the editing view for this record:

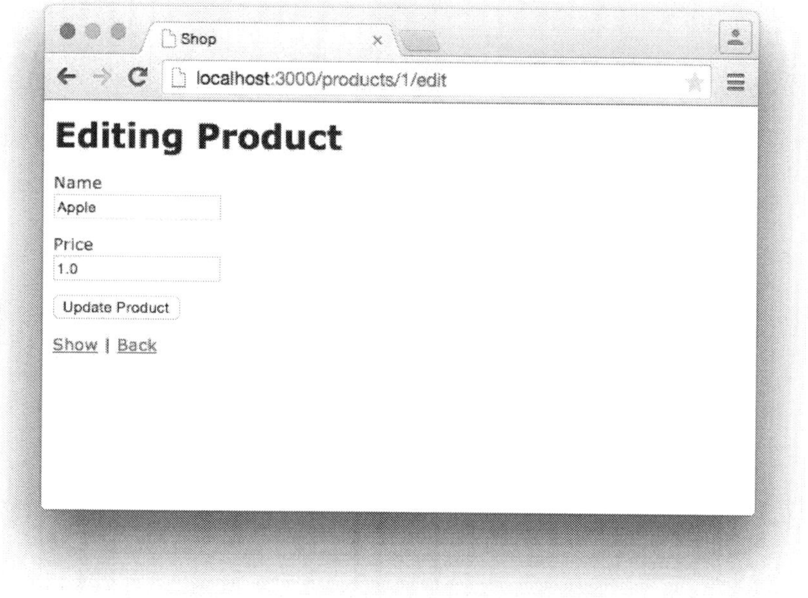

Figure 4. Products edit

And if you click *Destroy* on the Index page, you can delete a record after confirming the message that pops up.

Isn't that cool?! Within less than 10 minutes, you have written a Web application that allows you to *c*reate, *r*ead/*r*etrieve, *u*pdate and *d*elete/*d*estroy records CRUD. That is the scaffolding magic. You can save a lot of time.

Where Are the Views?

You can probably guess, but let's have a look at the directory app/views/products anyway:

```
$ tree app/views/products/
app/views/products/
├────── _form.html.erb
├────── edit.html.erb
├────── index.html.erb
├────── index.json.jbuilder
├────── new.html.erb
├────── show.html.erb
└────── show.json.jbuilder
```

There are two different file extensions. The html.erb is for HTML requests and the json.jbuilder is for JSON requests.

For index, edit, new and show the corresponding views are located there. As new and edit both require a form for editing the data, this is stored in the partial _form.html.erb in accordance with the principle of DRY (*D*on't *R*epeat *Y*ourself) and integrated in new.html.erb and edit.html.erb with a <%= render 'form' %>.

Let's open the file app/views/products/index.html.erb:

```erb
<p id="notice"><%= notice %></p>

<h1>Listing Products</h1>

<table>
  <thead>
    <tr>
      <th>Name</th>
      <th>Price</th>
      <th colspan="3"></th>
    </tr>
  </thead>

  <tbody>
    <% @products.each do |product| %>
      <tr>
        <td><%= product.name %></td>
        <td><%= product.price %></td>
        <td><%= link_to 'Show', product %></td>
        <td><%= link_to 'Edit', edit_product_path(product) %></td>
        <td><%= link_to 'Destroy', product, method: :delete, data: { confirm:
        'Are you sure?' } %></td>
      </tr>
    <% end %>
  </tbody>
</table>

<br>

<%= link_to 'New Product', new_product_path %>
```

You are now an old hand when it comes to ERB, so you'll be able to read and understand the code without any problems.

link_to

In the views generated by the scaffold generator, you first came across the helper `link_to`. This creates `<a hre ⋯>` links. You can of course also enter a link manually via `<a href="⋯">` in the erb, but for links within a Rails project, `link_to` is more practical, because you can use the names of the routes as a target. The code becomes much easier to read. In the above example, there are the following routes:

```
$ rails routes
       Prefix Verb   URI Pattern                Controller#Action
     products GET    /products(.:format)        products#index
              POST   /products(.:format)        products#create
  new_product GET    /products/new(.:format)    products#new
 edit_product GET    /products/:id/edit(.:format) products#edit
      product GET    /products/:id(.:format)    products#show
              PATCH  /products/:id(.:format)    products#update
              PUT    /products/:id(.:format)    products#update
              DELETE /products/:id(.:format)    products#destroy
```

The first part of this route is the name of the route. With a new call, this is `new_product`. A link to `new_product` looks like this in the erb code (you can see it at the end of the file `app/views/products/index.html.erb`):

```
<%= link_to 'New Product', new_product_path %>
```

In the HTML code of the generated page (http://localhost:3000/products) you can see the result:

```
<%= link_to 'New Product', new_product_path %>
```

With link_to you can also link to resources within a RESTful resource. Again, you can find examples for this in app/views/products/index.html.erb. In the table, a show, an edit and a destroy link is rendered for each product:

```
<tbody>
  <% @products.each do |product| %>
    <tr>
      <td><%= product.name %></td>
      <td><%= product.price %></td>
      <td><%= link_to 'Show', product %></td>
      <td><%= link_to 'Edit', edit_product_path(product) %></td>
      <td><%= link_to 'Destroy', product, method: :delete, data: { confirm:
      'Are you sure?' } %></td>
    </tr>
  <% end %>
</tbody>
```

From the resource and the selected route, Rails automatically determines the required URL and the required HTTP verb (in other words, whether it is a POST, GET, PUT or DELETE). For index and show calls, you need to observe the difference between singular and plural. link_to 'Show', product links to a single record and link_to 'Show', products_path links to the index view.

Whether the name of the route is used with or without the suffix _path in link_to depends on whether Rails can 'derive'' the route from the other specified information. If only one object is specified (in our example, the variable 'product), then Rails automatically assumes that it is a show route.

Examples:

ERD-Code	Explanation
link_to 'Show', Product.first	Link to the first product.
link_to 'New Product', new_product_path	Link to the Web interface where a new product can be created.
link_to 'Edit', edit_product_path(Product.first)	Link to the form where the first product can be edited.
link_to 'Destroy', Product.first, method: :delete	Link to deleting the first product.

form_for

In the partial used by new and edit, app/views/products/_form.html.erb, you will find the following code for the product form:

```
<%= form_for(@product) do |f| %>
  <% if @product.errors.any? %>
    <div id="error_explanation">
      <h2><%= pluralize(@product.errors.count, "error") %> prohibited this
      product from being saved:</h2>

      <ul>
      <% @product.errors.full_messages.each do |message| %>
        <li><%= message %></li>
      <% end %>
      </ul>
    </div>
  <% end %>

  <div class="field">
    <%= f.label :name %><br>
    <%= f.text_field :name %>
  </div>
  <div class="field">
    <%= f.label :price %><br>
    <%= f.text_field :price %>
  </div>
  <div class="actions">
    <%= f.submit %>
  </div>
<% end %>
```

In a block, the helper form_for takes care of creating the HTML form via which the user can enter the data for the record or edit it. If you delete a complete `<div class="field">` element here, this can no longer be used for input in the web interface. I am not going to comment on all possible form field variations at this point. The most frequently used ones will appear in examples later on and be explained then (if they are not self-explanatory).

You can find an overview of all form helpers at http://guides.rubyonrails.org/form_helpers.html

When using validations in the model, any validation errors that occur are displayed in the following code at the head of the form:

```
<% if @product.errors.any? %>
    <div id="error_explanation">
      <h2><%= pluralize(@product.errors.count, "error") %> prohibited this
      product from being saved:</h2>

      <ul>
      <% @product.errors.full_messages.each do |message| %>
        <li><%= message %></li>
      <% end %>
      </ul>
    </div>
  <% end %>
```

Let's add a small validation to the app/models/product.rb model:

app/models/product.rb

```
class Product < ActiveRecord::Base
  validates :name,
            presence: true
end
```

When ever somebody wants to save a product which doesn't have a name Rails will show this Flash Error:

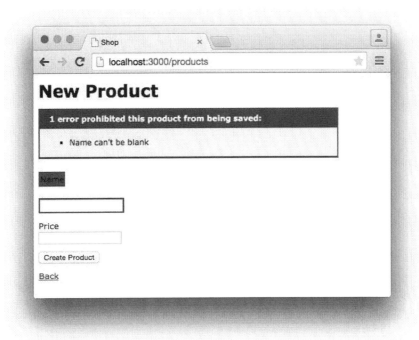

Figure 5. Products error flash

Access via JSON

By default, Rails' scaffolding generates not just access via HTML for human users, but also a direct interface for machines. The same methods index, show, new, create, update and destroy can be called via this interface, but in a format that is easier to read for machines. As an example, we will demonstrate the index action via which all data can be read in one go. With the same idea, data can be removed (destroy) or edited (update).

JSON (see wikipedia.org/wiki/Json) seems to be the new cool kid. So we use JSON.

If you do not require machine-readable access to data, you can remove these lines in the file Gemfile (followed by the command bundle).

Gemfile

```
# Build JSON APIs with ease. Read more: https://github.com/rails/jbuilder
gem 'jbuilder', '~> 2.0'
```

Of course you can delete the format.json lines manually too. But please don't forget to delete the JSON view files too.

JSON as Default

Right at the beginning of `app/controllers/products_controller.rb` you will find the entry for the index action:

app/controllers/products_controller.rb

```
# GET /products
# GET /products.json
def index
  @products = Product.all
end
```

The code is straightforward. In the instance variable `@products`, all products are saved. The view `app/views/products/index.json.jbuilder` contains the following code to render the JSON:

app/views/products/index.json.jbuilder

```
json.array!(@products) do |product|
  json.extract! product, :id, :name, :price
  json.url product_url(product, format: :json)
end
```

You can use your browser to fetch the JSON output. Just open http://localhost:3000/products.json and view the result. I installed a JSON view extension in my Chrome browser to get a nicer format.

Figure 6. Products index json

If you do not want the JSON output, you need to delete the `json.jbuilder` files.

If you ever need a JSON and XML interface in a Rails application, you just need to specify both variants in the controller in the block `respond_to`. Here is an example with the `app/controllers/products_controller.rb` in the index action:

app/controllers/products_controller.rb

```
# GET /products
# GET /products.json
# GET /products.xml
def index
  @products = product.all

  respond_to do |format|
    format.html # index.html.erb
    format.json { render json: @products }
    format.xml { render xml: @products }
  end
end
```

When Should You Use Scaffolding?

You should never use scaffolding just for the sake of it. There are Rails developers who never use scaffolding and always build everything manually. I find scaffolding quite useful for quickly getting into a new project. But it is always just the beginning.

Example for a Minimal Project

Let's assume we need a web page quickly with which we can list products and represent them individually. But we do not require an editing or deleting function. In that case, a large part of the code created via scaffold would be useless and have to be deleted. Let's try it out as follows:

```
$ rails new read-only-shop
  [...]
$ cd read-only-shop
$ rails generate scaffold product name 'price:decimal{7,2}'
  [...]
$ rails db:migrate
  [...]
```

Now create the db/seeds.rb with some demo products:

db/seeds.rb

```
Product.create(name: 'Apple', price: 1)
Product.create(name: 'Orange', price: 1)
Product.create(name: 'Pineapple', price: 2.4)
Product.create(name: 'Marble cake', price: 3)
```

And populate it with this data:

```
$ rails db:seed
```

As we only need index and show, we should delete the not required views:

```
$ rm app/views/products/_form.html.erb
$ rm app/views/products/new.html.erb
$ rm app/views/products/edit.html.erb
```

The json.jbuilder views are not needed either:

```
$ rm app/views/products/*.json.jbuilder
```

The file app/controllers/products_controller.rb can be simplified with an editor. It should look like this:

app/controllers/products_controller.rb

```
class ProductsController < ApplicationController
  # GET /products
  def index
    @products = Product.all
  end

  # GET /products/1
  def show
    @product = Product.find(params[:id])
  end
end
```

We only need the routes for index and show. Please open the file config/routes.rb and edit it as follows:

config/routes.rb

```
Rails.application.routes.draw do
  resources :products, only: [:index, :show]
end
```

A rails routes shows us that really only index and show are routed now:

```
$ rails routes
   Prefix Verb URI Pattern            Controller#Action
 products GET  /products(.:format)      products#index
  product GET  /products/:id(.:format) products#show
```

If we now start the server rails server and go to the URL http://localhost:3000/products, we get an error message.

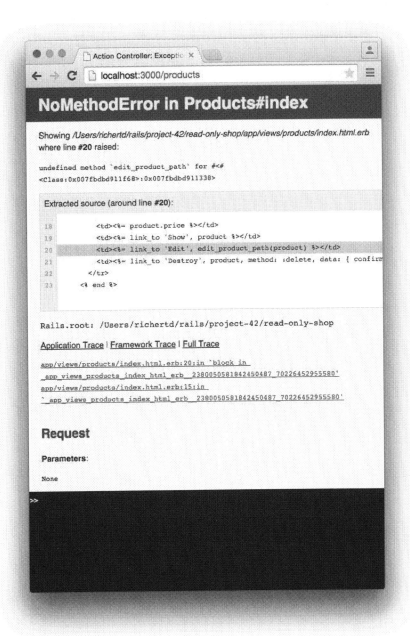

Figure 7. Products index json

The same message will be displayed in the log:

```
$ rails server
=> Booting Puma
=> Rails 5.0.0 application starting in development on http://localhost:3000
[...]

Started GET "/products" for ::1 at 2015-04-19 17:19:34 +0200
  ActiveRecord::SchemaMigration Load (0.1ms)  SELECT "schema_migrations".*
  FROM "schema_migrations"
Processing by ProductsController#index as HTML
  Product Load (0.2ms)  SELECT "products".* FROM "products"
  Rendered products/index.html.erb within layouts/application (22.3ms)
Completed 500 Internal Server Error in 55ms (ActiveRecord: 0.7ms)

ActionView::Template::Error (undefined method `edit_product_path' for
<<Class:0x007fa95920b278>:0x007fa959209ea0>):
    17:        <td><%= product.name %></td>
    18:        <td><%= product.price %></td>
    19:        <td><%= link_to 'Show', product %></td>
    20:        <td><%= link_to 'Edit', edit_product_path(product) %></td>
    21:        <td><%= link_to 'Destroy', product, method: :delete, data: {
    confirm: 'Are you sure?' } %></td>
    22:      </tr>
    23:    <% end %>
  app/views/products/index.html.erb:20:in `block in
  _app_views_products_index_html_erb3218631573957912904_70182660610380'
  app/views/products/index.html.erb:15:in
  `_app_views_products_index_html_erb3218631573957912904_70182660610380'
[...]
```

The error message states that we call an undefined method `edit_product_path` in the view
app/views/products/index.html.erb. As we only route index and show now, there are no more edit, destroy or
new methods any more. So we need to adapt the file app/views/products/index.html.erb in the editor as follows:

app/views/products/index.html.erb

```
<table>
  <thead>
    <tr>
      <th>Name</th>
      <th>Price</th>
      <th></th>
    </tr>
  </thead>

  <tbody>
    <% @products.each do |product| %>
      <tr>
        <td><%= product.name %></td>
        <td><%= product.price %></td>
        <td><%= link_to 'Show', product %></td>
      </tr>
    <% end %>
  </tbody>
</table>
```

And while we are at it, we also edit the app/views/products/show.html.erb accordingly:

```erb
<p>
  <strong>Name:</strong>
  <%= @product.name %>
</p>

<p>
  <strong>Price:</strong>
  <%= @product.price %>
</p>

<%= link_to 'Back', products_path %>
```

Now our application is finished. Start the Rails server with `rails server` and open the URL
http://localhost:3000/products in the browser.

Figure 8. ReadOnlyProducts index

 In this example, I am not commenting on the required changes in the tests, as this is not
an exercise for test driven development but meant to demonstrate a way of working
with scaffolding. TDD developers will quickly be able to adapt the tests.

Conclusion

Have a go and try it out. Try working with scaffolds one time and without them the next. Then you will soon
get a feel for whether it fits into your working method or not. I find that scaffolding makes my work much
easier for standard applications.

Routes

Introduction

In "Creating HTML Dynamically with erb" and "Scatfolding and REST" we came across *routes*. The configuration in config/routes.rb defines what happens in the Rails application when a user of a Rails application fetches a URL. A route can be static and dynamic and pass any dynamic values with variables to the controller. If several routes apply to a URL, the one that is listed at the top of config/routes.rb wins.

 If you do not have much time, you can skip this chapter for now   and get back to it later if you have any specific questions.

Let's first build a test Rails application so we can experiment:

```
$ rails new shop
  [...]
$ cd shop
```

With rails routes we can display the routes of a project. Let's try it straight away in the freshly created project:

```
$ rails routes
You don't have any routes defined!

Please add some routes in config/routes.rb.

For more information about routes, see the Rails guide:
http://guides.rubyonrails.org/routing.html.
```

That's what I call a good error message. It's a new Rails project, there are no routes yet.

HTTP GET Requests for Singular Resources

As you might know the HTTP protocol uses different so called verbs to access content on the web server (e.g. GET to request a page or POST to send a form to the server). First we'll have a look at GET requests.

Create a controller with three pages:

```
$ rails generate controller Home index ping pong
      create  app/controllers/home_controller.rb
       route  get "home/pong"
       route  get "home/ping"
       route  get "home/index"
      [...]
```

Now rails routes lists a route for these three pages:

```
$ rails routes
     Prefix Verb URI Pattern           Controller#Action
 home_index GET  /home/index(.:format) home#index
  home_ping GET  /home/ping(.:format)  home#ping
  home_pong GET  /home/pong(.:format)  home#pong
```

The pages can be accessed at the following URLs after starting the Rails server with `rails server`:

- http://localhost:3000/home/index

  for `home_index GET /home/index(.:format) home#index`

- http://localhost:3000/home/ping

  for `home_ping GET /home/ping(.:format) home#ping`

- http://localhost:3000/home/pong

  for `home_pong GET /home/pong(.:format) home#pong`

Figure 9. Home ping

With the output `home#index`, Rails tells us that the route `home/index` goes into the controller home and there to the action/method `index`. These routes are defined in the file `config/routes.rb`. `rails generate controller Home index ping pong` has automatically inserted the following lines there:

config/routes.rb

```
get "home/index"
get "home/ping"
get "home/pong"
```

Naming a Route

A route should also always have an internal name which doesn't change. In the section "HTTP Get Requests for Singular Resources" there is the following route:

```
home_pong GET /home/pong(.:format)   home#pong
```

This route has the automatically created name `home_pong`. Generally, you should always try to work with the name of the route within a Rails application. So you would point a `link_to` to `home_pong` and not to /home/pong. This has the big advantage that you can later edit (in the best case, optimize) the routing for visitors externally and do not need to make any changes internally in the application. Of course, you need to enter the old names with :as in that case.

as

If you want to define the name of a route yourself, you can do so with :as. For example, the line

```
get "home/pong", as: 'different_name'
```

results in the route

```
different_name GET  /home/pong(.:format)  home#pong
```

to

With to you can define an other destination for a rout. For example, the line

```
get "home/applepie", to: "home#ping"
```

results in the route

```
home_applepie GET  /home/applepie(.:format) home#ping
```

Parameters

The routing engine can not just assign fixed routes but also pass parameters which are part of the URL. A typical example would be date specifications (e.g. http://example.com/2010/12/ for all December postings).

To demonstrate this, let's create a mini blog application:

```
$ rails new blog
  [...]
$ cd blog
$ rails generate scaffold post subject content published_on:date
  [...]
$ rails db:migrate
  [...]
```

As example data in the db/seeds.rb we take:

db/seeds.rb

```
Post.create(subject: 'A test', published_on: '01.10.2011')
Post.create(subject: 'Another test', published_on: '01.10.2011')
Post.create(subject: 'And yet one more test', published_on: '02.10.2011')
Post.create(subject: 'Last test', published_on: '01.11.2011')
Post.create(subject: 'Very final test', published_on: '01.11.2012')
```

With rails db:seed we populate the database with this data:

```
$ rails db:seed
```

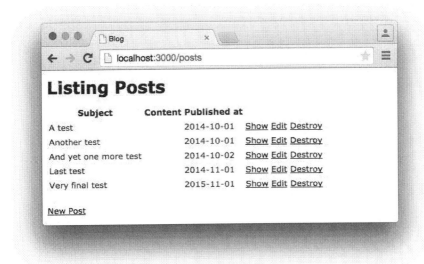

Figure 10. Posts index

If we now start the Rails server with `rails         server` and go to the page http://localhost:3000/posts in the browser, we will see this:

For this kind of blog it would of course be very useful if you could render all entries for the year 2010 with the URL http://localhost:3000/2010/ and all entries for October 1st 2010 with http://localhost:3000/2010/10/01. We can do this by using optional parameters. Please enter the following configuration in the `config/routes.rb`:

config/routes.rb

```
Blog::Application.routes.draw do
  resources :posts

  get ':year(/:month(/:day))', to: 'posts#index'
end
```

The round brackets represent optional parameters. In this case, you have to specify the year, but not necessarily the month or day. `rails routes` shows the new route at the last line:

```
$ rails routes
    Prefix Verb   URI Pattern                        Controller#Action
     posts GET    /posts(.:format)                   posts#index
           POST   /posts(.:format)                   posts#create
  new_post GET    /posts/new(.:format)               posts#new
 edit_post GET    /posts/:id/edit(.:format)          posts#edit
      post GET    /posts/:id(.:format)               posts#show
           PATCH  /posts/:id(.:format)               posts#update
           PUT    /posts/:id(.:format)               posts#update
           DELETE /posts/:id(.:format)               posts#destroy
           GET    /:year(/:month(/:day))(.:format)   posts#index
```

If we do not change anything else, we still get the same result when calling http://localhost:3000/2011/ and http://localhost:3000/2011/10/01 as we did with http://localhost:3000/posts. But have a look at the output of rails server for the request http://localhost:3000/2011

```
Started GET "/2011" for 127.0.0.1 at 2015-04-24 17:50:30 +0200
  ActiveRecord::SchemaMigration Load (0.2ms)  SELECT "schema_migrations".* FROM
"schema_migrations"
Processing by PostsController#index as HTML
  Parameters: {"year"=>"2011"}
  Post Load (0.3ms)  SELECT "posts".* FROM "posts"
  Rendered posts/index.html.erb within layouts/application (9.7ms)
Completed 200 OK in 2263ms (Views: 2243.0ms | ActiveRecord: 0.6ms)
```

The route has been recognised and an "year" ⇒ "2011" has been assigned to the hash params (written misleadingly as Parameters in the output). Going to the URL http://localhost:3000/2010/12/24 results in the following output, as expected:

```
Started GET "/2010/12/24" for 127.0.0.1 at 2015-04-24 17:52:12 +0200
Processing by PostsController#index as HTML
  Parameters: {"year"=>"2010", "month"=>"12", "day"=>"24"}
  Post Load (0.2ms)  SELECT "posts".* FROM "posts"
  Rendered posts/index.html.erb within layouts/application (2.3ms)
Completed 200 OK in 33ms (Views: 31.9ms | ActiveRecord: 0.2ms)
```

In case of the URL http://localhost:3000/2010/12/24, the following values have been saved in the hash params: "year"⇒"2010", "month"⇒"12", "day"⇒"24".

In the controller, we can access params[] to access the values defined in the URL. We simply need to adapt the index method in app/controllers/posts_controller.rb to output the posts entered for the corresponding date, month or year:

app/controllers/posts_controller.rb

```ruby
# GET /posts
# GET /posts.json
def index
  # Check if the URL requests a date.
  if Date.valid_date? params[:year].to_i, params[:month].to_i, params[:day].to_i
    start_date = Date.parse("#{params[:day]}.#{params[:month]}.#{params[:year]}")
    end_date = start_date

  # Check if the URL requests a month
  elsif Date.valid_date? params[:year].to_i, params[:month].to_i, 1
    start_date = Date.parse("1.#{params[:month]}.#{params[:year]}")
    end_date = start_date.end_of_month

  # Check if the URL requests a year
  elsif params[:year] && Date.valid_date?(params[:year].to_i, 1, 1)
    start_date = Date.parse("1.1.#{params[:year]}")
    end_date = start_date.end_of_year
  end

  if start_date && end_date
    @posts = Post.where(published_on: start_date..end_date)
  else
    @posts = Post.all
  end
end
```

If we now go to http://localhost:3000/2011/10/01 , we can see all posts of October 1st 2011.

Figure 11. Posts 2011-10-01

Constraints

In the section "Parameters" I showed you how you can read out parameters from the URL and pass them to the controller. Unfortunately, the entry defined there in the config/routes.rb

```
get ':year(/:month(/:day))', to: 'posts#index'
```

has one important disadvantage: it does not verify the individual elements. For example, the URL http://localhost:3000/just/an/example will be matched just the same and then of course results in an error:

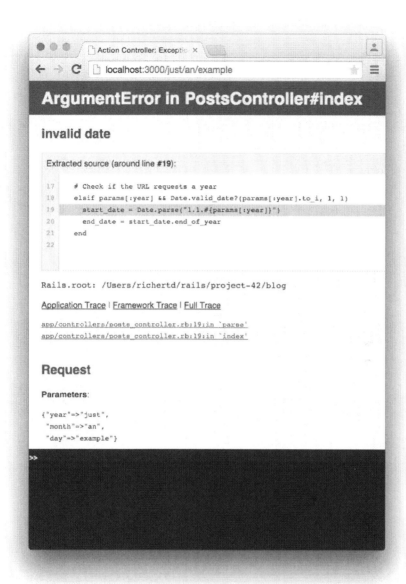

Figure 12. Fehlermeldung

In the log output in `log/development.log` we can see the following entry:

```
Started GET "/just/an/example" for ::1 at 2015-04-24 17:59:30 +0200
Processing by PostsController#index as HTML
  Parameters: {"year"=>"just", "month"=>"an", "day"=>"example"}
Completed 500 Internal Server Error in 2ms (ActiveRecord: 0.0ms)

ArgumentError (invalid date):
  app/controllers/posts_controller.rb:19:in `parse'
  app/controllers/posts_controller.rb:19:in `index'
```

Obviously, `Date.parse( "example.an.just")` cannot work. A date is made up of numbers, not letters.

Constraints can define the content of the URL more precisely via regular expressions. In the case of our blog, the `config/routes.rb` with contraints would look like this:

config/routes.rb

```
Blog::Application.routes.draw do
  resources :posts

  get ':year(/:month(/:day))', to: 'posts#index', constraints: { year:
  /\d{4}/, month: /\d{2}/, day: /\d{2}/ }
end
```

 Please note that you cannot use regex anchors such as "^" in regular   expressions in a constraint.

If we go to the URL again with this configuration, Rails gives us an error message "No route matches":

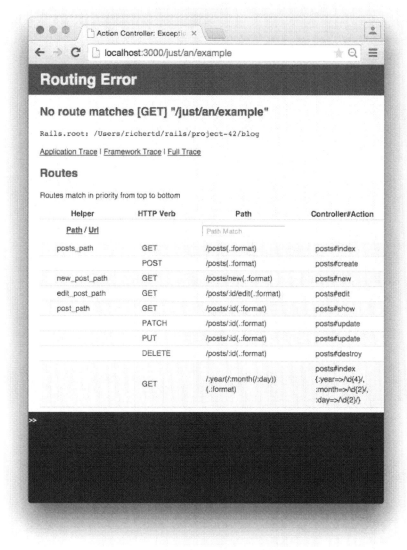

Figure 13. No route error

Redirects

Our current application answers request in the format YYYY/MM/DD (4 digits for the year, 2 digits for the month and 2 digits for the day). That is ok for machines but maybe a human would request a single digit month (like January) and a single digit day without adding the extra 0 to make it two digits. We can fix that with a couple of redirect rules which catch these URLs and redirect them to the correct ones.

config/routes.rb

```
Blog::Application.routes.draw do
  resources :posts

  get ':year/:month/:day', to: redirect("/%{year}/0%{month}/0%{day}"),
  constraints: { year: /\d{4}/, month: /\d{1}/, day: /\d{1}/ }
  get ':year/:month/:day', to: redirect("/%{year}/0%{month}/%{day}"),
  constraints: { year: /\d{4}/, month: /\d{1}/, day: /\d{2}/ }
  get ':year/:month/:day', to: redirect("/%{year}/%{month}/0%{day}"),
  constraints: { year: /\d{4}/, month: /\d{2}/, day: /\d{1}/ }
  get ':year/:month', to: redirect("/%{year}/0%{month}"), constraints: { year:
  /\d{4}/, month: /\d{1}/ }

  get ':year(/:month(/:day))', to: 'posts#index', constraints: { year:
  /\d{4}/, month: /\d{2}/, day: /\d{2}/ }
end
```

With this set of redirect rules, we can ensure that a user of the page can also enter single-digit days and months and still ends up in the right place, or is redirected to the correct format.

 Redirects in the `config/routes.rb` are by default http redirects with the code 301 ("Moved Permanently"). So even search engines will profit from this.

root :to ⇒ `welcome#index'

Lets switch back to our previous created shop-project.

```
$ cd ../shop
```

In the default `config/routes.rb` file you will find the following comment quite a long way down:

config/routes.rb

```
# You can have the root of your site routed with "root"
# root 'welcome#index'
```

If you comment out the last line there, you can define your http://localhost:3000/ with it. Let's put it on `home#index:

config/routes.rb

```
Shop::Application.routes.draw do
  get "home/index"
  get "home/ping"
  get "home/pong"
  root 'home#index'
end
```

Our new routes:

```
$ rails routes
    Prefix Verb URI Pattern           Controller#Action
home_index GET  /home/index(.:format) home#index
 home_ping GET  /home/ping(.:format)  home#ping
 home_pong GET  /home/pong(.:format)  home#pong
      root GET  /
```

If we go to the root URL http://localhost:3000 we now see home#index.

Figure 14. home index

resources

resources provides routes for a RESTful resource. Let's try it with the mini blog application:

```
$ rails new blog
  [...]
$ cd blog
$ rails generate scaffold post subject content published_on:date
  [...]
$ rails db:migrate
  [...]
```

The scaffold generator automatically creates a resources route in the config/routes.rb:

config/routes.rb

```
Blog::Application.routes.draw do
  resources :posts
end
```

 New routes are always added at the beginning of config/routes.rb by   rails generate scripts.

The resulting routes:

```
$ rails routes
    Prefix Verb   URI Pattern             Controller#Action
     posts GET    /posts(.:format)        posts#index
           POST   /posts(.:format)        posts#create
  new_post GET    /posts/new(.:format)    posts#new
 edit_post GET    /posts/:id/edit(.:format) posts#edit
      post GET    /posts/:id(.:format)    posts#show
           PATCH  /posts/:id(.:format)    posts#update
           PUT    /posts/:id(.:format)    posts#update
           DELETE /posts/:id(.:format)    posts#destroy
```

You have already encountered these RESTful routes in the chapter "Scaffolding and REST". They are required for displaying and editing records.

Selecting Specific Routes with only: or except:

If you only want to use specific routes from the finished set of RESTful routes, you can limit them with :only or :except.

The following config/routes.rb defines only the routes for index and show:

config/routes.rb

```
Blog::Application.routes.draw do
  resources :posts, only: [:index, :show]
end
```

With rails routes we can check the result:

```
$ rails routes
Prefix Verb URI Pattern          Controller#Action
 posts GET  /posts(.:format)     posts#index
  post GET  /posts/:id(.:format) posts#show
```

except works exactly the other way round:

config/routes.rb

```
Blog::Application.routes.draw do
  resources :posts, except: [:index, :show]
end
```

Now all routes except for index and show are possible:

```
$ rails routes
    Prefix Verb   URI Pattern             Controller#Action
     posts POST   /posts(.:format)        posts#create
  new_post GET    /posts/new(.:format)    posts#new
 edit_post GET    /posts/:id/edit(.:format) posts#edit
      post PATCH  /posts/:id(.:format)    posts#update
           PUT    /posts/:id(.:format)    posts#update
           DELETE /posts/:id(.:format)    posts#destroy
```

When using only and except, please make sure you also adapt the views generated by the scaffold generator. For example, there is a link on the index page to the new view with `<%= link_to 'New Post', new_post_path %>` but this view no longer exists in the above only example.

Nested Resources

Nested resources refer to routes of resources that work with an association. These can be addressed precisely via routes. Let's create a second resource, comment:

```
$ rails generate scaffold comment post_id:integer content
  [...]
$ rails db:migrate
  [...]
```

Now we associate the two resources. In the file app/models/post.rb, we add a has_many:

app/models/post.rb

```
class Post < ActiveRecord::Base
  has_many :comments
end
```

And in the file app/models/comment.rb, its counterpart belongs_to:

app/models/comment.rb

```
class Comment < ActiveRecord::Base
  belongs_to :post
end
```

The routes generated by the scaffold generator look like this:

```
$ rails routes
      Prefix Verb   URI Pattern                  Controller#Action
    comments GET    /comments(.:format)          comments#index
             POST   /comments(.:format)          comments#create
 new_comment GET    /comments/new(.:format)      comments#new
edit_comment GET    /comments/:id/edit(.:format) comments#edit
     comment GET    /comments/:id(.:format)      comments#show
             PATCH  /comments/:id(.:format)      comments#update
             PUT    /comments/:id(.:format)      comments#update
             DELETE /comments/:id(.:format)      comments#destroy
       posts POST   /posts(.:format)             posts#create
    new_post GET    /posts/new(.:format)         posts#new
   edit_post GET    /posts/:id/edit(.:format)    posts#edit
        post PATCH  /posts/:id(.:format)         posts#update
             PUT    /posts/:id(.:format)         posts#update
             DELETE /posts/:id(.:format)         posts#destroy
```

So we can get the first post with /posts/1 and all the comments with /comments. By using nesting, we can get all comments with the ID 1 via /posts/1/ comments. We need to change the config/routes.rb:

config/routes.rb

```ruby
Blog::Application.routes.draw do
  resources :posts do
    resources :comments
  end
end
```

This gives us the desired routes:

```
$ rails routes
           Prefix Verb   URI Pattern                                Controller#Action
    post_comments GET    /posts/:post_id/comments(.:format)         comments#index
                  POST   /posts/:post_id/comments(.:format)         comments#create
 new_post_comment GET    /posts/:post_id/comments/new(.:format)     comments#new
edit_post_comment GET    /posts/:post_id/comments/:id/edit(.:format) comments#edit
     post_comment GET    /posts/:post_id/comments/:id(.:format)     comments#show
                  PATCH  /posts/:post_id/comments/:id(.:format)     comments#update
                  PUT    /posts/:post_id/comments/:id(.:format)     comments#update
                  DELETE /posts/:post_id/comments/:id(.:format)     comments#destroy
            posts GET    /posts(.:format)                           posts#index
                  POST   /posts(.:format)                           posts#create
         new_post GET    /posts/new(.:format)                       posts#new
        edit_post GET    /posts/:id/edit(.:format)                  posts#edit
             post GET    /posts/:id(.:format)                       posts#show
                  PATCH  /posts/:id(.:format)                       posts#update
                  PUT    /posts/:id(.:format)                       posts#update
                  DELETE /posts/:id(.:format)                       posts#destroy
```

But we still need to make some changes in the file app/controllers/comments_controller.rb. This ensures that only the Comments of the specified Post can be displayed or changed:

app/controllers/comments_controller.rb

```ruby
class CommentsController < ApplicationController
  before_action :set_post
  before_action :set_comment, only: [:show, :edit, :update, :destroy]

  # GET /comments
  # GET /comments.json
  def index
    @comments = Comment.all
  end

  # GET /comments/1
  # GET /comments/1.json
  def show
  end

  # GET /comments/new
  def new
    @comment = @post.comments.build
  end

  # GET /comments/1/edit
  def edit
  end
```

```ruby
# POST /comments
# POST /comments.json
def create
  @comment = @post.comments.build(comment_params)

  respond_to do |format|
    if @comment.save
      format.html { redirect_to @comment, notice: 'Comment was successfully
      created.' }
      format.json { render action: 'show', status: :created, location:
      @comment }
    else
      format.html { render action: 'new' }
      format.json { render json: @comment.errors, status:
      :unprocessable_entity }
    end
  end
end

# PATCH/PUT /comments/1
# PATCH/PUT /comments/1.json
def update
  respond_to do |format|
    if @comment.update(comment_params)
      format.html { redirect_to @comment, notice: 'Comment was successfully
      updated.' }
      format.json { head :no_content }
    else
      format.html { render action: 'edit' }
      format.json { render json: @comment.errors, status:
      :unprocessable_entity }
    end
  end
end

# DELETE /comments/1
# DELETE /comments/1.json
def destroy
  @comment.destroy
  respond_to do |format|
    format.html { redirect_to comments_url }
    format.json { head :no_content }
  end
end

private
  def set_post
    @post = Post.find(params[:post_id])
  end

  # Use callbacks to share common setup or constraints between actions.
  def set_comment
    @comment = @post.comments.find(params[:id])
  end

  # Never trust parameters from the scary internet, only allow the white
  # list through.
  def comment_params
    params.require(:comment).permit(:post_id, :content)
  end
```

```
  end
```

Unfortunately, this is only half the story, because the views still link to the old routes. So we need to adapt each view in accordance with the nested route.

Please note that you need to change the form_for call to form_for([@post, @comment]).

app/views/comments/_form.html.erb

```erb
<%= form_for([@post, @comment]) do |f| %>
  <% if @comment.errors.any? %>
    <div id="error_explanation">
      <h2><%= pluralize(@comment.errors.count, "error") %> prohibited this
      comment from being saved:</h2>

      <ul>
      <% @comment.errors.full_messages.each do |msg| %>
        <li><%= msg %></li>
      <% end %>
      </ul>
    </div>
  <% end %>

  <div class="field">
    <%= f.label :content %><br />
    <%= f.text_field :content %>
  </div>
  <div class="actions">
    <%= f.submit %>
  </div>
<% end %>
```

app/views/comments/edit.html.erb

```erb
<h1>Editing comment</h1>

<%= render 'form' %>

<%= link_to 'Show', [@post, @comment] %> |
<%= link_to 'Back', post_comments_path(@post) %>
```

app/views/comments/index.html.erb

```erb
<h1>Listing comments</h1>

<table>
  <thead>
    <tr>
      <th>Post</th>
      <th>Content</th>
      <th colspan="3"></th>
    </tr>
  </thead>

  <tbody>
    <% @comments.each do |comment| %>
      <tr>
        <td><%= comment.post_id %></td>
        <td><%= comment.content %></td>
        <td><%= link_to 'Show', [@post, comment] %></td>
        <td><%= link_to 'Edit', edit_post_comment_path(@post, comment) %></td>
        <td><%= link_to 'Destroy', [@post, comment], method: :delete, data: {
        confirm: 'Are you sure?' } %></td>
      </tr>
    <% end %>
  </tbody>
</table>

<br>

<%= link_to 'New Comment', new_post_comment_path(@post) %>
```

app/views/comments/new.html.erb

```erb
<h1>New comment</h1>

<%= render 'form' %>

<%= link_to 'Back', post_comments_path(@post) %>
```

app/views/comments/show.html.erb

```erb
<p id="notice"><%= notice %></p>

<p>
  <b>Post:</b>
  <%= @comment.post_id %>
</p>

<p>
  <b>Content:</b>
  <%= @comment.content %>
</p>

<%= link_to 'Edit', edit_post_comment_path(@post, @comment) %> |
<%= link_to 'Back', post_comments_path(@post) %>
```

Please go ahead and have a go at experimenting with the URLs listed under rails routes. You can now generate a new post with /posts/new and a new comment for this post with /posts/:post_id/comments/new.

If you want to see all comments of the first post you can access that with the URL http://localhost:3000/posts/1/comments. It would look like this:

Figure 15. listing comments

Shallow Nesting

Sometimes it is a better option to use shallow nesting. For our example the config/routes.rb would contain the following routes:

config/routes.rb

```
Blog::Application.routes.draw do
  resources :posts do
    resources :comments, only: [:index, :new, :create]
  end

  resources :comments, except: [:index, :new, :create]
end
```

That would lead to a less messy rails routes output:

```
$ rails routes
         Prefix Verb   URI Pattern                             Controller#Action
  post_comments GET    /posts/:post_id/comments(.:format)       comments#index
                POST   /posts/:post_id/comments(.:format)       comments#create
new_post_comment GET   /posts/:post_id/comments/new(.:format)  comments#new
          posts GET    /posts(.:format)                         posts#index
                POST   /posts(.:format)                         posts#create
       new_post GET    /posts/new(.:format)                     posts#new
      edit_post GET    /posts/:id/edit(.:format)                posts#edit
           post GET    /posts/:id(.:format)                     posts#show
                PATCH  /posts/:id(.:format)                     posts#update
                PUT    /posts/:id(.:format)                     posts#update
                DELETE /posts/:id(.:format)                     posts#destroy
   edit_comment GET    /comments/:id/edit(.:format)             comments#edit
        comment GET    /comments/:id(.:format)                  comments#show
                PATCH  /comments/:id(.:format)                  comments#update
                PUT    /comments/:id(.:format)                  comments#update
                DELETE /comments/:id(.:format)                  comments#destroy
```

Shallow nesting trys to combine the best of two worlds. And because it is often used there is a shortcut. You can use the following config/routes.rb to achieve it:

config/routes.rb

```
Blog::Application.routes.draw do
  resources :posts do
    resources :comments, shallow: true
  end
end
```

Comments on Nested Resources

Generally, you should never nest more deeply than one level and nested resources should feel natural. After a while, you will get a feel for it. In my opinion, the most important point about RESTful routes is that they should feel logical. If you phone a fellow Rails programmer and say "I've got a resource post and a resource comment here", then both parties should immediately be clear on how you address these resources via REST and how you can nest them.

Further Information on Routes

The topic routes is far more complex than we can address here. For example, you can also involve other HTTP methods/verbs. The official routing documentation http://guides.rubyonrails.org/routing.html will give you a lot of information an examples for these features and edge cases.

Bundler and Gems

Gems constitute the package management in the world of Ruby.

 If you do not have much time, you can skip this chapter for now and get back to it later if you have any specific questions.

If a Ruby developer wants to offer a specific feature or a certain program or collection of programs to other Ruby developers, he can create a "gem" from these. This gem can then be installed via `gem install`.

 Have a look at https://www.ruby-toolbox.com to get an overview of the existing gems.

In a Rails project, different gems are used and a developer can also add further gems. The programm `bundle` helps the developer to install all these gems in the right version and to take into account dependencies. In older Rails versions, you as developer had to always call a `bundle install` after a `rails new`. Now, this is done automatically within `rails new`.

The file `Gemfile` generated by `rails new` indicates which gems are to be installed by Bundler:

```
source 'https://rubygems.org'

# Bundle edge Rails instead: gem 'rails', github: 'rails/rails'
gem 'rails', '>= 5.0.0', '< 5.1'
# Use sqlite3 as the database for Active Record
gem 'sqlite3'
# Use Uglifier as compressor for JavaScript assets
gem 'uglifier', '>= 1.3.0'
# Use CoffeeScript for .coffee assets and views
gem 'coffee-rails', '~> 4.1.0'
# See https://github.com/rails/execjs#readme for more supported runtimes
# gem 'therubyracer', platforms: :ruby

# Use jquery as the JavaScript library
gem 'jquery-rails'
# Turbolinks makes following links in your web application faster. Read more:
https://github.com/rails/turbolinks
gem 'turbolinks'
# Build JSON APIs with ease. Read more: https://github.com/rails/jbuilder
gem 'jbuilder', '~> 2.0'
# Use Puma as the app server
gem 'puma'

# Use ActiveModel has_secure_password
# gem 'bcrypt', '~> 3.1.7'

# Use Capistrano for deployment
# gem 'capistrano-rails', group: :development

group :development, :test do
  # Call 'byebug' anywhere in the code to stop execution and get a debugger console
  gem 'byebug'
end

group :development do
  # Access an IRB console on exception pages or by using <%= console %> in views
  gem 'web-console', '~> 3.0'
  # Spring speeds up development by keeping your application running in the background. Read
more: https://github.com/rails/spring
  gem 'spring'
end

# Windows does not include zoneinfo files, so bundle the tzinfo-data gem
gem 'tzinfo-data', platforms: [:mingw, :mswin, :x64_mingw, :jruby]
```

The format used is easy to explain: the word gem is followed by the name of the gem and then, if required, a specification of the version of the gem.

For example, the line gem 'rails', '5.0.0' stands for "install the gem with the name rails in the version 5.0.0".

With ~> before the version number you can determine that the newest version after this version number should be installed. As a result, the last digit is incremented, so for example gem 'rails', '~> 4.0.0' would correspondingly install a Rails 4.0.1, but not a 4.1 (for the latter, you would need to specify gem 'rails', '~> 4.1').

You have the option of installing certain gems only in certain environments. To do so, you need to enclose the corresponding lines in a `group :name do` loop.

Apart from the file `Gemfile` there is also the file `Gemfile.lock` and the exact versions of the installed gems are listed there. In the above example, it looks like this:

Gemfile.lock

```
GEM
  remote: https://rubygems.org/
  specs:
    actioncable (5.0.0.1)
      actionpack (= 5.0.0.1)
      celluloid (~> 0.17.2)
      coffee-rails (~> 4.1.0)
      em-hiredis (~> 0.3.0)
      faye-websocket (~> 0.10.0)
      redis (~> 3.0)
      websocket-driver (~> 0.6.1)
    actionmailer (5.0.0.1)
      actionpack (= 5.0.0.1)
      actionview (= 5.0.0.1)
      activejob (= 5.0.0.1)
      mail (~> 2.5, >= 2.5.4)
      rails-dom-testing (~> 1.0, >= 1.0.5)
      [...]
```

The advantage of `Gemfile.lock` is that it makes it possible for several developers to work on the same Rails project independently from one another and to still be sure that they are all working with the same gem versions. If a file is `Gemfile.lock`, this will be used by the Bundler. This is also useful for deploying the Rails project later on a web server.

Thanks to this mechanism you can use and develop several Rails projects with different gem version numbers in parallel.

bundle update

With `bundle update` you can update gems to new versions. As an example, I have a Rails project with the Rails version 4.2.1:

```
$ rails -v
Rails 4.2.1
$
```

In the file `Gemfile`, this version is listed:

Gemfile

```
source 'https://rubygems.org'

# Bundle edge Rails instead: gem 'rails', github: 'rails/rails'
gem 'rails', '4.2.1'
[...]
```

And also in the `Gemfile.lock`:

```
$ grep 'rails' Gemfile.lock
  [...]
  rails (= 4.2.1)
  [...]
$
```

Assumed we are working with rails 4.2.0 and we want to update to rails 4.2.4. Then we have to change the Gemfile from this:

Gemfile

```
[...]
gem 'rails', '4.2.0'
[...]
```

to this:

Gemfile

```
[...]
gem 'rails', '4.2.4'
[...]
```

After this change, you can use bundle update rails to install the new Rails version (required dependencies are automatically taken into account by Bundler):

```
$ bundle update rails
  [...]
$ rails -v
Rails 4.2.4
$
```

 After every gem update, you should first run rake test to make sure that a new gem version does not add any unwanted side effects.

bundle outdated

If you want to know which of the gems used by your Rails project are now available in a new version, you can do this via the command bundle outdated. Example:

```
$ bundle outdated
Fetching gem metadata from https://rubygems.org/...........
Fetching version metadata from https://rubygems.org/...
Fetching dependency metadata from https://rubygems.org/..
Resolving dependencies....

Outdated gems included in the bundle:
  * hiredis (newest 0.6.1, installed 0.5.2)
  * mime-types (newest 3.0, installed 2.99)
  * mini_portile2 (newest 2.1.0, installed 2.0.0)
```

To update them you'll have to change the version numbers in Gemfile and run a bundle update.

bundle exec

bundle exec is required whenever a program such as rake is used in a Rails project and is present in a different version than the rest of the system. The resulting error message is always easy to implement:

```
You have already activated rake 0.10, but your Gemfile requires rake 0.9.2.2.
Using bundle exec may solve this.
```

In this case, it helps to invoke the command with a preceding bundle exec:

```
$ bundle exec rake db:migrate
```

binstubs

In some environments, using bundle exec is too complicated. In that case, you can install programs with the correct version via bundle install --binstubs in the directory bin:

```
$ bundle install --binstubs
Using rake 10.4.2
Using i18n 0.7.0
[...]
Using web-console 2.1.2
Bundle complete! 12 Gemfile dependencies, 54 gems now installed.
Use bundle show [gemname] to see where a bundled gem is installed.
```

Afterwards, you can always use these programs. Example:

```
$ bin/rake db:migrate
==  CreateUsers: migrating ====================================================
-- create_table(:users)
   -> 0.0018s
==  CreateUsers: migrated (0.0019s) ===========================================
```

Further Information on Bundler

The topic Bundler is far more complex than can be described here. If you want to find out more on Bundler, please visit the following websites to find further information:

- http://railscasts.com/episodes/201-bundler-revised
- http://gembundler.com/

Forms

The Data-Input Workflow

To understand forms we take a look at the data workflow. Understanding it better will help to understand the work of forms.

Example application:

```
$ rails new testapp
[...]
$ cd testapp
$ rails generate scaffold Person first_name last_name
[...]
$ rails db:migrate
[...]
$ rails server
=> Booting Puma
=> Rails 5.0.0.1 application starting in development on http://localhost:3000
[...]
```

Most times we create forms by using the Scaffold. Let's go through the flow the data

Request the people#new form

When we request the http://localhost:3000/people/new URL the router answers the following route:

```
new_person GET    /people/new(.:format)    people#new
```

The controller `app/controllers/people_controller.rb` runs this code:

app/controllers/people_controller.rb

```
# GET /people/new
def new
  @person = Person.new
end
```

So a new Instance of `Person` is created and stored in the instance variable `@person`.

Rails takes `@person` and starts processing the view file `app/views/people/new.html.erb`

app/views/people/new.html.erb

```
<h1>New Person</h1>

<%= render 'form', person: @person %>

<%= link_to 'Back', people_path %>
```

`render 'form'` renders the file `app/views/people/_form.html.erb` and sets the local variable `person` with the content of `@person`.

```erb
<%= form_for(person) do |f| %>
  <% if person.errors.any? %>
    <div id="error_explanation">
      <h2><%= pluralize(person.errors.count, "error") %> prohibited this person from being
saved:</h2>

      <ul>
      <% person.errors.full_messages.each do |message| %>
        <li><%= message %></li>
      <% end %>
      </ul>
    </div>
  <% end %>

  <div class="field">
    <%= f.label :first_name %>
    <%= f.text_field :first_name %>
  </div>

  <div class="field">
    <%= f.label :last_name %>
    <%= f.text_field :last_name %>
  </div>

  <div class="actions">
    <%= f.submit %>
  </div>
<% end %>
```

`form_for(person)` embeddeds the two `text_fields` `:first_name` and `:last_name` plus a `submit` Button.

The resulting HTML:

```html
[...]
<form class="new_person" id="new_person" action="/people" accept-charset="UTF-8" method=
"post"><input name="utf8" type="hidden" value="&#x2713;" /><input type="hidden"
name="authenticity_token" value="nMTs[...]vmeBw==" />

  <div class="field">
    <label for="person_first_name">First name</label>
    <input type="text" name="person[first_name]" id="person_first_name" />
  </div>

  <div class="field">
    <label for="person_last_name">Last name</label>
    <input type="text" name="person[last_name]" id="person_last_name" />
  </div>

  <div class="actions">
    <input type="submit" name="commit" value="Create Person" data-disable-with="Create Person"
/>
  </div>
</form>
[...]
```

This form uses the `post` method to upload the data to the server.

Push the Data to the Server

We enter "Stefan" in the first_name field and "Wintermeyer" in the last_name field and click the submit button. The browser uses the post method to uploads the data to the URL /people. The log shows:

```
Started POST "/people" for ::1 at 2016-01-27 18:47:19 +0100
Processing by PeopleController#create as HTML
  Parameters: {"utf8"=>"✓",
"authenticity_token"=>"DtI0HIHVB7lOIu76YuI1f1byUrDhs89B0ti3fkT9oJVRiljnAdKPsmDeuvir9DZ+6eCoIkX3V
gza15a8pjX4qw==", "person"=>{"first_name"=>"Stefan", "last_name"=>"Wintermeyer"},
"commit"=>"Create Person"}
   (0.1ms)  begin transaction
  SQL (0.3ms)  INSERT INTO "people" ("first_name", "last_name", "created_at", "updated_at")
VALUES (?, ?, ?, ?)  [["first_name", "Stefan"], ["last_name", "Wintermeyer"], ["created_at",
2016-01-27 19:47:19 UTC], ["updated_at", 2016-01-27 19:47:19 UTC]]
   (0.9ms)  commit transaction
Redirected to http://localhost:3000/people/1
Completed 302 Found in 7ms (ActiveRecord: 1.3ms)
```

What happened in Rails?

The router answers the request with this route

```
POST    /people(.:format)          people#create
```

The controller app/controllers/people_controller.rb runs this code

app/controllers/people_controller.rb

```
# POST /people
# POST /people.json
def create
  @person = Person.new(person_params)

  respond_to do |format|
    if @person.save
      format.html { redirect_to @person, notice: 'Person was successfully created.' }
      format.json { render :show, status: :created, location: @person }
    else
      format.html { render :new }
      format.json { render json: @person.errors, status: :unprocessable_entity }
    end
  end
end
[...]

# Never trust parameters from the scary internet, only allow the white list through.
def person_params
  params.require(:person).permit(:first_name, :last_name)
end
```

A new instance variable @person is created. It represents a new Person which was created with the params that were send from the browser to the Rails application. The params are checked in the person_params method which is a whitelist. That is done so the user can not just inject params which we don't want to be injected.

Once @person is saved a redirect_to @person is triggered. That would be http://localhost:3000/people/1 in this example.

Present the new Data

The redirect to http://localhost:3000/people/1 is traceable in the log file

```
Started GET "/people/1" for ::1 at 2016-01-27 18:47:19 +0100
Processing by PeopleController#show as HTML
  Parameters: {"id"=>"1"}
  Person Load (0.2ms)  SELECT  "people".* FROM "people" WHERE "people"."id" = ? LIMIT ?  [["id",
1], ["LIMIT", 1]]
  Rendered people/show.html.erb within layouts/application (2.0ms)
Completed 200 OK in 55ms (Views: 49.3ms | ActiveRecord: 0.2ms)
```

The router answers to this request with

```
person GET    /people/:id(.:format)      people#show
```

Which gets handled be the show method in app/controllers/people_controller.rb

Generic Forms

A form doesn't have to be hardwired to an ActiveRecord object. You can use the form_tag helper to create a form by yourself. I use the example of http://guides.rubyonrails.org/form_helpers.html (which is the official Rails guide about forms) to show how to create a search form which is not connected to a model:

```
<%= form_tag("/search", method: "get") do %>
  <%= label_tag(:q, "Search for:") %>
  <%= text_field_tag(:q) %>
  <%= submit_tag("Search") %>
<% end %>
```

It results in this HTML code:

```
<form accept-charset="UTF-8" action="/search" method="get">
  <label for="q">Search for:</label>
  <input id="q" name="q" type="text" />
  <input name="commit" type="submit" value="Search" />
</form>
```

To handle this you'd have to create a new route in config/routes.rb and write a method in a controller to handle it.

FormTagHelper

There is not just a helper for text fields. Have a look at the official API documentation for all FormTagHelpers at http://api.rubyonrails.org/classes/ActionView/Helpers/FormTagHelper.html to get an overview. Because we use Scaffold to create a form there is no need to memorize them. It is just important to know where to look in case you need something else.

Alternatives

Many Rails developer use Simple Form as an alternative to the standard way of defining forms. It is worth a try because you can really safe time and most of the times it's just easier. Simple Form is available as a Gem at https://github.com/plataformatec/simple_form

Tests

Introduction

I have been programming for 35 years and most of the time I have managed quite well without test-driven development (TDD). I am not going to be mad at you if you decide to just skip this chapter. You can create Rails applications without tests and are not likely to get any bad karma as a result (at least, I hope not - but you can never be entirely sure with the whole karma thing).

But if you should decide to go for TDD, then I can promise you that it is an enlightenment. The basic idea of TDD is that you write a test for each programming function to check this function. In the pure TDD teaching, this test is written before the actual programming. Yes, you will have a lot more to do initially. But later, you can run all the tests and see that the application works exactly as you wanted it to. The read advantage only becomes apparent after a few weeks or months, when you look at the project again and write an extension or new variation. Then you can safely change the code and check it still works properly by running the tests. This avoids a situation where you find yourself saying "oops, that went a bit wrong, I just didn't think of this particular problem".

Often, the advantage of TDD already becomes evident when writing a program. Tests can reveal many careless mistakes that you would otherwise only have stumbled across much later on.

This chapter is a brief overview of the topic test-driven development with Rails. If you have tasted blood and want to find out more, you can dive into the official Rails documentation at http://guides.rubyonrails.org/testing.html.

 TDD is just like driving a car. The only way to learn it is by doing it.

Example for a User in a Web Shop

Let's start with a user scaffold in an imaginary web shop:

```
$ rails new webshop
  [...]
$ cd webshop
$ rails generate scaffold user login_name first_name last_name birthday:date
      [...]
      invoke    test_unit
      create      test/models/user_test.rb
      create      test/fixtures/users.yml
      [...]
      invoke    test_unit
      create      test/controllers/users_controller_test.rb
      invoke    helper
      create      app/helpers/users_helper.rb
      invoke      test_unit
      [...]
$ rails db:migrate
      [...]
```

You already know all about scaffolds (if not, please go and read the chapter "Scaffolding and REST" first) so you know what the application we have just created does. The scaffold created a few tests (they are easy to recognise because the word test is in the file name).

The complete test suite of a Rails project is processed with the command rails test. Let's have a go and see what a test produces at this stage of development:

```
$ rails test
Running via Spring preloader in process 48169
Run options: --seed 30780

# Running:

.......

Finished in 2.128604s, 3.2885 runs/s, 5.6375 assertions/s.

7 runs, 12 assertions, 0 failures, 0 errors, 0 skips
```

The output 7 runs, 12 assertions, 0 failures, 0 errors, 0 skips looks good. By default, a test will run
correctly in a standard scaffold.

Let's now edit the app/models/user.rb and insert a few validations (if these are not entirely clear to you, please
read the section "Validation"):

app/models/user.rb

```
class User < ApplicationRecord
  validates :login_name,
            presence: true,
            length: { minimum: 10 }

  validates :last_name,
            presence: true
end
```

Then we execute rails test again:

```
$ rails test
Running via Spring preloader in process 48284
Run options: --seed 61281

# Running:

"User.count" didn't change by 1.
Expected: 3
  Actual: 2

bin/rails test test/controllers/users_controller_test.rb:19

.....

Finished in 0.305897s, 22.8835 runs/s, 32.6908 assertions/s.

7 runs, 10 assertions, 1 failures, 0 errors, 0 skips
```

Boom! This time we have 1 failures. The error happens in the should create user and the should update user.
The explanation for this is in our validation. The example data created by the scaffold generator went through
in the first rails test (without validation). The errors only occurred the second time (with validation).

This example data is created as _fixtures_tests tests in YAML format in the directory test/fixtures/. Let's have
a look at the example data for User in the file test/fixtures/users.yml:

test/fixtures/users.yml

```
one:
  login_name: MyString
  first_name: MyString
  last_name: MyString
  birthday: 2015-12-27

two:
  login_name: MyString
  first_name: MyString
  last_name: MyString
  birthday: 2015-12-27
```

There are two example records there that do not fulfill the requirements of our validation. The login_name should have a length of at least 10. Let's change the login_name in test/fixtures/users.yml accordingly:

test/fixtures/users.yml

```
one:
  login_name: MyString12
  first_name: MyString
  last_name: MyString
  birthday: 2015-12-27

two:
  login_name: MyString12
  first_name: MyString
  last_name: MyString
  birthday: 2015-12-27
```

Now, a rails test completes without any errors again:

```
$ rails test
Running via Spring preloader in process 48169
Run options: --seed 3341

# Running:

.......

Finished in 0.326051s, 21.4690 runs/s, 39.8711 assertions/s.

7 runs, 12 assertions, 0 failures, 0 errors, 0 skips
```

Now we know that valid data has to be contained in the test/fixtures/users.yml so that the standard test created via scaffold will succeed. But nothing more. Next step is to change the test/fixtures/users.yml to a minimum (for example, we do not need a first_name):

test/fixtures/users.yml

```
one:
  login_name: MyString12
  last_name: Mulder

two:
  login_name: MyString12
  last_name: Scully
```

To be on the safe side, let's do another `rake test` after making our changes (you really can't do that often enough):

```
$ rails test

# Running:

.......

Finished in 0.336391s, 20.8091 runs/s, 38.6455 assertions/s.

7 runs, 12 assertions, 0 failures, 0 errors, 0 skips
```

 All fixtures are loaded into the database when a test is   started. You need to keep this in mind for your test,   especially if you use `uniqueness` in your validation.

Functional Tests

Let's take a closer look at the point where the original errors occurred:

```
"User.count" didn't change by 1.
Expected: 3
  Actual: 2

bin/rails test test/controllers/users_controller_test.rb:19
```

In the `UsersControllerTest` the User could not be created. The controller tests are located in the directory `test/functional/`. Let's now take a good look at the file `test/controllers/users_controller_test.rb`

```ruby
require 'test_helper'

class UsersControllerTest < ActionDispatch::IntegrationTest
  setup do
    @user = users(:one)
  end

  test "should get index" do
    get users_url
    assert_response :success
  end

  test "should get new" do
    get new_user_url
    assert_response :success
  end

  test "should create user" do
    assert_difference('User.count') do
      post users_url, params: { user: { birthday: @user.birthday, first_name: @user.first_name,
last_name: @user.last_name, login_name: @user.login_name } }
    end

    assert_redirected_to user_path(User.last)
  end

  [...]
end
```

At the beginning, we find a setup instruction:

```ruby
setup do
  @user = users(:one)
end
```

These three lines of code mean that for the start of each individual test, an instance @user with the data of the item one from the file test/fixtures/users.yml is created. setup is a predefined callback that - if present - is started by Rails before each test. The opposite of setup is teardown. A teardown - if present - is called automatically after each test.

For every test (in other words, at each run of rails test), a   fresh and therefore empty test database is created automatically. This   is a different database than the one that you access by default via   rails console (that is the development database). The databases are   defined in the configuration file config/database.yml. If you want to   do debugging, you can access the test database with   rails console test.

This functional test then tests various web page functions. First, accessing the index page:

```ruby
test "should get index" do
  get users_url
  assert_response :success
end
```

The command get users_url accesses the page /users. assert_response :success means that the page was delivered.

Let's look more closely at the should create user problem from earlier.

```
test "should create user" do
  assert_difference('User.count') do
    post users_url, params: { user: { birthday: @user.birthday, first_name: @user.first_name,
last_name: @user.last_name, login_name: @user.login_name } }
  end

  assert_redirected_to user_path(User.last)
end
```

The block assert_difference('User.count') do ⋯ end expects a change by the code contained within it. User.count after should result in +1.

The last line assert_redirected_to user_path(User.last) checks if after the newly created record the redirection to the corresponding view show occurs.

Without describing each individual functional test line by line, it's becoming clear what these tests do: they execute real queries to the Web interface (or actually to the controllers) and so they can be used for testing the controllers.

Unit Tests

For testing the validations that we have entered in app/models/user.rb, units tests are more suitable. Unlike the functional tests, these test only the model, not the controller's work.

The unit tests are located in the directory test/models/. But a look into the file test/models/user_test.rb is rather sobering:

test/models/user_test.rb

```
require 'test_helper'

class UserTest < ActiveSupport::TestCase
  # test "the truth" do
  #   assert true
  # end
end
```

By default, scaffold only writes a commented-out dummy test.

A unit test always consists of the following structure:

```
test "an assertion" do
  assert something_is_true_or_false
end
```

The word assert already indicates that we are dealing with an assertion in this context. If this assertion is true, the test will complete and all is well. If this assertion is false, the test fails and we have an error in the program (you can specify the output of the error as string at the end of the assert line).

If you have a look at guides.rubyonrails.org/testing.html you'll see that there are some other assert variations. Here are a few examples:

- assert(boolean, [msg])

- assert_equal(obj1, obj2, [msg])
- assert_not_equal(obj1, obj2, [msg])
- assert_same(obj1, obj2, [msg])
- assert_not_same(obj1, obj2, [msg])
- assert_nil(obj, [msg])
- assert_not_nil(obj, [msg])
- assert_match(regexp, string , [msg])
- assert_no_match(regexp, string , [msg])

Let's breathe some life into the first test in the test/unit/user_test.rb:

test/unit/user_test.rb

```
require 'test_helper'

class UserTest < ActiveSupport::TestCase
  test 'a user with no attributes is not valid' do
    user = User.new
    assert_not user.save, 'Saved a user with no attributes.'
  end
end
```

This test checks if a newly created User that does not contain any data is valid (it shouldn't be).

So a rails test then completes immediately:

```
$ rails test:units
Running via Spring preloader in process 48169
Run options: --seed 43319

# Running:

.

Finished in 0.043224s, 23.1353 runs/s, 23.1353 assertions/s.

8 runs, 13 assertions, 0 failures, 0 errors, 0 skips
```

Now we integrate two asserts in a test to check if the two fixture entries in the test/fixtures/users.yml are really valid:

```
require 'test_helper'

class UserTest < ActiveSupport::TestCase
  test 'an empty user is not valid' do
    assert !User.new.valid?, 'Saved an empty user.'
  end

  test "the two fixture users are valid" do
    assert User.new(last_name: users(:one).last_name, login_name:
    users(:one).login_name ).valid?, 'First fixture is not valid.'
    assert User.new(last_name: users(:two).last_name, login_name:
    users(:two).login_name ).valid?, 'Second fixture is not valid.'
  end
end
```

Then once more a rails test:

```
$ rails test:units
Running via Spring preloader in process 48169
Run options: --seed 11674

# Running:

.........

Finished in 0.388814s, 23.1473 runs/s, 38.5789 assertions/s.

9 runs, 15 assertions, 0 failures, 0 errors, 0 skips
```

Fixtures

With *fixtures* you can generate example data for tests. The default format for this is YAML. The files for this can be found in the directory test/fixtures/ and are automatically created with rails generate scaffold. But of course you can also define your own files. All fixtures are loaded anew into the test database by default with every test.

Examples for alternative formats (e.g. CSV) can be found at api.rubyonrails.org/classes/ActiveRecord/Fixtures.html.

Static Fixtures

The simplest variant for fixtures is static data. The fixture for User used in "Example for a User in a Web Shop" statically looks as follows:

test/fixtures/users.yml

```
one:
   login_name: fox.mulder
   last_name: Mulder

two:
   login_name: dana.scully
   last_name: Scully
```

You simple write the data in YAML format into the corresponding file.

Fixtures with ERB

Static YAML fixtures are sometimes too unintelligent. In these cases, you can work with ERB.

If we want to dynamically enter today's day 20 years ago for the birthdays, then we can simply do it with ERB in test/fixtures/users.yml

```
one:
  login_name: fox.mulder
  last_name: Mulder
  birthday: <%= 20.years.ago.to_s(:db) %>

two:
  login_name: dana.scully
  last_name: Scully
  birthday: <%= 20.years.ago.to_s(:db) %>
```

Integration Tests

Integration tests are tests that work like functional tests but can go over several controllers and additionally analyze the content of a generated view. So you can use them to recreate complex workflows within the Rails application. As an example, we will write an integration test that tries to create a new user via the Web GUI, but omits the login_name and consequently gets corresponding flash error messages.

A rake generate scaffold generates unit and functional tests, but not integration tests. You can either do this manually in the directory test/integration/ or more comfortably with rails generate integration_test. So let's create an integration test:

```
$ rails generate integration_test invalid_new_user_workflow
Running via Spring preloader in process 48532
      invoke  test_unit
      create    test/integration/invalid_new_user_workflow_test.rb
```

We now populate this file test/integration/invalid_new_user_workflow_test.rb with the following test:

test/integration/invalid_new_user_workflow_test.rb

```ruby
require 'test_helper'

class InvalidNewUserWorkflowTest < ActionDispatch::IntegrationTest
  fixtures :all

  test 'try to create a new user without a login' do
    @user = users(:one)

    get '/users/new'
    assert_response :success

    post users_url, params: { user: { last_name: @user.last_name } }
    assert_equal '/users', path
    assert_select 'li', "Login name can't be blank"
    assert_select 'li', "Login name is too short (minimum is 10 characters)"
  end
end
```

Let's run all tests:

```
$ rails test
Running via Spring preloader in process 48169
Run options: --seed 47618

# Running:

..........

Finished in 0.278271s, 3.5936 runs/s, 14.3745 assertions/s.

10 runs, 19 assertions, 0 failures, 0 errors, 0 skips
```

The example clearly shows that you can program much without manually using a web browser to try it out. Once you have written a test for the corresponding workflow, you can rely in future on the fact that it will run through and you don't have to try it out manually in the browser as well.

rails stats

rails stats With `rails stats` you get an overview of your Rails project. For our example, it looks like this:

```
$ rails stats
+----------------------+-------+-------+---------+---------+-----+-------+
| Name                 | Lines |  LOC  | Classes | Methods | M/C | LOC/M |
+----------------------+-------+-------+---------+---------+-----+-------+
| Controllers          |    79 |    53 |       2 |       9 |   4 |     3 |
| Helpers              |     4 |     4 |       0 |       0 |   0 |     0 |
| Jobs                 |     2 |     2 |       1 |       0 |   0 |     0 |
| Models               |    11 |    10 |       2 |       0 |   0 |     0 |
| Mailers              |     4 |     4 |       1 |       0 |   0 |     0 |
| Javascripts          |    30 |     0 |       0 |       0 |   0 |     0 |
| Libraries            |     0 |     0 |       0 |       0 |   0 |     0 |
| Tasks                |     0 |     0 |       0 |       0 |   0 |     0 |
| Controller tests     |    48 |    38 |       1 |       7 |   7 |     3 |
| Helper tests         |     0 |     0 |       0 |       0 |   0 |     0 |
| Model tests          |    15 |    13 |       1 |       2 |   2 |     4 |
| Mailer tests         |     0 |     0 |       0 |       0 |   0 |     0 |
| Integration tests    |    17 |    13 |       1 |       1 |   1 |    11 |
+----------------------+-------+-------+---------+---------+-----+-------+
| Total                |   210 |   137 |       9 |      19 |   2 |     5 |
+----------------------+-------+-------+---------+---------+-----+-------+
  Code LOC: 73    Test LOC: 64    Code to Test Ratio: 1:0.9
```

In this project, we have a total of 73 LOC (Lines Of Code) in the controllers, helpers and models. Plus we have a total of 64 LOC for tests. This gives us a test relation of 1:1.0.9. Logically, this does not say anything about the quality of tests.

More on Testing

The most important link on the topic testing is surely the URL http://guides.rubyonrails.org/testing.html. There you will also find several good examples on this topic.

No other topic is the subject of much discussion in the Rails community as the topic testing. There are very many alternative test tools. One very popular one is RSpec (see http://rspec.info/). I am deliberately not going to discuss these alternatives here, because this book is mainly about helping you understand Rails, not the thousands of extra tools with which you can build your personal Rails development environment.

Cookies and Sessions

Cookies

With a cookie, you can store information on the web browser's system, in form of strings as key-value pairs that the web server has previously sent to this browser. The information is later sent back from the browser to the server in the HTTP header. A cookie (if configured accordingly) is deleted from the browser system neither by restarting the browser nor by restarting the whole system. Of course, the browser's user can manually delete the cookie.

 A browser does not have to accept cookies and it does not have to save them either. But we live in a world where almost every page uses cookies. So most users will have enabled the cookie functionality. For more information on cookies, please visit Wikipedia at http://en.wikipedia.org/wiki/Http_cookie.

A cookie can only have a limited size (the maximum is 4 kB). You should remember that the information of the saved cookies is sent from the browser to the server. So you should only use cookies for storing small amounts of data (for example, a customer id) to avoid the protocol overhead becoming too big.

Rails provides a hash with the name cookies[] that we can use transparently. Rails automatically takes care of the technological details in the background.

To demonstrate how cookies work, we are going to build a Rails application that places a cookie on a page, reads it out on another page and displays the content, and the cookie is deleted on a third page.

```
$ rails new cookie_jar
  [...]
$ cd cookie_jar
$ rails generate controller home set_cookies show_cookies delete_cookies
  [...]
```

We populate the controller file app/controllers/home_controller.rb as follows:

app/controllers/home_controller.rb

```
class HomeController < ApplicationController
  def set_cookies
    cookies[:user_name]      = "Smith"
    cookies[:customer_number] = "1234567890"
  end

  def show_cookies
    @user_name       = cookies[:user_name]
    @customer_number = cookies[:customer_number]
  end

  def delete_cookies
    cookies.delete :user_name
    cookies.delete :customer_number
  end
end
```

And the view file app/views/home/show_cookies.html.erb as follows:

app/views/home/show_cookies.html.erb

```
<table>
  <tr>
    <td>User Name:</td>
    <td><%= @user_name %></td>
  </tr>
  <tr>
    <td>Customer Number:</td>
    <td><%= @customer_number %></td>
  </tr>
</table>
```

Start the Rails server with `rails server` and go to the URL http://localhost:3000/home/show_cookies in your browser. You will not see any values.

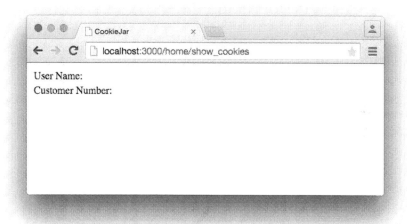

Figure 16. Show Cookies empty

Now go to the URL http://localhost:3000/home/set_cookies and then back to http://localhost:3000/home/show_cookies. Now you will see the values that we have set in the method set_cookies.

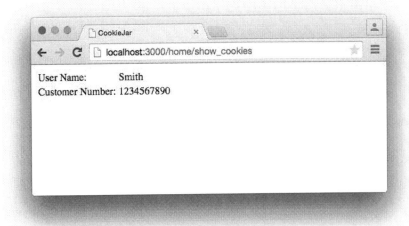

Figure 17. Show Cookies set

By requesting the page http://localhost:3000/home/delete_cookies you can delete the cookies again.

The cookies you have placed in this way stay alive in the browser until you close the browser completely.

 The content of a cookie in the browser is easy to be read   and to be manipulated by a tech-savvy user. It's not   encrypted, so it should not contain any passwords or similar data. Nor is it advisable to save shopping baskets in an   unsigned cookie, otherwise the user could change the prices   in this shopping basket himself.

Permanent Cookies

Cookies are normally set to give the application a way of recognizing users when they visit again later. Between these visits to the website, much time can go by and the user may well close the browser in the meantime. To store cookies for longer than the current browser session, you can use the method permanent. Our above example can be expanded by adding this method in the app/controllers/home_controller.rb:

app/controllers/home_controller.rb

```ruby
class HomeController < ApplicationController
  def set_cookies
    cookies.permanent[:user_name]    = "Smith"
    cookies.permanent[:customer_number] = "1234567890"
  end

  def show_cookies
    @user_name    = cookies[:user_name]
    @customer_number = cookies[:customer_number]
  end

  def delete_cookies
    cookies.delete :user_name
    cookies.delete :customer_number
  end
end
```

"permanent" here does not really mean permanent. You cannot set a cookie permanently. When you set a cookie, it always needs a "valid until" stamp that the browser can use to automatically delete old cookies. With the method permanent this value is set to today's date in 20 years. This is practically the same as permanent.

Signed Cookies

With normally placed cookies, you have no option on the application side to find out if the user of the application has changed the cookie. This can quickly lead to security problems, as changing the content of a cookie in the browser is no great mystery. The solution is signing the cookies with a key that is only known to us. This key is automatically created via a random generator with each rails new and is located in the file config/secrets.yml:

config/secrets.yml

```
development:
  secret_key_base: f4c3[...]095b

test:
  secret_key_base: d6ef[...]052a

# Do not keep production secrets in the repository,
# instead read values from the environment.
production:
  secret_key_base: <%= ENV["SECRET_KEY_BASE"] %>
```

As mentioned in the comment over the production key it is not a good idea to store the production key in the source code of your project. It's better to store it as an environment variable and let the Rails project read it from there.

To sign cookies, you can use the method signed. You have to use it for writing and reading the cookie. Our above example can be expanded by adding this method in the app/controllers/home_controller.rb:

app/controllers/home_controller.rb

```
class HomeController < ApplicationController
  def set_cookies
    cookies.permanent.signed[:user_name]       = "Smith"
    cookies.permanent.signed[:customer_number] = "1234567890"
  end

  def show_cookies
    @user_name       = cookies.signed[:user_name]
    @customer_number = cookies.signed[:customer_number]
  end

  def delete_cookies
    cookies.delete :user_name
    cookies.delete :customer_number
  end
end
```

The content of the cookie is now encrypted every time you set the cookie. The name of the cookie can still be read by the user, but not the value.

Sessions

As HTTP is a stateless protocol, we encounter special problems when developing applications. An individual web page has no connection to the next web page and they do not know of one another. But as you want to register only once on many websites, not over and over again on each individual page, this can pose a problem. The solution is called session and Rails offers it to the programmer transparently as a session[] hash. Rails automatically creates a new session for each new visitor of the web page. This session is saved by default as cookie and so it is subject to the 4 kB limit. But you can also store the sessions in the database (see the section "Saving Sessions in the Database"). An independent and unique session ID is created automatically and the cookie is deleted by default when the web browser is closed.

The beauty of a Rails session is that we can not just save strings there as with cookies, but any object, hashes and arrays. So you can for example use it to conveniently implement a shopping cart in an online shop.

Breadcrumbs via Session

As an example, we create an application with a controller and three views. When a view is visited, the previously visited views are displayed in a little list.

The basic application:

```
$ rails new breadcrumbs
  [...]
$ cd breadcrumbs
$ rails generate controller Home ping pong index
  [...]
```

First we create a method with which we can save the last three URLs in the session and set an instance variable @breadcrumbs, to be able to neatly retrieve the values in the view. To that end, we set up a before_filter in the app/controllers/home_controller.rb:

```ruby
class HomeController < ApplicationController
  before_filter :set_breadcrumbs

  def ping
  end

  def pong
  end

  def index
  end

  private
  def set_breadcrumbs
    if session[:breadcrumbs]
      @breadcrumbs = session[:breadcrumbs]
    else
      @breadcrumbs = Array.new
    end

    @breadcrumbs.push(request.url)

    if @breadcrumbs.count > 4
      # shift removes the first element
      @breadcrumbs.shift
    end

    session[:breadcrumbs] = @breadcrumbs
  end
end
```

Now we use the app/views/layouts/application.html.erb to display these last entries at the top of each page:

app/views/layouts/application.html.erb

```
<!DOCTYPE html>
<html>
  <head>
    <title>Breadcrumbs</title>
    <%= csrf_meta_tags %>
    <%= action_cable_meta_tag %>

    <%= stylesheet_link_tag    'application', media: 'all', 'data-turbolinks-track' => true %>
    <%= javascript_include_tag 'application', 'data-turbolinks-track' => true %>
  </head>

  <% if @breadcrumbs && @breadcrumbs.any? %>
    <h3>Surf History</h3>
    <ul>
      <% @breadcrumbs[0..2].each do |breadcrumb| %>
        <li><%= link_to breadcrumb, breadcrumb %></li>
      <% end %>
    </ul>
  <% end %>

  <body>
    <%= yield %>
  </body>
</html>
```

Now you can start the Rails server with `rails server` and go to http://localhost:3000/home/ping, http://localhost:3000/home/pong or http://localhost:3000/home/index and at the top you will then always see the pages that you have visited before. Of course, this only works on the second page, because you do not yet have a history on the first page you visit.

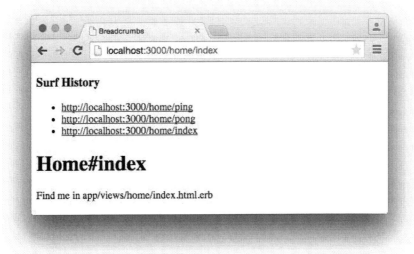

Figure 18. Breadcrumbs session example

reset_session

Occasionally, there are situations where you want to reset a session (in other words, delete the current session and start again with a new, fresh session). For example, if you log out of a web application, the session will be reset. This is easily done and we can quickly integrate it into our breadcrumb application.

 With the switch "-s" the generator doesn't overwrite existing files. In this example that would be the `home_controller.rb` file.

```
$ rails generate controller Home reset -s
Running via Spring preloader in process 49668
      skip  app/controllers/home_controller.rb
     route  get 'home/reset'
    invoke  erb
     exist    app/views/home
    create    app/views/home/reset.html.erb
    invoke  test_unit
      skip    test/controllers/home_controller_test.rb
    invoke  helper
 identical    app/helpers/home_helper.rb
    invoke    test_unit
    invoke  assets
    invoke    coffee
 identical      app/assets/javascripts/home.coffee
    invoke    css
 identical      app/assets/stylesheets/home.css
```

The correspondingly expanded controller `app/controllers/home_controller.rb` then looks like this:

app/controllers/home_controller.rb

```ruby
class HomeController < ApplicationController
  before_filter :set_breadcrumbs

  def ping
  end

  def pong
  end

  def index
  end

  def reset
    reset_session
    @breadcrumbs = nil
  end

  private
  def set_breadcrumbs
    if session[:breadcrumbs]
      @breadcrumbs = session[:breadcrumbs]
    else
      @breadcrumbs = Array.new
    end

    @breadcrumbs.push(request.url)

    if @breadcrumbs.count > 4
      # shift removes the first element
      @breadcrumbs.shift
    end

    session[:breadcrumbs] = @breadcrumbs
  end
end
```

So you can delete the current session by going to the URL http://localhost:3000/home/reset.

 It's not just important to invoke reset_session, but you need to also set the instance variable @breadcrumbs to nil. Otherwise, the old breadcrumbs would still appear in the view.

Saving Sessions in the Database

Saving the entire session data in a cookie on the user's browser is not always the best solution. Amongst others, the limit of 4 kB can pose a problem. But it's no big obstacle, we can relocate the storing of the session from the cookie to the database with the Active Record Session Store gem (https://github.com/rails/activerecord-session_store). Then the session ID is of course still saved in a cookie, but the whole other session data is stored in the database on the server.

To install the gem we have to add the following line at the end of the file Gemfile

Gemfile

```ruby
gem 'activerecord-session_store'
```

After that we have to run `bundle install`

```
$ bundle install
[...]
```

After that we have to run `rails generate active_record:session_migration` and `rails db:migrate` to create the needed table in the database.

```
$ rails generate active_record:session_migration
      create  db/migrate/20150428183919_add_sessions_table.rb
$ rails db:migrate
== 20150428183919 AddSessionsTable: migrating ================================
-- create_table(:sessions)
   -> 0.0019s
-- add_index(:sessions, :session_id, {:unique=>true})
   -> 0.0008s
-- add_index(:sessions, :updated_at)
   -> 0.0008s
== 20150428183919 AddSessionsTable: migrated (0.0037s) ========================
```

After that we'll have to change the `session_store` in the file `config/initializers/session_store.rb` to `:active_record_store`.

config/initializers/session_store.rb

```
Rails.application.config.session_store :active_record_store, :key => '_my_app_session'
```

Job done. Now you need to start the server again with `rails server` and Rails saves all sessions in the database.

Active Job

Sometimes a specific piece of code takes a long time to run but doesn't need to run right away. An example is sending an e-mail after creating an order at the end of a online shopping workflow. It can take a couple of seconds to send an e-mail but you don't want your user to wait for that to happen within the controller. It makes more sense to use a queueing mechanism for these tasks.

Active Job provides such a queueing system. You can create jobs which are being processed asynchronous by active job.

Create a New Job

The quickest way to create a new job is the job generator. Lets create an example job which waits for 10 seconds and than logs an info message:

```
$ rails new shop
  [...]
$ cd shop
$ rails generate job example
      invoke  test_unit
      create    test/jobs/example_job_test.rb
      create    app/jobs/example_job.rb
$
```

All jobs are created in the app/jobs directory. Please change the app/jobs/example_job.rb file accordingly:

app/jobs/example_job.rb

```ruby
class ExampleJob < ApplicationJob
  queue_as :default

  def perform(*args)
    sleep 10
    logger.info "Just waited 10 seconds."
  end
end
```

You can test the job in your console with ExampleJob.perform_later which creates it:

```
$ rails console
Loading development environment (Rails 5.0.0)
>> ExampleJob.perform_later
Performing ExampleJob from Inline(default)
Just waited 10 seconds.
Performed ExampleJob from Inline(default) in 10014.5ms
Enqueued ExampleJob (Job ID: f0b6937d-c2b4-4685-afe3-d571044b57a0) to Inline(default)
=> #<ExampleJob:0x007ffa99a3f020 @arguments=[], @job_id="f0b6937d-c2b4-4685-afe3-d571044b57a0",
@queue_name="default", @priority=nil>
>> exit
$
```

The file log/development.log now contains the logging output.

A more concrete example of using jobs you'll find in the Action Mailer chapter where an e-mail gets send.

Set the time for future execution

The `set` method provides two arguments which can be used to set the execution of a job in the future:

- wait

```
ExampleJob.set(wait: 1.hour).perform_later
```

- wait_until

```
ExampleJob.set(wait_until: Date.tomorrow.noon).perform_later
```

== Configure the Job Server Backend

The page http://api.rubyonrails.org/classes/ActiveJob/QueueAdapters.html lists all available backends. To use one of them you have to install the needed gem. Here is an example for the use of the popular Sidekiq. To use the gem you have to add it to `Gemfile` and run a `bundle install` afterwards:

Gemfile

```
[...]
gem 'sidekiq'
```

In `config/application.rb` you can configure the use of it:

config/application.rb

```
require File.expand_path('../boot', __FILE__)

require 'rails/all'

# Require the gems listed in Gemfile, including any gems
# you've limited to :test, :development, or :production.
Bundler.require(*Rails.groups)

module Shop
  class Application < Rails::Application
    # Settings in config/environments/* take precedence over those specified here.
    # Application configuration should go into files in config/initializers
    # -- all .rb files in that directory are automatically loaded.

    config.active_job.queue_adapter = :sidekiq
  end
end
```

Action Mailer

Even if we mainly use Ruby on Rails to generate web pages, it sometimes is useful to be able to send an e-mail.

So let's go and build an example with minimal user management for a web shop that automatically sends an e-mail to the user when a new user is created:

```
$ rails new webshop
  [...]
$ cd webshop
$ rails generate scaffold User name email
  [...]
$ rails db:migrate
  [...]
```

For the user model we create a minimal validation in the app/models/user.rb, so that we can be sure that each user has a name and a syntactically correct e-mail address.

app/models/user.rb

```
class User < ApplicationRecord
  validates :name,
            presence: true

  validates :email,
            presence: true,
            format: { with: /\A([^@\s]+)@((?:[-a-z0-9]+\.)+[a-z]{2,})\Z/i }
end
```

There is a generator with the name mailer that creates the files required for mailing. First, we have a look at the output of the rails generate mailer, without passing any further arguments:

```
$ rails generate mailer
Usage:
  rails generate mailer NAME [method method] [options]

[...]

Example:
========
    rails generate mailer Notifications signup forgot_password invoice

    creates a Notifications mailer class, views, and test:
        Mailer:   app/mailers/notifications.rb
        Views:    app/views/notifications/signup.text.erb [...]
        Test:     test/mailers/notifications_test.rb
```

That is just what we expected. So let's now create the mailer notification:

```
$ rails generate mailer Notification new_account
      create  app/mailers/notification_mailer.rb
      invoke  erb
      create    app/views/notification_mailer
      create    app/views/notification_mailer/new_account.text.erb
      create    app/views/notification_mailer/new_account.html.erb
      invoke  test_unit
      create    test/mailers/notification_mailer_test.rb
      create    test/mailers/previews/notification_mailer_preview.rb
```

In the file app/mailers/notification_mailer.rb you will find the controller:

app/mailers/notification_mailer.rb

```
class NotificationMailer < ApplicationMailer

  # Subject can be set in your I18n file at config/locales/en.yml
  # with the following lookup:
  #
  #   en.notification_mailer.new_account.subject
  #
  def new_account
    @greeting = "Hi"

    mail to: "to@example.org"
  en
```

In it, we change the new_account method to accept a parameter with new_account(user)` and some code to use that to send the confirmation e-mail.

app/mailers/notification_mailer.rb

```
class NotificationMailer < ApplicationMailer
  def new_account(user)
    @user = user
    mail(to: user.email, subject: "Account #{user.name} is active")
  end
end
```

Now we create the view for this method. Actually we have to breath live into two files:

- app/views/notification_mailer/new_account.text.erb
- app/views/notification_mailer/new_account.html.erb

In case you want to send an non-HTML only e-mail you can delete the file app/views/notification_mailer/new_account.html.erb. Otherwise ActionMailer will generate an e-mail which can be read as a modern HTML or a traditional text one.

app/views/notification_mailer/new_account.text.erb

```
Hello <%= @user.name %>,

your new account is active.

Have a great day!
  A Robot
```

```
<p>Hello <%= @user.name %>,</p>
<p>your new account is active.</p>
<p>Have a great day!</br>
  A Robot</p>
```

As we want to send this e-mail after the create of a User, we still need add an `after_create` callback which triggers the delivery:

app/models/user.rb

```
class User < ApplicationRecord
  validates :name,
            presence: true

  validates :email,
            presence: true,
            format: { with: /\A([^@\s]+)@((?:[-a-z0-9]+\.)+[a-z]{2,})\Z/i }

  after_create :send_welcome_email

  private

  def send_welcome_email
    Notification.new_account(self).deliver_later
  end
end
```

Let's create a new User in the console:

```
$ rails console
Loading development environment (Rails 5.0.0)
>> User.create(name: 'Wintermeyer', email: 'stefan.wintermeyer@amooma.de')
   (0.1ms)  begin transaction
  SQL (0.3ms)  INSERT INTO "users" ("name", "email", "created_at", "updated_at") VALUES (?, ?,
?, ?)  [["name", "Wintermeyer"], ["email", "stefan.wintermeyer@amooma.de"], ["created_at", 2016-
01-25 19:05:40 UTC], ["updated_at", 2016-01-25 19:05:40 UTC]]
  User Load (0.1ms)  SELECT  "users".* FROM "users" WHERE "users"."id" = ? LIMIT ?  [["id", 1],
["LIMIT", 1]]
Performing ActionMailer::DeliveryJob from Inline(mailers) with arguments: "NotificationMailer",
"new_account", "deliver_now", <GlobalID:0x007fb7a4b41528 @uri=<URI::GID gid://webshop/User/1>>
  Rendered notification_mailer/new_account.html.erb within layouts/mailer (0.8ms)
  Rendered notification_mailer/new_account.text.erb within layouts/mailer (0.3ms)
NotificationMailer#new_account: processed outbound mail in 116.0ms
Sent mail to stefan.wintermeyer@amooma.de (7.9ms)
Date: Mon, 25 Jan 2016 19:05:40 +0100
From: from@example.com
To: stefan.wintermeyer@amooma.de
Message-ID: <56a639c46679d_e0c63fdbd043fa085071@Millennium-Falcon.local.mail>
Subject: Account Wintermeyer is active
Mime-Version: 1.0
Content-Type: multipart/alternative;
 boundary="--==_mimepart_56a639c4657a7_e0c63fdbd043fa084936";
 charset=UTF-8
Content-Transfer-Encoding: 7bit
```

```
-----==_mimepart_56a639c4657a7_e0c63fdbd043fa084936
Content-Type: text/plain;
 charset=UTF-8
Content-Transfer-Encoding: 7bit


Hello Wintermeyer,

your new account is active.

Have a great day!
  A Robot


-----==_mimepart_56a639c4657a7_e0c63fdbd043fa084936
Content-Type: text/html;
 charset=UTF-8
Content-Transfer-Encoding: 7bit

<!DOCTYPE html>
<html>
  <head>
    <meta http-equiv="Content-Type" content="text/html; charset=utf-8" />
    <style>
      /* Email styles need to be inline */
    </style>
  </head>

  <body>
    <p>Hello Wintermeyer,</p>
<p>your new account is active.</p>
<p>Have a great day!</br>
  A Robot</p>

  </body>
</html>

-----==_mimepart_56a639c4657a7_e0c63fdbd043fa084936--

Performed ActionMailer::DeliveryJob from Inline(mailers) in 127.08ms
Enqueued ActionMailer::DeliveryJob (Job ID: 589388e9-0e80-437d-8f1e-b4801d599460) to
Inline(mailers) with arguments: "NotificationMailer", "new_account", "deliver_now",
<GlobalID:0x007fb7a4c02110 @uri=<URI::GID gid://webshop/User/1>>
  (1.6ms)  commit transaction
=> #<User id: 1, name: "Wintermeyer", email: "stefan.wintermeyer@amooma.de", created_at: "2016-
01-25 19:05:40", updated_at: "2016-01-25 19:05:40">
>> exit
```

That was straightforward. In the development mode we see the e-mail in the log. In production mode it would be send to the configured SMTP gateway.

 Have a look at the files `app/views/layouts/mailer.html.erb` and `app/views/layouts/mailer.text.erb` to set a generic envelope (e.g. add CSS) for your e-mail content. It works like `app/views/layouts/application.html.erb` for HTML views.

Configuring the E-Mail Server

Rails can use a local `sendmail` or an external SMTP server for delivering the e-mails.

Sending via Local Sendmail

If you want to send the e-mails in the traditional way via local sendmail, then you need to insert the following lines into your configuration file config/environments/development.rb (for the development environment) or config/environments/production.rb (for your production environment):

config/environments/development.rb

```
config.action_mailer.delivery_method = :sendmail
config.action_mailer.perform_deliveries = true
config.action_mailer.raise_delivery_errors = true
```

Sending via Direct SMTP

If you want to send the e-mail directly via a SMTP server (for example Google Mail), then you need to insert the following lines into your configuration file config/environments/development.rb (for the development environment) or config/environments/production.rb (for your production environment):

config/environments/development.rb

```
config.action_mailer.delivery_method = :smtp
config.action_mailer.smtp_settings = {
  address:             "smtp.gmail.com",
  port:                587,
  domain:              'example.com',
  user_name:           '<username>',
  password:            '<password>',
  authentication:      'plain',
  enable_starttls_auto: true  }
```

Of course you need to adapt the values for :domain, :user_name and :password in accordance with your configuration.

Custom X-Header

If you feel the urge to integrate an additional X-header then this is no problem. Here is an example for expanding the file app/mailers/notification_mailer.rb:

app/mailers/notification_mailer.rb

```
class NotificationMailer < ApplicationMailer
  def new_account(user)
    @user = user
    headers["X-Priority"] = '3'
    mail(to: user.email, subject: "The account #{user.name} is active.")
  end
end
```

This means the sent e-mail would look like this:

```
Sent mail to stefan.wintermeyer@amooma.de (50ms)
Date: Wed, 30 May 2012 17:35:21 +0200
From: from@example.com
To: stefan.wintermeyer@amooma.de
Message-ID: <4fc63e39e356a_aa083fe366028cd8803c7@MacBook.local.mail>
Subject: The new account Wintermeyer is active.
Mime-Version: 1.0
Content-Type: text/plain;
 charset=UTF-8
Content-Transfer-Encoding: 7bit
X-Priority: 3

Hello Wintermeyer,

your new account is active.

Have a great day!
  A Robot
```

Attachments

E-mail attachments are also defined in the controller.

As an example we add in app/mailers/notification_mailer.rb the Rails image app/assets/images/rails.png to an e-mail as attachment:

app/mailers/notification_mailer.rb

```ruby
class NotificationMailer < ApplicationMailer
  def new_account(user)
    @user = user
    attachments['rails.png'] =
      File.read("#{Rails.root}/app/assets/images/rails.png")
    mail(to: user.email, subject: "The account #{user.name} is active.")
  end
end
```

Inline Attachments

For *inline attachments* in HTML e-mails, you need to use the method inline when calling attachments. In our example controller app/mailers/notification_mailer.rb:

app/mailers/notification_mailer.rb

```ruby
class NotificationMailer < ApplicationMailer
  def new_account(user)
    @user = user
    attachments.inline['rails.png'] =
      File.read("#{Rails.root}/app/assets/images/rails.png")
    mail(to: user.email, subject: "The account #{user.name} is active.")
  end
end
```

In the HTML e-mail, you can access the hash attachments[] via image_tag. In our example the app/views/notification_mailer/new_account.html.erb would look like this:

```
<!DOCTYPE html>
<html>
  <head>
    <meta content="text/html; charset=UTF-8" http-equiv="Content-Type" />
  </head>
  <body>
    <%= image_tag attachments['rails.png'].url, :alt => 'Rails Logo' %>
    <p>Hello <%= @user.name %>,</p>

    <p>your new account is active.</p>

    <p><i>Have a great day!</i></p>
    <p>A Robot</p>
  </body>
</html>
```

Further Information

The Rails online documentation has a very extensive entry on ActionMailer at http://guides.rubyonrails.org/action_mailer_basics.html.

Internationalization

Introduction

If you are in the lucky situation of only creating web pages in English only, then you can skip this chapter completely.

But even if you want to create a web page that only uses one language (other than English), you will need to dive into this chapter. It is not enough to just translate the views. Because already if you use scaffolding, you will need to take care of the English and therefore not yet translated validation errors.

The class I18n is responsible for anything to do with translation in the Rails application. It offers two important methods for this purpose:

- I18n.translate or I18n.t

  Takes care of inserting previously defined text blocks. These can contain variables.

- I18n.localize or I18n.l

  Takes care of adapting time and date specifications to the local format.

With I18n.locale you define the language you want to use in the current call. In the configuration file config/application.rb, the entry config.i18n.default_locale sets the default value for I18n.locale. If you do not make any changes there, this value is set by default to :en for English.

For special cases such as displaying numbers, currencies and times, there are special helpers available. For example, if you want to create a German web page, you can ensure that the number 1000.23 can be correctly displayed with a decimal comma as "1.000,23" on the German page and with a decimal point on an English web page as "1,000.23".

Let's create an example application which includes the rails-i18n gem by Sven Fuchs (https://github.com/svenfuchs/i18n). It provides a couple of language files with translations and format info.

```
$ rails new webshop
  [...]
$ cd webshop
$ echo "gem 'rails-i18n'" >> Gemfile
$ bundle
  [...]
$
```

In the console we can see the different output of a number depending on the language setting:

```
$ rails console
Loading development environment (Rails 5.0.0)
>> price = 1000.23
=> 1000.23
>> helper.number_to_currency(price, locale: :de)
=> "1.000,23 €"
>> helper.number_to_currency(price, locale: :en)
=> "$1,000.23"
>> helper.number_to_currency(price, locale: :fr)
=> "1 000,23 €"
>> exit
$
```

I18n.t

With I18n.t you can retrieve previously defined translations. The translations are saved by default in YAML format in the directory config/locales/. Technically, you do not have to use YAML as format.

In config/locales/ you can find an example file config/locales/en.yml with the following content:

config/locales/en.yml

```
en:
  hello: "Hello world"
```

In the Rails console we can try out how I18n.t works:

```
$ rails console
Loading development environment (Rails 5.0.0)
>> I18n.t :hello
=> "Hello world"
>> I18n.locale
=> :en
>> exit
$
```

Let's first create a config/locales/de.yml with the following content:

config/locales/de.yml

```
de:
  hello: "Hallo Welt"
```

Now you have to tell rails to load this file by adding one line in config/application.rb.

config/application.rb

```
config.i18n.load_path += Dir[Rails.root.join('my', 'locales',
'*.{rb,yml}').to_s]
```

In the console we can set the system language with I18n.locale = :de to German.

```
$ rails console
Loading development environment (Rails 5.0.0)
>> I18n.locale
=> :en
>> I18n.locale = :de
=> :de
>> I18n.t :hello
=> "Hallo Welt"
```

I18n.t looks by default for the entry in the language defined in I18n.locale. It does not matter if you are working with I18n.t or I18n.translate. Nor does it matter if you are searching for a symbol or a string:

```
>> I18n.locale = :en
=> :en
>> I18n.t :hello
=> "Hello world"
>> I18n.t 'hello'
=> "Hello world"
>> I18n.translate 'hello'
=> "Hello world"
```

If a translation does not exist, you get an error message that says translation missing:. This also applies if a translation is only missing in one language (then all other languages will work, but for the missing translation you will get the error message). In that case, you can define a default with default: 'any default value':

```
>> I18n.t 'asdfasdfasdf'
=> "translation missing: de.asdfasdfasdf"
>> I18n.t 'asdfasdfasdf', default: 'asdfasdfasdf'
=> "asdfasdfasdf"
>> exit
```

In the YAML structure you can also specify several levels. Please amend the config/locale/en.yml as follows:

config/locale/en.yml

```
en:
  hello: "Hello world"
  example:
    test: "A test"
  aaa:
    bbb:
      test: "An other test"
```

You can display the different levels within the string with dots or with a :scope for the symbols. You can also mix both options.

```
$ rails console
Loading development environment (Rails 5.0.0)
>> I18n.t 'example.test'
=> "A test"
>> I18n.t 'aaa.bbb.test'
=> "An other test"
>> I18n.t :test, scope: [:aaa, :bbb]
=> "An other test"
>> I18n.t :test, scope: 'aaa.bbb'
=> "An other test"
>> exit
$
```

It's up to you which structure you choose to save your translations in the YAML files. But the structure described in "A Rails Application in Only One Language: German" does make some things easier and that's why we are going to use it for this application as well.

Using I18n.t in the View

In the view, you can use I18n.t as follows:

```
<%= t :hello-world %>

<%= I18n.t :hello-world %>

<%= I18n.translate :hello-world %>

<%= I18n.t 'hello-world' %>

<%= I18n.t 'aaa.bbb.test' %>

<%= link_to I18n.t('views.destroy'), book, confirm:
I18n.t('views.are_you_sure'), method: :delete %>
```

Localized Views

In Rails, there is a useful option of saving several variations of a view as "localized views", each of which represents a different language. This technique is independent of the potential use of I18n.t in these views. The file name results from the view name, the language code (for example, de for German) and html.erb for ERB pages. Each of these are separated by a dot. So the German variation of the index.html.erb page would get the file name index.de.html.erb.

Your views directory could then look like this:

```
|-app
|---views
|-----products
|-------_form.html.erb
|-------_form.de.html.erb
|-------edit.html.erb
|-------edit.de.html.erb
|-------index.html.erb
|-------index.de.html.erb
|-------new.html.erb
|-------new.de.html.erb
|-------show.html.erb
|-------show.de.html.erb
|-----page
|-------index.html.erb
|-------index.de.html.erb
```

The language set with config.i18n.default_locale is used automatically if no language was encoded in the file name. In a new and not yet configured Rails project, this will be English. You can configure it in the file config/application.rb.

A Rails Application in Only One Language: German

In a Rails application aimed only at German users, it is unfortunately not enough to just translate all the views into German. The approach is in many respects similar to a multi-lingual Rails application (see the section xref:#multilingual-rails-application["Multilingual Rails Application"]). Correspondingly, there will be a certain amount of repetition. I am going to show you the steps you need to watch out for by using a simple application as example.

Let's go through all the changes using the example of this bibliography application:

```
$ rails new bibliography
  [...]
$ cd bibliography
$ rails generate scaffold book title number_of_pages:integer
  'price:decimal{7,2}'
  [...]
$ rake db:migrate
  [...]
$
```

To get examples for validation errors, please insert the following validations in the app/models/book.rb:

app/models/book.rb

```
class Book < ActiveRecord::Base
  validates :title,
            presence: true,
            uniqueness: true,
            length: { within: 2..255 }

  validates :price,
            presence: true,
            numericality: { greater_than: 0 }
end
```

Please search the configuration file config/application.rb for the value config.i18n.default_locale and set it to :de for German. In the same context, we then also insert two directories in the line above for the translations of the models and the views. This directory structure is not a technical requirement, but makes it easier to keep track of things if your application becomes big:

config/application.rb

```
config.i18n.load_path += Dir[Rails.root.join('config', 'locales', 'models',
'*', '*.yml').to_s]
config.i18n.load_path += Dir[Rails.root.join('config', 'locales', 'views',
'*', '*.yml').to_s]
config.i18n.default_locale = :de
```

You then still need to create the corresponding directories:

```
$ mkdir -p config/locales/models/book
$ mkdir -p config/locales/views/book
$
```

Now you need to generate a language configuration file for German or simply download a ready-made one by Sven Fuchs from his Github repository at https://github.com/svenfuchs/rails-i18n:

```
$ cd config/locales
$ curl -O
  https://raw.githubusercontent.com/svenfuchs/rails-i18n/master/rails/locale/de.yml
  % Total    % Received % Xferd  Average Speed   Time    Time     Time  Current
                                 Dload  Upload   Total   Spent    Left  Speed
100  5027  100  5027    0     0  14877      0 --:--:-- --:--:-- --:--:-- 14916
$
```

If you know how Bundler works, you can also insert the line gem 'rails-i18n' into the file Gemfile and then execute bundle install. This gives you all language files from the repository.

In the file config/locales/de.yml, you have all required formats and generic wordings for German that you need for a normal Rails application (for example, days of the week, currency symbols, etc). Have a look at it with your favorite editor to get a first impression.

Next, we need to tell Rails that a model book' is not called `book' in German, but `Buch'. The same applies to all attributes. So we create the file `config/locales/models/book/de.yml with the following structure. As side effect, we get the methods Model.model_name.human and Model.human_attribute_name(attribute), with which we can insert the model and attribute names in the view.

config/locales/models/book/de.yml

```
de:
  activerecord:
    models:
      book: 'Buch'
    attributes:
      book:
        title: 'Titel'
        number_of_pages: 'Seitenanzahl'
        price: 'Preis'
```

In the file config/locales/views/book/de.yml we insert a few values for the scaffold views:

config/locales/views/book/de.yml

```
de:
  views:
    show: Anzeigen
    edit: Editieren
    destroy: Löschen
    are_you_sure: Sind Sie sicher?
    back: Zurück
    edit: Editieren
    book:
      index:
        title: Bücherliste
        new: Neues Buch
      edit:
        title: Buch editieren
      new:
        title: Neues Buch
      flash_messages:
        book_was_successfully_created: 'Das Buch wurde angelegt.'
        book_was_successfully_updated: 'Das Buch wurde aktualisiert.'
```

Now we still need to integrate a "few" changes into the views. We use the I18n.t helper that can also be abbreviated with t in the view. I18n.t reads out the corresponding item from the YAML file. In the case of a purely monolingual German application, we could also write the German text directly into the view, but with this method we can more easily switch to multilingual use if required.

```erb
<%= form_for(@book) do |f| %>
  <% if @book.errors.any? %>
    <div id="error_explanation">
      <h2><%= t 'activerecord.errors.template.header', :model =>
      Book.model_name.human, :count => @book.errors.count %></h2>
      <ul>
      <% @book.errors.full_messages.each do |msg| %>
        <li><%= msg %></li>
      <% end %>
      </ul>
    </div>
  <% end %>

  <div class="field">
    <%= f.label :title %><br>
    <%= f.text_field :title %>
  </div>
  <div class="field">
    <%= f.label :number_of_pages %><br>
    <%= f.number_field :number_of_pages %>
  </div>
  <div class="field">
    <%= f.label :price %><br>
    <%= f.text_field :price %>
  </div>
  <div class="actions">
    <%= f.submit %>
  </div>
<% end %>
```

```erb
<h1><%= t 'views.book.edit.title' %></h1>

<%= render 'form' %>

<%= link_to I18n.t('views.show'), @book %> |
<%= link_to I18n.t('views.back'), books_path %>
```

app/views/books/index.html.erb

```erb
<h1><%= t 'views.book.index.title' %></h1>

<table>
  <thead>
    <tr>
      <th><%= Book.human_attribute_name(:title) %></th>
      <th><%= Book.human_attribute_name(:number_of_pages) %></th>
      <th><%= Book.human_attribute_name(:price) %></th>
      <th></th>
      <th></th>
      <th></th>
    </tr>
  </thead>

  <tbody>
    <% @books.each do |book| %>
      <tr>
        <td><%= book.title %></td>
        <td><%= number_with_delimiter(book.number_of_pages) %></td>
        <td><%= number_to_currency(book.price) %></td>
        <td><%= link_to I18n.t('views.show'), book %></td>
        <td><%= link_to I18n.t('views.edit'), edit_book_path(book) %></td>
        <td><%= link_to I18n.t('views.destroy'), book, method: :delete, data:
        { confirm: I18n.t('views.are_you_sure')} %></td>
      </tr>
    <% end %>
  </tbody>
</table>

<br>

<%= link_to I18n.t('views.book.index.new'), new_book_path %>
```

app/views/books/new.html.erb

```erb
<h1><%= t 'views.book.new.title' %></h1>

<%= render 'form' %>

<%= link_to I18n.t('views.back'), books_path %>
```

app/views/books/show.html.erb

```
<p id="notice"><%= notice %></p>

<p>
  <strong><%= Book.human_attribute_name(:title) %>:</strong>
  <%= @book.title %>
</p>

<p>
  <strong><%= Book.human_attribute_name(:number_of_pages) %>:</strong>
  <%= number_with_delimiter(@book.number_of_pages) %>
</p>

<p>
  <strong><%= Book.human_attribute_name(:price) %>:</strong>
  <%= number_to_currency(@book.price) %>
</p>

<%= link_to I18n.t('views.edit'), edit_book_path(@book) %> |
<%= link_to I18n.t('views.back'), books_path %>
```

 In the show and index view, I integrated the helpers `number_with_delimiter` and `number_to_currency` so the numbers are represented more attractively for the user.

Right at the end, we still need to adapt a few flash messages in the controller app/controllers/books_controller.rb:

app/controllers/books_controller.rb

```
class BooksController < ApplicationController
  before_action :set_book, only: [:show, :edit, :update, :destroy]

  # GET /books
  # GET /books.json
  def index
    @books = Book.all
  end

  # GET /books/1
  # GET /books/1.json
  def show
  end

  # GET /books/new
  def new
    @book = Book.new
  end

  # GET /books/1/edit
  def edit
  end

  # POST /books
  # POST /books.json
  def create
    @book = Book.new(book_params)

    respond_to do |format|
```

```ruby
      if @book.save
        format.html { redirect_to @book, notice:
        I18n.t('views.book.flash_messages.book_was_successfully_created') }
        format.json { render action: 'show', status: :created, location: @book }
      else
        format.html { render action: 'new' }
        format.json { render json: @book.errors, status: :unprocessable_entity }
      end
    end
  end

  # PATCH/PUT /books/1
  # PATCH/PUT /books/1.json
  def update
    respond_to do |format|
      if @book.update(book_params)
        format.html { redirect_to @book, notice:
        I18n.t('views.book.flash_messages.book_was_successfully_updated') }
        format.json { head :no_content }
      else
        format.html { render action: 'edit' }
        format.json { render json: @book.errors, status: :unprocessable_entity
        }
      end
    end
  end

  # DELETE /books/1
  # DELETE /books/1.json
  def destroy
    @book.destroy
    respond_to do |format|
      format.html { redirect_to books_url }
      format.json { head :no_content }
    end
  end

  private
    # Use callbacks to share common setup or constraints between actions.
    def set_book
      @book = Book.find(params[:id])
    end

    # Never trust parameters from the scary internet, only allow the white list through.
    def book_params
      params.require(:book).permit(:title, :number_of_pages, :price)
    end
end
```

Now you can use the views generated by the scaffold generator entirely in German. The structure of the YAML files shown here can of course be adapted to your own preferences. The texts in the views and the controller are displayed with I18n.t. At this point you could of course also integrate the German text directly if the application is purely in German.

Paths in German

Our bibliography is completely in German, but the URLs are still in English. If we want to make all books available at the URL http://localhost:3000/buecher instead of the URL http://localhost:3000/books then we need to add the following entry to the config/routes.rb:

config/routes.rb

```
Bibliography::Application.routes.draw do
  resources :books, path: 'buecher', path_names: { new: 'neu', edit:
  'editieren' }
end
```

As a result, we then have the following new paths:

```
$ rake routes
(in /Users/xyz/rails/project-42/bibliography)
    Prefix Verb   URI Pattern                      Controller#Action
     books GET    /buecher(.:format)               books#index
           POST   /buecher(.:format)               books#create
  new_book GET    /buecher/neu(.:format)           books#new
 edit_book GET    /buecher/:id/editieren(.:format) books#edit
      book GET    /buecher/:id(.:format)           books#show
           PATCH  /buecher/:id(.:format)           books#update
           PUT    /buecher/:id(.:format)           books#update
           DELETE /buecher/:id(.:format)           books#destroy
$
```

The brilliant thing with Rails routes is that you do not need to do anything else. The rest is managed transparently by the routing engine.

Multilingual Rails Application

The approach for multilingual Rails applications is very similar to the monoligual, all-German Rails application described in the section "A Rails Application in Only One Language: German". But we need to define YAML language files for all required languages and tell the Rails application which language it should currently use. We do this via I18n.locale.

Using I18n.locale for Defining the Default Language

Of course, a Rails application has to know in which language a web page should be represented. I18n.locale saves the current language and can be read by the application. I am going to show you this with a mini web shop example:

```
$ rails new webshop
  [...]
$ cd webshop
$
```

This web shop gets a homepage:

```
$ rails generate controller Page index
  [...]
$
```

We still need to enter it as root page in the config/routes.rb:

config/routes.rb

```
Webshop::Application.routes.draw do
  get "page/index"
  root 'page#index'
end
```

We populate the `app/views/page/index.html.erb` with the following example:

app/views/page/index.html.erb

```
<h1>Example Webshop</h1>
<p>Welcome to this webshop.</p>

<p>
<strong>I18n.locale:</strong>
<%= I18n.locale %>
</p>
```

If we start the Rails server with `rails server` and go to http://localhost:3000/ in the browser, then we see the following web page:

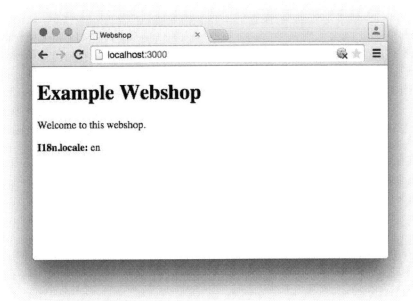

Figure 19. I18n ganze seite page index

As you can see, the default is set to "en" for English. Stop the Rails server with CTRL-C and change the setting for the default language to German in the file `config/application.rb`:

config/application.rb

```
config.i18n.default_locale = :de
```

If you then start the Rails server and again go to http://localhost:3000/ in the web browser, you will see the following web page:

image::screenshots/chapter10/i18n_ganze_seite_page_index_default_locale_de.png[I18n ganze seite page index default locale de,title="I18n ganze seite page index default locale de"]

The web page has not changed, but as output of `<%= I18n.locale %>` you now get "de' for German (Deutsch), not "en' for English as before.

Please stop the Rails server with CTRL-C and change the setting for the default language to en for English in the file `config/application.rb`:

config/application.rb

```
# The default locale is :en and all translations from config/locales/*.rb,yml
# are auto loaded.
# config.i18n.load_path += Dir[Rails.root.join('my', 'locales',
# '*.{rb,yml}').to_s]
config.i18n.default_locale = :en
```

We now know how to set the default for `I18n.locale` in the entire application, but that only gets half the job done. A user wants to be able to choose his own language. There are various ways of achieving this. To make things clearer, we need a second page that displays a German text.

Please create the file `app/views/page/index.de.html.erb` with the following content:

app/views/page/index.de.html.erb

```
<h1>Beispiel Webshop</h1>
<p>Willkommen in diesem Webshop.</p>

<p>
<strong>I18n.locale:</strong>
<%= I18n.locale %>
</p>
```

Setting I18n.locale via URL Path Prefix

The more stylish way of setting the language is to add it as prefix to the URL. This enables search engines to manage different language versions better. We want http://localhost:3000/de to display the German version of our homepage and http://localhost:3000/en the English version. The first step is adapting the `config/routes.rb`

config/routes.rb

```
Webshop::Application.routes.draw do
  scope ':locale', locale: /en|de/ do
    get "page/index"
    get '/', to: 'page#index'
  end

  root 'page#index'
end
```

Next, we need to set a `before_action` in the `app/controllers/application_controller.rb`. This filter sets the parameter locale set by the route as `I18n.locale`:

app/controllers/application_controller.rb

```ruby
class ApplicationController < ActionController::Base
  # Prevent CSRF attacks by raising an exception.
  # For APIs, you may want to use :null_session instead.
  protect_from_forgery with: :exception

  before_action :set_locale

  private
  def set_locale
    I18n.locale = params[:locale] || I18n.default_locale
  end
end
```

Now you have to allow the new locales to be loaded. Add this line to your `config/application.rb`

config/application.rb

```ruby
config.i18n.available_locales = [:en, :de]
```

To test it, start Rails with `rails server` and go to the URL http://localhost:3000/de.

Figure 20. I18n root de

Of course we can also go to http://localhost:3000/de/page/index:

Figure 21. I18n de page index

If we go to http://localhost:3000/en and http://localhost:3000/en/page/index we get the English version of each page.

But now we have a problem: by using the prefix, we initially get to a page with the correct language, but what if we want to link from that page to another page in our Rails project? Then we would need to manually insert the prefix into the link. Who wants that? Obviously there is a clever solution for this problem. We can set global default parameters for URL generation by defining a method called default_url_options in our controller.

So we just need to add this method in app/controllers/application_controller.rb:

app/controllers/application_controller.rb

```ruby
class ApplicationController < ActionController::Base
  # Prevent CSRF attacks by raising an exception.
  # For APIs, you may want to use :null_session instead.
  protect_from_forgery with: :exception

  before_action :set_locale

  def default_url_options
    { locale: I18n.locale }
  end

  private
  def set_locale
    I18n.locale = params[:locale] || I18n.default_locale
  end
end
```

As a result, all links created with link_to and url_for (on which link_to is based) are automatically expanded by the parameter locale. You do not need to do anything else. All links generated via the scaffold generator are automatically changed accordingly.

Navigation Example

To give the user the option of switching easily between the different language versions, it makes sense to offer two links at the top of the web page. We don't want the current language to be displayed as active link. This can be achieved as follows for all views in the file app/views/layouts/application.html.erb:

app/views/layouts/application.html.erb

```
<!DOCTYPE html>
<html>
<head>
  <title>Webshop</title>
  <%= stylesheet_link_tag    'application', media: 'all',
  'data-turbolinks-track' => true %>
  <%= javascript_include_tag 'application', 'data-turbolinks-track' => true %>
  <%= csrf_meta_tags %>
</head>
<body>

<p>
<%= link_to_unless I18n.locale == :en, "English", locale: :en %>
|
<%= link_to_unless I18n.locale == :de, "Deutsch", locale: :de %>
</p>

<%= yield %>

</body>
</html>
```

The navigation is then displayed at the top of the page.

Figure 22. I18n url prefix

Setting I18n.locale via Accept Language HTTP Header of Browser

When a user goes to your web page for the first time, you ideally want to immediately display the web page in the correct language for that user. To do this, you can read out the accept language field in the HTTP header. In every web browser, the user can set his preferred language (see http://www.w3.org/International/questions/qa-lang-priorities). The browser automatically informs the web server and consequently Ruby on Rails of this value.

Please edit the `app/controllers/application_controller.rb` as follows:

app/controllers/application_controller.rb

```ruby
class ApplicationController < ActionController::Base
  # Prevent CSRF attacks by raising an exception.
  # For APIs, you may want to use :null_session instead.
  protect_from_forgery with: :exception

  before_action :set_locale

  private
  def extract_locale_from_accept_language_header
    http_accept_language =
    request.env['HTTP_ACCEPT_LANGUAGE'].scan(/^[a-z]{2}/).first
    if ['de', 'en'].include? http_accept_language
      http_accept_language
    else
      'en'
    end
  end

  def set_locale
    I18n.locale = extract_locale_from_accept_language_header ||
    I18n.default_locale
  end
end
```

And please do not forget to clean the settings from the section "I18n.locale via URL Path Prefix" out of the `config/routes.rb`:

config/routes.rb

```ruby
Webshop::Application.routes.draw do
  get "page/index"
  root 'page#index'
end
```

Now you always get the output in the language defined in the web browser. Please note that `request.env['HTTP_ACCEPT_LANGUAGE'].scan(/^[a-z]{2}/).first` does not catch all cases. For example, you should make sure that you support the specified language in your Rails application in the first place. There are some ready-made gems that can easily do this job for you. Have a look at https://www.ruby-toolbox.com/categories/i18n#http_accept_language to find them.

Saving I18n.locale in a Session

Often you want to save the value of I18n.locale in a session.

 The approach described here for sessions will of course work just the same with cookies.

To set the value, let's create a controller in our web shop as example: the controller SetLanguage with the two actions english and german:

```
$ rails generate controller SetLanguage english german
  [...]
$
```

In the file `app/controllers/set_language_controller.rb` we populate the two actions as follows:

app/controllers/set_language_controller.rb

```ruby
class SetLanguageController < ApplicationController
  def english
    I18n.locale = :en
    set_session_and_redirect
  end

  def german
    I18n.locale = :de
    set_session_and_redirect
  end

  private
  def set_session_and_redirect
    session[:locale] = I18n.locale
    redirect_to :back
    rescue ActionController::RedirectBackError
      redirect_to :root
  end
end
```

Finally, we also want to adapt the `set_locale` methods in the file `app/controllers/application_controller.rb`:

app/controllers/application_controller.rb

```ruby
class ApplicationController < ActionController::Base
  # Prevent CSRF attacks by raising an exception.
  # For APIs, you may want to use :null_session instead.
  protect_from_forgery with: :exception

  before_filter :set_locale

  private
  def set_locale
    I18n.locale = session[:locale] || I18n.default_locale
    session[:locale] = I18n.locale
  end
end
```

After starting Rails with `rails server`, you can now set the language to German by going to the URL http://localhost:3000/set_language/german and to English by going to http://localhost:3000/set_language/english.

Navigation Example

To give the user the option of switching easily between the different language versions, it makes sense to offer two links at the top of the web page. We don't want the current language to be displayed as active link. This can be achieved as follows for all views in the file `app/views/layouts/application.html.erb`:

```
<!DOCTYPE html>
<html>
<head>
  <title>Webshop</title>
  <%= stylesheet_link_tag    "application", media: "all",
  "data-turbolinks-track" => true %>
  <%= javascript_include_tag "application", "data-turbolinks-track" => true %>
  <%= csrf_meta_tags %>
</head>
<body>

<p>
<%= link_to_unless I18n.locale == :en, "English", set_language_english_path %>
|
<%= link_to_unless I18n.locale == :de, "Deutsch", set_language_german_path %>
</p>

<%= yield %>

</body>
</html>
```

The navigation is then displayed at the top of the page.

Figure 23. I18n locale navigation

Setting I18n.locale via Domain Extension

If you have several domains with the extensions typical for the corresponding languages, you can of course also use these extensions to set the language. For example, if a user visits the page http://www.example.com he would see the English version, if he goes to http://www.example.de then the German version would be displayed.

To achieve this, we would need to go into the `app/controllers/application_controller.rb` and insert a `before_action` that analyses the accessed domain and sets the `I18n.locale`:

app/controllers/application_controller.rb

```ruby
class ApplicationController < ActionController::Base
  # Prevent CSRF attacks by raising an exception.
  # For APIs, you may want to use :null_session instead.
  protect_from_forgery with: :exception

  before_action :set_locale

  private
  def set_locale
    case request.host.split('.').last
    when 'de'
      I18n.locale = :de
    when 'com'
      I18n.locale = :en
    else
      I18n.locale = I18n.default_locale
    end
  end
end
```

To test this functionality, you can add the following items on your Linux or Mac OS X development system in the file /etc/hosts:

/etc/hosts

```
localhost www.example.com
localhost www.example.de
```

Then you can go to the URL http://www.example.com:3000 and http://www.example.de:3000 and you will see the corresponding language versions.

Which Approach is the Best?

I believe that a combination of the approaches described above will lead to the best result. When I first visit a web page I am happy if I find that the accept language HTTP header of my browser is read and implemented correctly. But it is also nice to be able to change the language later on in the user configuration (in particular for badly translated pages, English language is often better). And ultimately it has to be said that a page that is easy to represent is worth a lot for a search engine, and this also goes for the languages. Rails gives you the option of easily using all variations and even enables you to combine them together.

Multilingual Scaffolds

As an example, we use a mini webshop in which we translate a product scaffold. The aim is to make the application available in German and English.

The Rails application:

```
$ rails new webshop
  [...]
$ cd webshop
$ rails generate scaffold Product name description 'price:decimal{7,2}'
  [...]
$ rake db:migrate
  [...]
$
```

We define the product model in the app/models/product.rb

app/models/product.rb

```
class Product < ActiveRecord::Base
  validates :name,
            presence: true,
            uniqueness: true,
            length: { within: 2..255 }

  validates :price,
            presence: true,
            numericality: { greater_than: 0 }
end
```

When selecting the language for the user, we use the URL prefix variation described in the section "Setting I18n.locale via URL Path Prefix". We use the following app/controllers/application_controller.rb

app/controllers/application_controller.rb

```
class ApplicationController < ActionController::Base
  # Prevent CSRF attacks by raising an exception.
  # For APIs, you may want to use :null_session instead.
  protect_from_forgery with: :exception

  before_action :set_locale

  def default_url_options
    { locale: I18n.locale }
  end

  private
  def set_locale
    I18n.locale = params[:locale] || I18n.default_locale
  end
end
```

This is the config/routes.rb

config/routes.rb

```ruby
Webshop::Application.routes.draw do
  scope ':locale', locale: /en|de/ do
    resources :products
    get '/', to: 'products#index'
  end

  root 'products#index'
end
```

Then we insert the links for the navigation in the `app/views/layouts/application.html.erb`:

app/views/layouts/application.html.erb

```erb
<!DOCTYPE html>
<html>
<head>
  <title>Webshop</title>
  <%= stylesheet_link_tag    "application", media: "all",
  "data-turbolinks-track" => true %>
  <%= javascript_include_tag "application", "data-turbolinks-track" => true %>
  <%= csrf_meta_tags %>
</head>
<body>

<p>
<%= link_to_unless I18n.locale == :en, "English", locale: :en %>
|
<%= link_to_unless I18n.locale == :de, "Deutsch", locale: :de %>
</p>

<%= yield %>

</body>
</html>
```

Start the Rails server with `rails server`.

```
$ rails server
=> Rails 4.2.1 application starting in development on http://localhost:3000
=> Run rails server -h for more startup options
=> Ctrl-C to shutdown server
[2015-04-30 15:26:06] INFO  WEBrick 1.3.1
[2015-04-30 15:26:06] INFO  ruby 2.2.0 (2014-12-25) [x86_64-darwin14]
[2015-04-30 15:26:06] INFO  WEBrick::HTTPServer#start: pid=45201 port=3000
```

If we go to http://localhost:3000 we see the normal English page.

Figure 24. I18n basis version

If we click the option German, nothing changes on the page, apart from the language navigation right at the top.

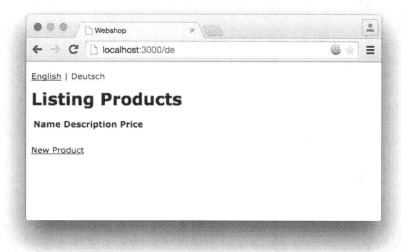

Figure 25. I18n basis version de

Now we still need to find a way of translating the individual elements of this page appropriately and as generically as possible.

Text Blocks in YAML Format

Now we need to define the individual text blocks for I18n.t. The corresponding directories still have to be created first:

```
$ mkdir -p config/locales/models/product
$ mkdir -p config/locales/views/product
$
```

To make sure that the YAML files created there are indeed read in automatically, you need to insert the following lines in the file config/application.rb:

config/application.rb

```
# The default locale is :en and all translations from config/locales/*.rb,yml
# are auto loaded.
config.i18n.load_path += Dir[Rails.root.join('config', 'locales', 'models',
'*', '*.yml').to_s]
config.i18n.load_path += Dir[Rails.root.join('config', 'locales', 'views',
'*', '*.yml').to_s]
config.i18n.default_locale = :en
```

German

Please create the file config/locales/models/product/de.yml with the following content.

config/locales/models/product/de.yml

```
de:
  activerecord:
    models:
      product: 'Produkt'
    attributes:
      product:
        name: 'Name'
        description: 'Beschreibung'
        price: 'Preis'
```

In the file config/locales/views/product/de.yml we insert a few values for the scaffold views:

config/locales/views/product/de.yml

```
de:
  views:
    show: Anzeigen
    edit: Editieren
    destroy: Löschen
    are_you_sure: Sind Sie sicher?
    back: Zurück
    edit: Editieren
    product:
      index:
        title: Liste aller Produkte
        new_product: Neues Produkt
      edit:
        title: Produkt editieren
      new:
        title: Neues Produkt
      flash_messages:
        product_was_successfully_created: 'Das Produkt wurde angelegt.'
        product_was_successfully_updated: 'Das Produkt wurde aktualisiert.'
```

Finally, we copy a ready-made default translation by Sven Fuchs from his github repository
https://github.com/svenfuchs/rails-i18n:

```
$ cd config/locales/
$ curl -O https://raw.githubusercontent.com/svenfuchs/rails-i18n/master/rails/locale/de.yml
  % Total    % Received % Xferd  Average Speed   Time    Time     Time  Current
                                 Dload  Upload   Total   Spent    Left  Speed
100  5027  100  5027    0     0  15756      0 --:--:-- --:--:-- --:--:-- 15758
$
```

 If you know how Bundler works you can also insert the line `gem 'rails-i18n'` into the
file `Gemfile` and then execute `bundle install`. This gives you all language files from the
repository.

The file `config/locales/de.yml` contains all required formats and generic phrases for German that we need for
a normal Rails application (for example days of the week, currency symbols, etc). Use your favorite editor to
have a look in there to get an impression.

English

As most things are already present in the system for English, we just need to insert a few values for the
scaffold views in the file `config/locales/views/product/en.yml`:

config/locales/views/product/en.yml

```
en:
  views:
    show: Show
    edit: Edit
    destroy: Delete
    are_you_sure: Are you sure?
    back: Back
    edit: Edit
    product:
      index:
        title: List of all products
        new_product: New product
      edit:
        title: Edit Product
      new:
        title: New product
      flash_messages:
        product_was_successfully_created: 'Product was created.'
        product_was_successfully_updated: 'Product was updated.'
```

Equipping Views with I18n.t

Please edit the listed view files as specified.

_form.html.erb

In the file `app/views/products/_form.html.erb` we need to change the display of the validation errors in the top
section to `I18n.t`. The names of form errors are automatically read in from `activerecord.attributes.product`:

```erb
<%= form_for(@product) do |f| %>
  <% if @product.errors.any? %>
    <div id="error_explanation">
      <h2><%= t 'activerecord.errors.template.header', model:
      Product.model_name.human, count: @product.errors.count %></h2>

      <ul>
      <% @product.errors.full_messages.each do |msg| %>
        <li><%= msg %></li>
      <% end %>
      </ul>
    </div>
  <% end %>

  <div class="field">
    <%= f.label :name %><br>
    <%= f.text_field :name %>
  </div>
  <div class="field">
    <%= f.label :description %><br>
    <%= f.text_field :description %>
  </div>
  <div class="field">
    <%= f.label :price %><br>
    <%= f.text_field :price %>
  </div>
  <div class="actions">
    <%= f.submit %>
  </div>
<% end %>
```

edit.html.erb

In the file app/views/products/edit.html.erb we need to integrate the heading and the links at the bottom of the page with I18n.t:

app/views/products/edit.html.erb

```erb
<h1><%= t 'views.product.edit.title' %></h1>

<%= render 'form' %>

<%= link_to I18n.t('views.show'), @product %> |
<%= link_to I18n.t('views.back'), products_path %>
```

index.html.erb

In the file app/views/products/index.html.erb we need to change practically every line. In the table header I use human_attribute_name(), but you could also do it directly with I18n.t. The price of the product is specified with the helper number_to_currency. In a real application, we would have to specify a defined currency at this point as well.

app/views/products/index.html.erb

```erb
<h1><%= t 'views.product.index.listing_products' %></h1>

<table>
  <thead>
    <tr>
      <th><%= Product.human_attribute_name(:name) %></th>
      <th><%= Product.human_attribute_name(:description) %></th>
      <th><%= Product.human_attribute_name(:price) %></th>
      <th></th>
      <th></th>
      <th></th>
    </tr>
  </thead>

  <tbody>
    <% @products.each do |product| %>
      <tr>
        <td><%= product.name %></td>
        <td><%= product.description %></td>
        <td><%= number_to_currency(product.price) %></td>
        <td><%= link_to I18n.t('views.show'), product %></td>
        <td><%= link_to I18n.t('views.edit'), edit_product_path(product)
        %></td>
        <td><%= link_to I18n.t('views.destroy'), product, method: :delete,
        data: { confirm: I18n.t('views.are_you_sure')} %></td>
      </tr>
    <% end %>
  </tbody>
</table>

<br>

<%= link_to I18n.t('views.product.index.new_product'), new_product_path %>
```

new.html.erb

In the app/views/products/new.html.erb we need to adapt the heading and the link:

app/views/products/new.html.erb

```erb
<h1><%= t 'views.product.new.title' %></h1>

<%= render 'form' %>

<%= link_to I18n.t('views.back'), products_path %>
```

show.html.erb

In the app/views/products/show.html.erb we again use human_attribute_name() for the attributes. Plus the links need to be translated with I18n.t. As with the index view, we again use number_to_currency() to show the price in formatted form:

```erb
<p id="notice"><%= notice %></p>

<p>
  <strong><%= Product.human_attribute_name(:name) %>:</strong>
  <%= @product.name %>
</p>

<p>
  <strong><%= Product.human_attribute_name(:description) %>:</strong>
  <%= @product.description %>
</p>

<p>
  <strong><%= Product.human_attribute_name(:price) %>:</strong>
  <%= number_to_currency(@product.price) %>
</p>

<%= link_to I18n.t('views.edit'), edit_product_path(@product) %> |
<%= link_to I18n.t('views.back'), products_path %>
```

Translating Flash Messages in the Controller

Finally, we need to translate the two flash messages in the app/controllers/products_controller.rb for creating (create) and updating (update) records, again via I18n.t:

app/controllers/products_controller.rb

```ruby
class ProductsController < ApplicationController
  before_action :set_product, only: [:show, :edit, :update, :destroy]

  # GET /products
  # GET /products.json
  def index
    @products = Product.all
  end

  # GET /products/1
  # GET /products/1.json
  def show
  end

  # GET /products/new
  def new
    @product = Product.new
  end

  # GET /products/1/edit
  def edit
  end

  # POST /products
  # POST /products.json
  def create
    @product = Product.new(product_params)

    respond_to do |format|
      if @product.save
```

```
      format.html { redirect_to @product, notice:
      I18n.t('views.product.flash_messages.product_was_successfully_created')
      }
      format.json { render action: 'show', status: :created, location:
      @product }
    else
      format.html { render action: 'new' }
      format.json { render json: @product.errors, status:
      :unprocessable_entity }
    end
  end
end

# PATCH/PUT /products/1
# PATCH/PUT /products/1.json
def update
  respond_to do |format|
    if @product.update(product_params)
      format.html { redirect_to @product, notice:
      I18n.t('views.product.flash_messages.product_was_successfully_updated')
      }
      format.json { head :no_content }
    else
      format.html { render action: 'edit' }
      format.json { render json: @product.errors, status:
      :unprocessable_entity }
    end
  end
end

# DELETE /products/1
# DELETE /products/1.json
def destroy
  @product.destroy
  respond_to do |format|
    format.html { redirect_to products_url }
    format.json { head :no_content }
  end
end

private
  # Use callbacks to share common setup or constraints between actions.
  def set_product
    @product = Product.find(params[:id])
  end

  # Never trust parameters from the scary internet, only allow the white
  # list through.
  def product_params
    params.require(:product).permit(:name, :description, :price)
  end
end
```

The Result

Now you can use the scaffold products both in German and in English. You can switch the language via the link at the top of the page.

Further Information

The best source of information on this topic can be found in the Rails documentation at http://guides.rubyonrails.org/i18n.html. This also shows how you can operate other backends for defining the translations.

As so often, Railscasts.com offers a whole range of Railscasts on the topic I18n: http://railscasts.com/episodes?utf8=%E2%9C%93&search=i18n

Asset Pipeline

The asset pipeline offers the Rails developer the opportunity of delivering CSS, JavaScript and image files to the browser more optimally - in other words, in a more compressed form and therefore more quickly. Different CSS files are combined into one big file and delivered to the browser with a fingerprint in the file name. This fingerprinting enables the browser and any proxy in between to optimally cache the data, so the browser can load these files more quickly.

 In case you are running on HTTP/2 is might be a good idea to   break up this flow into smaller chunks to maximize caching.   I will detail this in future versions of this book because   most systems are still running on HTTP/1.1.

Within the asset pipeline, you can program CSS, SASS, JavaScript and CoffeeScript extensively and clearly, in order to let them be delivered later as automatically compressed CSS and JavaScript files.

As an example we use once more our web shop with a product scaffold:

```
$ rails new webshop
  [...]
$ cd webshop
$ rails generate scaffold product name 'price:decimal{7,2}'
  [...]
$ rake db:migrate
  [...]
$
```

In the directory app/assets you will then find the following files:

```
app/assets/
├──── config
│     └──── manifest.js
├──── images
├──── javascripts
│     ├──── application.js
│     ├──── cable.coffee
│     └──── channels
└──── stylesheets
      └──── application.css
```

The files app/assets/javascripts/application.js and app/assets/stylesheets/application.css are what is referred to as manifest files. They automatically include the other files in the relevant directory.

application.js

The file app/assets/javascripts/application.js has the following content:

app/assets/javascripts/application.js

```
// [...]
//= require jquery
//= require jquery_ujs
//= require turbolinks
//= require_tree .
```

In the application.js, the jQuery files defined in the jquery gem are automatically integrated (for further information on jQuery, please visit http://jquery.com/). Plus all other files in this directory are integrated via require_tree . as shown above.

The not yet optimized result can be viewed in the development environment at the URL http://localhost:3000/assets/application.js.

application.css

The file app/assets/stylesheets/application.css has the following content:

app/assets/stylesheets/application.css

```
/*
 * [...]
*= require_tree .
*= require_self
*/
```

With the command require_tree . all files in this directory are automatically integrated.

rails assets:precompile

When using the asset pipeline, you need to remember that you have to precompile the assets before starting the Rails server in the production environment. This happens via the command rails assets:precompile:

```
$ rails assets:precompile
I, [2015-12-01T12:08:50.495102 #54978]  INFO -- : Writing
/Users/xyz/webshop/public/assets/application-de26[...]fb6c.js
I, [2015-12-01T12:08:50.555494 #54978]  INFO -- : Writing
/Users/xyz/webshop/public/assets/application-2ce5[...]f443.css
```

If you forget to do this, you will find the following error message in the log:

```
ActionView::Template::Error (application.css isn't precompiled)
```

The files created by rails assets:precompile appear in the directory public/assets

```
public/assets
├──── application-12b3c7dd74e9de7cbb1efa76a6d.css
├──── application-12b3c7dd74e9de7cbb1efa76a6d.css.gz
├──── application-723d1be6cc74abb1cec24276d681.js
├──── application-723d1be6cc74abb1cec24276d681.js.gz
└──── manifest-720d2116dee3d83d194ffd9d0957c21c.json
```

Go ahead and use your favorite editor to have a look at the created css and js files. You will find minimized and optimized code. If the web server supports it, the zipped gz files are delivered directly, which speeds things up a bit more.

The difference in file size is enormous. The file application.js created in the development
environment has a file size of 296 KB. The file js.gz created by rails assets:precompile is
only 88 KB. Users of cellphones in particular will be grateful for smaller file sizes.

 The speed advantage incidentally lies not just in the file size, but also in the fact that only
one file is downloaded, not several. The HTTP/1.1 overhead for loading a file is time-
consuming. Things are changing with HTTP/2. I'll update this chapter accordingly in future
editions of this book.

The Fingerprint

The fingerprint in the file name consists of a hash sum generated from the content of the relevant file. This
fingerprint ensures optimal caching and prevents an old cache being used if any changes are made to the
content. A simple but very effective method.

Coding Links to an Asset

All files below the directory app/assets are delivered in normal form by the Rails server. For example, you can
go to the URL http://localhost:3000/assets/rails.png to view the Rails logo saved under
app/assets/images/rails.png and to http://localhost:3000/assets/application.js to view the content of
app/assets/javascripts/application.js. The Rails image rails.png is delivered 1:1 and the file application.js
is first created by the asset pipeline.

But you should never enter these files as hard-wired in a view. To make the most of the asset pipeline, you
must use the helpers described here.

Coding Link to an Image

You can retrieve an image via the helper image_tag. This is what it would look like in the view for the file
app/assets/images/rails.png:

```
<%= image_tag "rails.png" %>
```

In development mode, the following HTML code results from this:

```
<img alt="Rails" src="/assets/rails.png" />
```

In production mode, you get an HTML code that points to a precompiled file with fingerprint:

```
<img alt="Rails" src="/assets/rails-be8732dac73d845ac5b142c8fb5f9fb0.png" />
```

Coding Link to a JavaScript File

You can use the helper javascript_include_tag to retrieve a JavaScript file compiled by the asset pipeline. This
is what it would look like in the view for the file app/assets/javascripts/application.js:

```
<%= javascript_include_tag "application" %>
```

In development mode, the following HTML code results from this:

```
<link href="/assets/application.css?body=1" media="all" rel="stylesheet"
type="text/css" />
<link href="/assets/products.css?body=1" media="all" rel="stylesheet"
type="text/css" />
<link href="/assets/scaffolds.css?body=1" media="all" rel="stylesheet"
type="text/css" />
```

In production mode, you get an HTML code that points to a precompiled file with fingerprint:

```
<link href="/assets/application-0149f820dbdd285aa65e241569d8c256.css"
media="all" rel="stylesheet" type="text/css" />
```

Coding Link to a CSS File

A stylesheet compiled by the asset pipeline can be retrieved via the helper stylesheet_link_tag. In the view, it would look like this for the file app/assets/stylesheets/application.css:

```
<%= stylesheet_link_tag "application" %>
```

In development mode, the following HTML code results from this:

```
<script src="/assets/jquery.js?body=1" type="text/javascript"></script>
<script src="/assets/jquery_ujs.js?body=1" type="text/javascript"></script>
<script src="/assets/products.js?body=1" type="text/javascript"></script>
<script src="/assets/application.js?body=1" type="text/javascript"></script>
```

In production mode, you get an HTML code that points to a precompiled file with fingerprint:

```
<script src="/assets/application-f8ca698e63b86d217c88772a65d2d20e.js"
type="text/javascript"></script>
```

Defaults in the application.html.erb

Incidentally, the file app/views/layouts/application.html.erb that the scaffold generator creates by default already contains the coding links for these JavaScript and stylesheet files:

```erb
<!DOCTYPE html>
<html>
  <head>
    <title>Webshop</title>
    <%= csrf_meta_tags %>
    <%= action_cable_meta_tag %>

    <%= stylesheet_link_tag    'application', media: 'all', 'data-turbolinks-track' => true %>
    <%= javascript_include_tag 'application', 'data-turbolinks-track' => true %>
  </head>

  <body>
    <%= yield %>
  </body>
</html>
```

JavaScript

The focus of this chapter is not on explaining JavaScript. The aim is to show you as a Rails programmer how you can integrate JavaScript in a Rails application. Correspondingly, the chapters do not explain JavaScript in detail. I am assuming that you can read and understand JavaScript. If not, it may be better to skip this chapter. You can happily get by without JavaScript.

jQuery

By default, Rails 5 uses the jQuery Javascript library (http://jquery.com/). If you do not require this library, you should delete the following lines from the file app/assets/javascripts/application.js within the asset pipeline (see the section "Asset Pipeline"):

```
//= require jquery
//= require jquery_ujs
```

With jQuery, you can implement animations and Ajax interactions on your web page relatively easily.

You will find a good introduction to this topic in the jQuery documentation at http://learn.jquery.com/

CoffeeScript

For many Rails developers, CoffeeScript is the best thing invented since the introduction of sliced bread. CoffeeScript is a simple programming language that is converted to JavaScript via the asset pipeline. I am going to use JavaScript and CoffeeScript in this chapter. If you would like to know more about CoffeeScript, please look at the CoffeeScript documentation at http://coffeescript.org/ and as so often there is also an excellent Railscast on CoffeeScript available at http://railscasts.com/episodes/267-coffeescript-basics.

JavaScript Helpers

For using JavaScript in the view, there are some useful helpers available.

javascript_tag

The easiest way of using JavaScript one-liners in a view is via javascript_tag.

With the following line in the view, you can execute an alert when the page is accessed:

```
<%= javascript_tag "alert('Just an example.')" %>
```

The HTML code generated is this:

```
<script type="text/javascript">
//<![CDATA[
alert('Just an example.')
//]]>
</script>
```

link_to_function

The helper link_to_function creates a link whose onclick handler executes a JavaScript.

Again, here is a example for an alert. The ERB code in the view looks like this:

```
<%= link_to_function "trigger alert", "alert('Just an example.')" %>
```

The generated HTML code:

```
<a href="#" onclick="alert('Just an example.'); return false;">trigger
alert</a>
```

button_to_function

The helper `button_to_function` creates a button whose `onclick` handler executes a JavaScript.

Once more the example with the alert. The ERB code in the view looks like this:

```
<%= button_to_function "trigger alert", "alert('Just an example.')" %>
```

The generated HTML code:

```
<input onclick="alert('Just an example.');" type="button" value="trigger
alert" />
```

Example

The easiest way of explaining how you go about programming with JavaScript and the asset pipeline in a Rails project is by using a little example. As always, the main focus is not on creating an amazingly meaningful application. ;-)

Changing Form Depending on Input

Let's build a room reservation system where you can book a single or double room and then have to enter either one or two guest names in the same form. The basic structure:

```
$ rails new hotel
  [...]
$ cd hotel
$ rails generate scaffold reservation start:date end:date
  room_type:string guest_name1 guest_name2
  [...]
$ rails db:migrate
  [...]
$ rails server
  [...]
```

With this setup we get a very spartanic and totally unnormalized http://localhost:3000/reservations/new

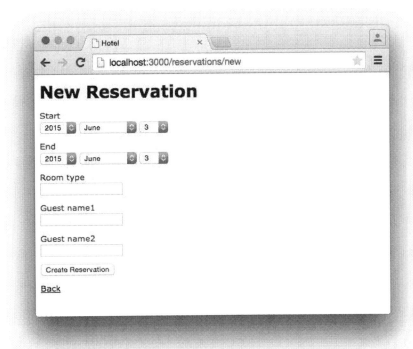

Figure 26. Hotel basic form

That is not userfriendly. The aim is to display the following page when you go to http://localhost:3000/reservations/new:

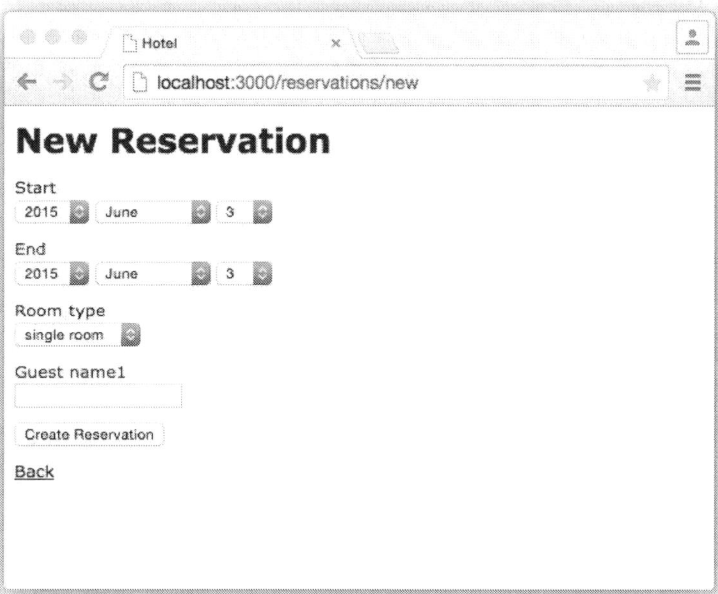

Figure 27. Hotel single room form

As soon as the user selects a double room instead of a single, we want a second name field to appear:

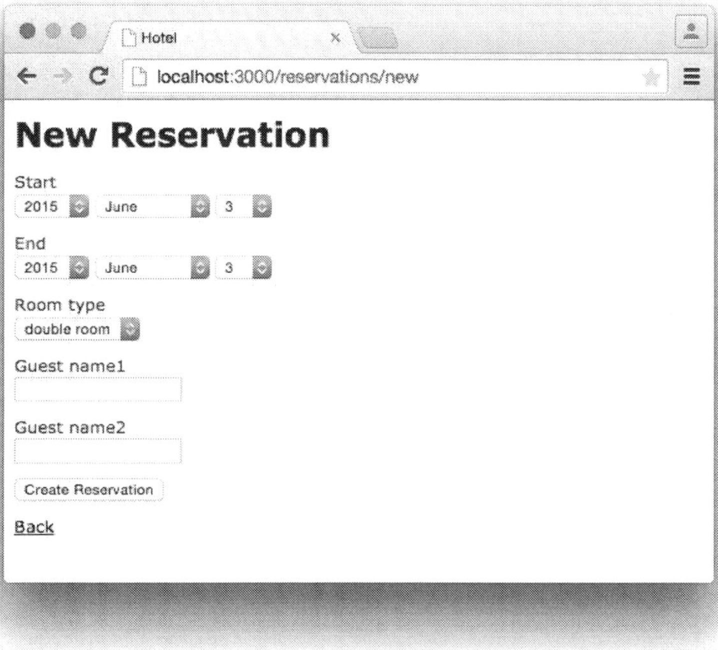

Figure 28. Hotel double room form

So I am changing two things in the app/views/reservations/_form.html.erb:

- Set the room_type via a dropdown box.

app/views/reservations/_form.html.erb

```
[...]
<div class="field">
  <%= f.select :room_type, options_for_select(['single room', 'double room']) %>
</div>
[...]
```

- In the div element around the second name, I set an ID `second_name`.

app/views/reservations/_form.html.erb

```
[...]
<div class="field" id='second_name'>
  <%= f.label :guest_name2 %>
  <%= f.text_field :guest_name2 %>
</div>
[...]
```

In the file app/assets/javascripts/reservations.js.coffee I define the CoffeeScript code that toggles the element with the ID second_name between visible (show) or invisible (hide) depending on the content of reservation_room_type:

app/assets/javascripts/reservations.js.coffee

```
ready = ->
  $('#second_name').hide()
  $('#reservation_room_type').change ->
    room_type = $('#reservation_room_type :selected').text()
    if room_type == 'single room'
      $('#second_name').hide()
    else
      $('#second_name').show()

$(document).ready(ready)
$(document).on('page:load', ready)
```

 In the real world, you would surely integrate the guest names in a 1:n has_many association, but in this example we just want to demonstrate how you can change the content of a form via JavaScript.

Caching

Where caching of web applications is concerned, most people tend to wait until they encounter performance problems. Then the admin first looks at the database and adds an index here and there. If that does not help, he has a look at the views and adds fragment caching. But this is not the best approach for working with caches. The aim of this chapter is to help you understand how key based cache expiration works. You can then use this approach to plan new applications already on the database structure level in such a way that you can cache optimally during development.

There are two main arguments for using caching:

- The application becomes faster for the user. A faster web page results in happier users which results in a better conversion rate.

- You need less hardware for the web server, because you require less resources for processing the queries. On average, a well cached system only needs a fifth of the processing power of a non-cached system. Quite often, it's even less.

 If these two arguments are irrelevant for you, then you don't   need to read this chapter.

We are going to look at three different caching methods:

- HTTP caching

  This is the sledge hammer among the caching methods and the ultimate performance weapon. In particular, web pages that are intended for mobile devices (for example iPhone) should try to make the most of HTTP caching. If you use a combination of key based cache expiration and HTTP caching, you save a huge amount of processing time on the server and also bandwidth.

- Page caching

  This is the screwdriver among the caching methods. You can get a lot of performance out of the system, but it is not as good as HTTP caching.

- Fragment caching

  The tweezers among the caching methods, so to speak. But don't underestimate it.

 The aim is to optimally combine all three methods.

A Simple Example Application

To try out the caching methods, we need an example application. We are going to use a simple phone book with a model for the company and a model for the employees of the company.

 Please consider: if the processing power you save (shown later)   is already so significant in such a simple application, it will   be even more significant in a more complex application with   more complex views.

We create the new Rails app:

```
$ rails new phone_book
  [...]
$ cd phone_book
$ rails generate scaffold company name
  [...]
$ rails generate scaffold employee company:references
  last_name first_name phone_number
  [...]
$ rails db:migrate
  [...]
```

Models

We insert a few rudimentary rules in the two models:

app/models/company.rb

```ruby
class Company < ApplicationRecord
  validates :name,
            presence: true,
            uniqueness: true

  has_many :employees, dependent: :destroy

  def to_s
    name
  end
end
```

app/models/employee.rb

```ruby
class Employee < ApplicationRecord
  belongs_to :company, touch: true

  validates :first_name,
            presence: true

  validates :last_name,
            presence: true

  validates :company,
            presence: true

  def to_s
    "#{first_name} #{last_name}"
  end
end
```

Views

We change the following two company views to list the number of employees in the Index view and all the employees in the Show view.

app/views/companies/index.html.erb

```
[...]
<table>
  <thead>
    <tr>
      <th>Name</th>
      <th>Number of employees</th>
      <th colspan="3"></th>
    </tr>
  </thead>

  <tbody>
    <% @companies.each do |company| %>
      <tr>
        <td><%= company.name %></td>
        <td><%= company.employees.count %></td>
        [...]
      </tr>
    <% end %>
  </tbody>
</table>
[...]
```

app/views/companies/show.html.erb

```
<p id="notice"><%= notice %></p>

<p>
  <strong>Name:</strong>
  <%= @company.name %>
</p>

<% if @company.employees.any? %>
<h1>Employees</h1>

<table>
  <thead>
    <tr>
      <th>Last name</th>
      <th>First name</th>
      <th>Phone number</th>
    </tr>
  </thead>

  <tbody>
    <% @company.employees.each do |employee| %>
      <tr>
        <td><%= employee.last_name %></td>
        <td><%= employee.first_name %></td>
        <td><%= employee.phone_number %></td>
      </tr>
    <% end %>
  </tbody>
</table>
<% end %>
```

Example Data

To easily populate the database, we use the Faker gem (see http://faker.rubyforge.org/). With Faker, you can generate random names and phone numbers. Please add the following line in the Gemfile:

Gemfile

```
gem 'faker'
```

Then start a bundle install:

```
$ bundle install
[...]
```

With the db/seeds.rb we create 30 companies with a random number of employees in each case:

db/seeds.rb

```
30.times do
  company = Company.new(:name => Faker::Company.name)
  if company.save
    SecureRandom.random_number(100).times do
      company.employees.create(
        first_name:    Faker::Name.first_name,
        last_name:     Faker::Name.last_name,
        phone_number:  Faker::PhoneNumber.phone_number
      )
    end
  end
end
```

We populate it via rails db:seed

```
$ rails db:seed
```

You can start the application with rails server and retrieve the example data with a web browser by going to the URLs http://localhost:3000/companies and http://localhost:3000/companies/1.

Normal Speed of the Pages to Optimize

In this chapter, we optimize the following web pages. Start the Rails application in development mode with rails server. The relevant numbers of course depend on the hardware you are using.

```
$ rails server
=> Booting Puma
=> Rails 5.0.0.1 application starting in development on http://localhost:3000
[...]
```

To access the web pages, we use the command line tool curl (http://curl.haxx.se/). Of course you can also access the web pages with other web browsers. We look at the time shown in the Rails log for creating the page. In reality, you need to add the time it takes for the page to be delivered to the web browser.

List of All Companies (Index View)

At the URL http://localhost:3000/companies the user can see a list of all saved companies with the relevant number of employees.

Generating the page takes 89ms.

```
Completed 200 OK in 89ms (Views: 79.0ms | ActiveRecord: 9.6ms)
```

Detailed View of a Single Company (Show View)

At the URL http://localhost:3000/companies/1 the user can see the details of the first company with all employees.

Generating the page takes 51ms.

```
Completed 200 OK in 51ms (Views: 48.9ms | ActiveRecord: 0.9ms)
```

HTTP Caching

HTTP caching attempts to reuse already loaded web pages or files. For example, if you visit a web page such as http://www.nytimes.com or http://www.wired.com several times a day to read the latest news, then certain elements of that page (for example, the logo image at the top of the page) will not be loaded again on your second visit. Your browser already has these files in the local cache, which saves loading time and bandwidth.

Within the Rails framework, our aim is answering the question "Has a page changed?" already in the controller. Because normally, most of the time is spent on rendering the page in the view. I'd like to repeat that: Most of the time is spent on rendering the page in the view!

Last-Modified

The web browser knows when it has downloaded a resource (e.g. a web page) and then placed it into it's cache. At a second request it can pass this information to the web server in an If-Modified-Since: header. The web server can then compare this information to the corresponding file and either deliver a newer version or return an HTTP 304 Not Modified code as response. In case of a 304, the web browser delivers the cached version. Now you are going to say, "That's all very well for images, but it won't help me at all for dynamically generated web pages such as the Index view of the companies." But you are underestimating the power of Rails.

 Please modify the times used in the examples in accordance with your own circumstances.

Please edit the show method in the controller file app/controllers/companies_controller.rb as follows :

app/controllers/companies_controller.rb

```
# GET /companies/1
# GET /companies/1.json
def show
  fresh_when last_modified: @company.updated_at
end
```

After restarting the Rails application, we have a look at the HTTP header of http://localhost:3000/companies/1:

```
$ curl -I http://localhost:3000/companies/1
HTTP/1.1 200 OK
X-Frame-Options: SAMEORIGIN
X-XSS-Protection: 1; mode=block
X-Content-Type-Options: nosniff
Last-Modified: Sun, 03 May 2015 18:38:05 GMT
[...]
```

The Last-Modified entry in the HTTP header was generated by fresh_when in the controller. If we later go to the same web page and specify this time as well, then we do not get the web page back, but a 304 Not Modified message:

```
$ curl -I http://localhost:3000/companies/1 --header 'If-Modified-Since: Sun,
03 May 2015 18:38:05 GMT'
HTTP/1.1 304 Not Modified
 [...]
```

In the Rails log, we find this:

```
Started HEAD "/companies/1" for 127.0.0.1 at 2015-05-03 20:51:02 +0200
Processing by CompaniesController#show as /
  Parameters: {"id"=>"1"}
  Company Load (0.1ms)  SELECT  "companies".* FROM "companies" WHERE
  "companies"."id" = ? LIMIT 1  [["id", 1]]
Completed 304 Not Modified in 2ms (ActiveRecord: 0.1ms)
```

Rails took 2ms to answer this request, compared to the 51ms of the standard variation. This is much faster! So you have used less resources on the server. And saved a massive amount of bandwidth. The user will be able to see the page much more quickly.

Etag

Sometimes the update_at field of a particular object is not meaningful on its own. For example, if you have a web page where users can log in and this page then generates web page contents based on a role model, it can happen that user A as admin is able to see an Edit link that is not displayed to user B as normal user. In such a scenario, the Last-Modified header explained in section "Last Modified" does not help.

In these cases, we can use the etag header. The etag is generated by the web server and delivered when the web page is first visited. If the user visits the same URL again, the browser can then check if the corresponding web page has changed by sending a If-None-Match: query to the web server.

Please edit the index and show methods in the controller file app/controllers/companies_controller.rb as follows:

```
# GET /companies
# GET /companies.json
def index
  @companies = Company.all
  fresh_when etag: @companies
end

# GET /companies/1
# GET /companies/1.json
def show
  fresh_when etag: @company
end
```

A special Rails feature comes into play for the etag: Rails automatically sets a new CSRF token for each new visitor of the website. This prevents cross-site request forgery attacks (see wikipedia.org/wiki/Cross_site_request_forgery). But it also means that each new user of a web page gets a new etag for the same page. To ensure that the same users also get identical CSRF tokens, these are stored in a cookie by the web browser and consequently sent back to the web server every time the web page is visited. The curl we used for developing does not do this by default. But we can tell curl that we want to save all cookies in a file and transmit these cookies later if a request is received.

For saving, we use the -c cookies.txt parameter.

```
$ curl -I http://localhost:3000/companies -c cookies.txt
HTTP/1.1 200 OK
X-Frame-Options: SAMEORIGIN
X-Xss-Protection: 1; mode=block
X-Content-Type-Options: nosniff
Etag: "a8a30e6dcdb4380f169dd18911cd6a51"
  [...]
```

With the parameter -b cookies.txt, curl sends these cookies to the web server when a request arrives. Now we get the same etag for two subsequent requests:

```
$ curl -I http://localhost:3000/companies -b cookies.txt
HTTP/1.1 200 OK
X-Frame-Options: SAMEORIGIN
X-Xss-Protection: 1; mode=block
X-Content-Type-Options: nosniff
Etag: "a8a30e6dcdb4380f169dd18911cd6a51"
[...]

$ curl -I http://localhost:3000/companies -b cookies.txt
HTTP/1.1 200 OK
X-Frame-Options: SAMEORIGIN
X-Xss-Protection: 1; mode=block
X-Content-Type-Options: nosniff
Etag: "a8a30e6dcdb4380f169dd18911cd6a51"
[...]
```

We now use this etag to find out in the request with If-None-Match if the version we have cached is still up to date:

```
$ curl -I http://localhost:3000/companies -b cookies.txt --header
'If-None-Match: "a8a30e6dcdb4380f169dd18911cd6a51"'
HTTP/1.1 304 Not Modified
X-Frame-Options: SAMEORIGIN
X-Xss-Protection: 1; mode=block
X-Content-Type-Options: nosniff
Etag: "a8a30e6dcdb4380f169dd18911cd6a51"
[...]
```

We get a 304 Not Modified in response. Let's look at the Rails log:

```
Started HEAD "/companies" for 127.0.0.1 at 2015-05-03 21:00:01 +0200
Processing by CompaniesController#index as /
  Cache digest for app/views/companies/index.html.erb:
  5365a42330adb48b855f7488b0d25b29
  Company Load (0.2ms)  SELECT "companies".* FROM "companies"
Completed 304 Not Modified in 5ms (ActiveRecord: 0.2ms)
```

Rails only took 5ms to process the request. Almost 10 times as fast as the variation without cache! Plus we have saved bandwidth again. The user will be happy with the speedy web application.

current_user and Other Potential Parameters

As basis for generating an etag, we can not just pass an object, but also an array of objects. This way, we can solve the problem with the logged-in user. Let's assume that a logged-in user is output with the method current_user.

We only have to add etag { current_user.try :id } in the app/controllers/application_controller.rb to make sure that all etags in the application include the current_user.id which is nil in case nobody is logged in.

app/controllers/application_controller.rb

```
class ApplicationController < ActionController::Base
  # Prevent CSRF attacks by raising an exception.
  # For APIs, you may want to use :null_session instead.
  protect_from_forgery with: :exception

  etag { current_user.try :id }
end
```

You can chain other objects in this array too and use this approach to define when a page has not changed.

The Magic of touch

What happens if an Employee is edited or deleted? Then the show view and potentially also the index view would have to change as well. That is the reason for the line

```
belongs_to :company, touch: true
```

in the employee model. Every time an object of the class Employee is saved in edited form, and if touch: true is used, ActiveRecord updates the superordinate Company element in the database. The updated_at field is set to the current time. It is "touched".

This approach ensures that a correct content is delivered.

stale?

Up to now, we have always assumed that only HTML pages are delivered. So we were able to use fresh_when and then do without the respond_to do |format| block. But HTTP caching is not limited to HTML pages. Yet if we render JSON (for example) as well and want to deliver it via HTTP caching, we need to use the method stale?. Using stale? resembles using the method fresh_when. Example:

```
def show
  if stale? @company
    respond_to do |format|
      format.html
      format.json { render json: @company }
    end
  end
end
```

Using Proxies (public)

Up to now, we always assumed that we are using a cache on the web browser. But on the Internet, there are many proxies that are often closer to the user and can therefore useful for caching in case of non-personalized pages. If our example was a publicly accessible phone book, then we could activate the free services of the proxies with the parameter public: true in fresh_when or stale?.

Example:

```
# GET /companies/1
# GET /companies/1.json
def show
  fresh_when @company, public: true
end
```

We go to the web page and get the output:

```
$ curl -I http://localhost:3000/companies/1
HTTP/1.1 200 OK
X-Frame-Options: SAMEORIGIN
X-Xss-Protection: 1; mode=block
X-Content-Type-Options: nosniff
Etag: "915880f20b5c0c57aa6d0c955910b009"
Last-Modified: Sun, 03 May 2015 18:38:05 GMT
Content-Type: text/html; charset=utf-8
Cache-Control: public
[...]
```

The header Cache-Control: public tells all proxies that they can also cache this web page.

Using proxies always has to be done with great caution. On the one hand, they are brilliantly suited for delivering your own web page quickly to more users, but on the other, you have to be absolutely sure that no personalized pages are cached on public proxies. For example, CSRF tags and Flash messages should never end up in a public proxy. To be sure with the CSRF tags, it is a good idea to make the output of `csrf_meta_tag` in the default `app/views/layouts/application.html.erb` layout dependent on the question whether the page may be cached publicly or not:

```
<%= csrf_meta_tag unless response.cache_control[:public] %>
```

Cache-Control With Time Limit

When using `Etag` and `Last-Modified` we assume that the web browser definitely checks once more with the web server if the cached version of a web page is still current. This is a very safe approach.

But you can take the optimization one step further by predicting the future: if I am already sure when delivering the web page that this web page is not going to change in the next two minutes, hours or days, then I can tell the web browser this directly. It then does not need to check back again within this specified period of time. This overhead saving has advantages, especially with mobile web browsers with relatively high latency. Plus you also save server load on the web server.

In the output of the HTTP header, you may already have noticed the corresponding line in the `Etag` and `Last-Modified` examples:

```
Cache-Control: max-age=0, private, must-revalidate
```

The item `must-revalidate` tells the web browser that it should definitely check back with the web server to see if a web page has changed in the meantime. The second parameter `private` means that only the web browser is allowed to cache this page. Any proxies on the way are not permitted to cache this page.

If we decide for our phone book that the web page is going to stay unchanged for at least 2 minutes, then we can expand the code example by adding the method `expires_in`. The controller `app/controllers/companies.rb` would then contain the following code for the method show:

```
# GET /companies/1
# GET /companies/1.json
def show
  expires_in 2.minutes
  fresh_when @company, public: true
end
```

Now we get a different cache control information in response to a request:

```
$ curl -I http://localhost:3000/companies/1
HTTP/1.1 200 OK
X-Frame-Options: SAMEORIGIN
X-Xss-Protection: 1; mode=block
X-Content-Type-Options: nosniff
Date: Sun, 03 May 2015 19:13:20 GMT
Etag: "915880f20b5c0c57aa6d0c955910b009"
Last-Modified: Sun, 03 May 2015 18:38:05 GMT
Content-Type: text/html; charset=utf-8
Cache-Control: max-age=120, public
[...]
```

The two minutes are specified in seconds (max-age=120) and we no longer need must-revalidate. So in the next 120 seconds, the web browser does not need to check back with the web server to see if the content of this page has changed.

> This mechanism is also used by the asset pipeline. Assets created there in the production environment can be identified clearly by the checksum in the file name and can be cached for a very long time both in the web browser and in public proxies. That's why we have the following section in the nginx configuration file:
>
> ```
> location ^~ /assets/ {
>   gzip_static on;
>   expires max;
>   add_header Cache-Control public;
> }
> ```

Fragment Caching

With fragment caching you can cache individual parts of a view. You can safely use it in combination with HTTP-Caching and Page Caching. The advantages once again are a reduction of server load and faster web page generation, which means increased usability.

Please install a new example application (see "A Simple Example Application").

Enabling Fragment Caching in Development Mode

First, we need to go to the file config/environments/development.rb and set the item config.action_controller.perform_caching to true:

config/environments/development.rb

```
config.action_controller.perform_caching = true
```

Otherwise, we cannot try out the fragment caching in development mode. In production mode, fragment caching is enabled by default.

Caching Table of Index View

On the page http://localhost:3000/companies, a very computationally intensive table with all companies is rendered. We can cache this table as a whole. To do so, we need to enclose the table in a <% cache('name_of_cache') do %> ⋯ <% end %> block:

```
<% cache('name_of_cache') do %>

[...]

<% end %>
```

Please edit the file app/views/companies/index.html.erb as follows:

app/views/companies/index.html.erb

```
<h1>Listing companies</h1>

<% cache('table_of_all_companies') do %>
<table>
  <thead>
    <tr>
      <th>Name</th>
      <th>Number of employees</th>
      <th colspan="3"></th>
    </tr>
  </thead>

  <tbody>
    <% @companies.each do |company| %>
      <tr>
        <td><%= company.name %></td>
        <td><%= company.employees.count %></td>
        <td><%= link_to 'Show', company %></td>
        <td><%= link_to 'Edit', edit_company_path(company) %></td>
        <td><%= link_to 'Destroy', company, method: :delete, data: { confirm:
        'Are you sure?' } %></td>
      </tr>
    <% end %>
  </tbody>
</table>
<% end %>

<br />

<%= link_to 'New Company', new_company_path %>
```

Then you can start the Rails server with rails server and go to the URL http://localhost:3000/companies. In the development log, you will now see the following entry:

```
Write fragment views/table_of_all_companies/f29cc422be54f7b98dfb461505742e7b
(16.9ms)
  Rendered companies/index.html.erb within layouts/application (89.6ms)
Completed 200 OK in 291ms (Views: 261.7ms | ActiveRecord: 10.7ms)
```

Writing the cache took 16.9 ms. In total, rendering the page took 291 ms.

If you repeatedly go to the same page, you will get a different result in the log:

```
Read fragment views/table_of_all_companies/f29cc422be54f7b98dfb461505742e7b
(0.2ms)
  Rendered companies/index.html.erb within layouts/application (1.7ms)
Completed 200 OK in 36ms (Views: 35.6ms | ActiveRecord: 0.0ms)
```

Reading the cache took 0.2 ms and rendering the page in total 36ms. Only a fifth of the processing time!

Deleting Fragment Cache

With the method expire_fragment you can clear specific fragment caches. Basically, we can build this idea into the model in the same way as shown in the section "Deleting Page Caches Automatically".

The model file app/models/company.rb would then look like this:

app/models/company.rb

```
class Company < ActiveRecord::Base
  validates :name,
            presence: true,
            uniqueness: true

  has_many :employees, dependent: :destroy

  after_create   :expire_cache
  after_update   :expire_cache
  before_destroy :expire_cache

  def to_s
    name
  end

  def expire_cache
    ActionController::Base.new.expire_fragment('table_of_all_companies')
  end
end
```

As the number of employees also has an effect on this table, we would also have to expand the file app/models/employees.rb accordingly:

app/models/employees.rb

```ruby
class Employee < ActiveRecord::Base
  belongs_to :company, touch: true

  validates :first_name,
            presence: true

  validates :last_name,
            presence: true

  validates :company,
            presence: true

  after_create   :expire_cache
  after_update   :expire_cache
  before_destroy :expire_cache

  def to_s
    "#{first_name} #{last_name}"
  end

  def expire_cache
    ActionController::Base.new.expire_fragment('table_of_all_companies')
  end
end
```

Deleting specific fragment caches often involves a lot of effort in terms of programming. One, you often miss things and two, in big projects it's not easy to keep track of all the different cache names. Often it is easier to automatically create names via the method cache_key. These then expire automatically in the cache.

Auto-Expiring Caches

Managing fragment caching is rather complex with the naming convention used in the section "Caching Table of Index View". On the one hand, you can be sure that the cache does not have any superfluous ballast if you have programmed neatly, but on the other, it does not really matter. A cache is structured in such a way that it deletes old and no longer required elements on its own. If we use a mechanism that gives a fragment cache a unique name, as in the asset pipeline, then we would not need to go to all the trouble of deleting fragment caches.

That is precisely what the method cache_key is for. cache_key gives you a unique name for an element. Let's try it in the console. First, we get the always identical cache_key of the first company item two times in a row ("companies/1-20150503192915968370000"), then we touch the item (a touch sets the attribute updated_at to the current time) and finally we output the new cache_key ("companies/1-20150503192915968370000"):

```
$ rails console
Loading development environment (Rails 4.2.1)
>> Company.first.cache_key
  Company Load (0.2ms)  SELECT  "companies".* FROM "companies"  ORDER BY
  "companies"."id" ASC LIMIT 1
=> "companies/1-20150503192915968370000"
>> Company.first.cache_key
  Company Load (0.3ms)  SELECT  "companies".* FROM "companies"  ORDER BY
  "companies"."id" ASC LIMIT 1
=> "companies/1-20150503192915968370000"
>> Company.first.touch
  Company Load (0.2ms)  SELECT  "companies".* FROM "companies"  ORDER BY
  "companies"."id" ASC LIMIT 1
   (0.2ms)  begin transaction
  SQL (0.7ms)  UPDATE "companies" SET "updated_at" = '2015-05-03
  19:51:56.619048' WHERE "companies"."id" = ?  [["id", 1]]
   (1.1ms)  commit transaction
=> true
>> Company.first.cache_key
  Company Load (0.3ms)  SELECT  "companies".* FROM "companies"  ORDER BY
  "companies"."id" ASC LIMIT 1
=> "companies/1-20150503195156619048000"
>> exit
```

Let's use this knowledge to edit the index view in the file app/views/companies/index.html.erb:

app/views/companies/index.html.erb

```erb
<h1>Listing companies</h1>

<% cache(@companies) do %>
<table>
  <thead>
    <tr>
      <th>Name</th>
      <th>Number of employees</th>
      <th colspan="3"></th>
    </tr>
  </thead>

  <tbody>
    <% @companies.each do |company| %>
      <tr>
        <td><%= company.name %></td>
        <td><%= company.employees.count %></td>
        <td><%= link_to 'Show', company %></td>
        <td><%= link_to 'Edit', edit_company_path(company) %></td>
        <td><%= link_to 'Destroy', company, method: :delete, data: { confirm:
        'Are you sure?' } %></td>
      </tr>
    <% end %>
  </tbody>
</table>
<% end %>

<br />

<%= link_to 'New Company', new_company_path %>
```

Here, we not only use a fragment cache for the whole table, but also one for each line. So the initial call will take longer than before. But if any individual companies change, only one line has to be re-rendered in each case.

 There is no general answer to the question in how much detail you should use fragment caching. Just go ahead and experiment with it, then look in the log to see how long things take.

Change Code in the View results in an expired Cache

Rails tracks an MD5 sum of the view you use. So if you change the file (e.g. app/views/companies/index.html.erb) the MD5 changes and all old caches will expire.

Cache Store

The cache store manages the stored fragment caches. If not configured otherwise, this is the Rails MemoryStore. This cache store is good for developing, but less suitable for a production system because it acts independently for each Ruby on Rails process. So if you have several Ruby on Rails processes running in parallel in the production system, each process holds its own MemoryStore.

MemCacheStore

Most production systems use memcached (http://memcached.org/) as cache store. To enable memcached as cache store in the production system, you need to add the following line in the file config/environments/production.rb:

config/environments/production.rb

```
config.cache_store = :mem_cache_store
```

The combination of appropriately used auto-expiring caches and memcached is an excellent recipe for a successful web page.

For a description of how to install a Rails production system with memcached, please read the chapter "Web Server in Production Mode".

Other Cache Stores

In the official Rails documentation you will find a list of other cache stores at http://guides.rubyonrails.org/caching_with_rails.html#cache-stores.

Page Caching

Page Caching is extrem and was removed from the core of Rails 4.0. But it is still available as a gem.

 To do this you need a bit of knowledge to configure your Webserver (e.g. Nginx or Apache).

With page caching, it's all about placing a complete HTML page (in other words, the render result of a view) into a subdirectory of the public directory and to have it delivered directly from there by the web server (for example Nginx) whenever the web page is visited next. Additionally, you can also save a compressed gz version of the HTML page there. A production web server will automatically deliver files below public itself and can also be configured so that any gz files present are delivered directly.

In complex views that may take 500ms or even more for rendering, the amount of time you save is of course considerable. As web page operator, you once more save valuable server resources and can service more visitors with the same hardware. The web page user profits from a faster delivery of the web page.

When programming your Rails application, please ensure that you also update this page itself, or delete it! You will find a description in the section "Deleting Page Caches Automatically". Otherwise, you end up with an outdated cache later.

Please also ensure that page caching rejects all URL parameters by default. For example, if you try to go to http://localhost:3000/companies?search=abc this automatically becomes http://localhost:3000/companies. But that can easily be fixed with a better route logic.

Please install a fresh example application (see section "A Simple Example Application") and add the gem with the following line in Gemfile.

```
gem 'actionpack-page_caching'
```

Now install it with the command bundle install.

```
$ bundle install
[...]
```

Lastly you have to tell Rails where to store the cache files. Please add the following line in your config/application.rb file:

config/application.rb

```
config.action_controller.page_cache_directory =
"#{Rails.root.to_s}/public/deploy"
```

Activating Page Caching in Development Mode

First we need to go to the file config/environments/development.rb and set the item config.action_controller.perform_caching to true:

config/environments/development.rb

```
config.action_controller.perform_caching = true
```

Otherwise, we cannot try the page caching in development mode. In production mode, page caching is enabled by default.

Configure our Webserver

Know you have to tell your webserver (e.g. Nginx or Apache) that it should check the /public/deploy directory first before hitting the Rails application. You have to configure too, that it will deliver a gz file if one is available.

There is no one perfect way of doing it. You have to find the best way of doing it in your environment by youself.

As a quick and dirty hack for development you can set the page_cache_directory to public. Than your development system will deliver the cached page.

```
config.action_controller.page_cache_directory =
"#{Rails.root.to_s}/public"
```

Caching Company Index and Show View

Enabling page caching happens in the controller. If we want to cache the show view for Company, we need to go to the controller app/controllers/companies_controller.rb and enter the command caches_page :show at the top:

app/controllers/companies_controller.rb

```
class CompaniesController < ApplicationController
  caches_page :show

  [...]
```

Before starting the application, the public directory looks like this:

```
public/
├──── 404.html
├──── 422.html
├──── 500.html
├──── favicon.ico
└──── robots.txt
```

After starting the appliation with rails server and going to the URLs http://localhost:3000/companies and http://localhost:3000/companies/1 via a web browser, it looks like this:

```
public
├──── 404.html
├──── 422.html
├──── 500.html
├──── deploy
│       └──── companies
│              └──── 1.html
├──── favicon.ico
└──── robots.txt
```

The file public/deploy/companies/1.html has been created by page caching.

From now on, the web server will only deliver the cached versions when these pages are accessed.

gz Versions

If you use page cache, you should also cache directly zipped gz files. You can do this via the option :gzip ⇒ true or use a specific compression parameter as symbol instead of true (for example :best_compression).

The controller app/controllers/companies_controller.rb would then look like this at the beginning:

app/controllers/companies_controller.rb

```
class CompaniesController < ApplicationController
  caches_page :show, gzip: true

  [...]
```

This automatically saves a compressed and an uncompressed version of each page cache:

```
public
├───── 404.html
├───── 422.html
├───── 500.html
├───── deploy
│      └────── companies
│             ├────── 1.html
│             └────── 1.html.gz
├───── favicon.ico
└───── robots.txt
```

The File Extension .html

Rails saves the page accessed at http://localhost:3000/companies under the file name companies.html. So the upstream web server will find and deliver this file if you go to http://localhost:3000/companies.html, but not if you try to go to http://localhost:3000/companies, because the extension .html at the end of the URI is missing.

If you are using the Nginx server as described in the chapter "Web Server in Production Mode", the easiest way is adapting the try_files instruction in the Nginx configuration file as follows:

```
try_files $uri/index.html $uri $uri.html @unicorn;
```

Nginx then checks if a file with the extension .html of the currently accessed URI exists.

Deleting Page Caches Automatically

As soon as the data used in the view changes, the saved cache files have to be deleted. Otherwise, the cache would no longer be up to date.

According to the official Rails documentation, the solution for this problem is the class ActionController::Caching::Sweeper. But this approach, described at http://guides.rubyonrails.org/caching_with_rails.html#sweepers, has a big disadvantage: it is limited to actions that happen within the controller. So if an action is triggered via URL by the web browser, the corresponding cache is also changed or deleted. But if an object is deleted in the console, for example, the sweeper would not realize this. For that reason, I am going to show you an approach that does not use a sweeper, but works directly in the model with ActiveRecord callbacks.

In our phone book application, we always need to delete the cache for http://localhost:3000/companies and http://localhost:3000/companies/company_id when editing a company. When editing an employee, we also have to delete the corresponding cache for the relevant employee.

Models

Now we still need to fix the models so that the corresponding caches are deleted automatically as soon as an object is created, edited or deleted.

app/models/company.rb

```ruby
class Company < ActiveRecord::Base
  validates :name,
            presence: true,
            uniqueness: true

  has_many :employees, dependent: :destroy

  after_create  :expire_cache
  after_update  :expire_cache
  before_destroy :expire_cache

  def to_s
    name
  end

  def expire_cache
    ActionController::Base.expire_page(Rails.application.routes.url_helpers.company_path(self))
    ActionController::Base.expire_page(Rails.application.routes.url_helpers.companies_path)
  end

end
```

app/models/employee.rb

```ruby
class Employee < ActiveRecord::Base
  belongs_to :company, touch: true

  validates :first_name,
            presence: true

  validates :last_name,
            presence: true

  validates :company,
            presence: true

  after_create  :expire_cache
  after_update  :expire_cache
  before_destroy :expire_cache

  def to_s
    "#{first_name} #{last_name}"
  end

  def expire_cache
    ActionController::Base.expire_page(Rails.application.routes.url_helpers.employee_path(self))
    ActionController::Base.expire_page(Rails.application.routes.url_helpers.employees_path)
    self.company.expire_cache
  end

end
```

Preheating

Now that you have read your way through the caching chapter, here is a final tip: preheat your cache!

For example, if you have a web application in a company and you know that at 9 o'clock in the morning, all employees are going to log in and then access this web application, then it's a good idea to let your web server go through all those views a few hours in advance with cron-job. At night, your server is probably bored anyway.

Check out the behavior patterns of your users. With public web pages, this can be done for example via Google Analytics (http://www.google.com/analytics/). You will find that at certain times of the day, there is a lot more traffic going in. If you have a quiet phase prior to this, you can use it to warm up your cache.

The purpose of preheating is once more saving server ressources and achieving better quality for the user, as the web page is displayed more quickly.

Action Cable

Modern webpages are not just static. They often get updates from the server without interaction from the user. Your Twitter or GMail browser client will display new Tweets or E-Mails without you reloading the page. The server pushes the information. Action Cable provides the tools you need to use these mechanisms without diving deep into the technical aspects of websockets.

The standard Rails scaffold example used to be the "Blog in 15 Minutes" screencast by @dhh. Now there is a new standard example to show how easy Action Cable can be used: A chat application. I find that a bit too complex for the first step so we begin with a much lighter setup to get a feeling how Action Cable works.

Minimal Current Time Update Example

This app will display the current time and updates the same time to all old visitors of the page which are still online. So the first user gets the current time until the next user opens the same page. At that time the second user gets the current time and the first user gets the new time in addition to the already existing one.

We start with a fresh Rails application and a basic page controller which provides an index action:

```
$ rails new clock
  [...]
$ cd clock
$ rails generate controller page index
  [...]
$
```

To display the time we create a @current_time variable in the index action.

app/controllers/page_controller.rb

```
class PageController < ApplicationController
  def index
    @current_time = Time.now
  end
end
```

The view displays that @current_time with this code:

app/views/page/index.html.erb

```
<div id="messages">
  <p><%= @current_time %></p>
</div>
```

Lastly we update the routes so that everything happens on the index page:

config/routes.rb

```
Rails.application.routes.draw do
  get 'page/index'
  root 'page#index'
end
```

Start the Rails server:

```
$ rails server
=> Booting Puma
=> Rails 5.0.0 application starting in development on http://localhost:3000
[...]
```

Now you can visit http://localhost:3000 with your browser and get the current time displayed. Reloading the page will result in an update on the same page.

To use Action Cable we need to add some more code. Action Cable uses channels which can be subscribed be the web browser and which will be used to send updates to the page. So we need to create a clock channel which can be done with a generator:

```
$ rails generate channel clock
Running via Spring preloader in process 1844
      create  app/channels/clock_channel.rb
      create  app/assets/javascripts/channels/clock.coffee
$
```

The JavaScript part of Action Cable has to be activated. The code is already there. You just have to remove the `#`s.

app/assets/javascripts/cable.coffee

```
#= require action_cable
#= require_self
#= require_tree ./channels
#
@App ||= {}
App.cable = ActionCable.createConsumer()
```

In the page.coffee file we add code to handle the subscription to the ClockChannel and which processes updates which are pushed by Action Cable. Those updates will be appended the the <div> with the messages id.

app/assets/javascripts/page.coffee

```
App.room = App.cable.subscriptions.create "ClockChannel",
  received: (data) ->
    $('#messages').append data['message']
```

The ClockChannel need some basic configuration to work:

app/channels/clock_channel.rb

```
class ClockChannel < ApplicationCable::Channel
  def subscribed
    stream_from "clock_channel"
  end

  def unsubscribed
    # Any cleanup needed when channel is unsubscribed
  end
end
```

The update will get broadcast by the following code in the show action:

```
class PageController < ApplicationController
  def index
    @current_time = Time.now.to_s

    ActionCable.server.broadcast 'clock_channel', message: '<p>'+Time.now.to_s+'</p>'
  end
end
```

Lastly we have to mount a websocket server in the routes.rb:

config/routes.rb

```
Rails.application.routes.draw do
  get 'page/index'
  root 'page#index'

  mount ActionCable.server => '/cable'
end
```

After restarting the Rails web server you can play with the application. Open a couple of browser windows and visit http://localhost:3000/

You'll see the new time update in every open window below the former time updates.

The Chat Application

Now it's time to tackle the chat application. I'm not going to walk you through that step by step but add some information.

We create a new application with a message scaffold where the model stores the messages.

```
$ rails new chatroom
  [...]
$ cd chatroom
$ rails generate controller page index
  [...]
$ rails generate scaffold message content
  [...]
$ rails db:migrate
  [...]
$ rails generate channel room speak
  [...]
$ rails generate job MessageBroadcast
```

config/routes.rb

```
Rails.application.routes.draw do
  get 'page/index'
  root 'page#index'

  mount ActionCable.server => '/cable'
end
```

app/views/page/index.html.erb

```erb
<h1>Chat</h1>

<div id="messages">
  <%= render @messages %>
</div>

<form>
  <label>Say:</label><br>
  <input type="text" data-behavior="room_speaker">
</form>
```

app/views/messages/_message.html.erb

```erb
<div class="message">
  <p>
    <b><%= l Time.now, format: :short %>:</b>
    <%= message.content %>
  </p>
</div>
```

We display the last 5 messages on the index page:

app/controllers/page_controller.rb

```ruby
class PageController < ApplicationController
  def index
    @messages = Message.order(:created_at).
                        reverse_order.
                        limit(5).
                        reverse
  end
end
```

app/assets/javascripts/cable.coffee

```coffee
#= require action_cable
#= require_self
#= require_tree ./channels
#
@App ||= {}
App.cable = ActionCable.createConsumer()
```

app/channels/room_channel.rb

```ruby
class RoomChannel < ApplicationCable::Channel
  def subscribed
    stream_from "room_channel"
  end

  def unsubscribed
  end

  def speak(data)
    Message.create! content: data['message']
  end
end
```

app/assets/javascripts/page.coffee

```coffee
App.room = App.cable.subscriptions.create "RoomChannel",
  connected: ->
    # Called when the subscription is ready for use on the server

  disconnected: ->
    # Called when the subscription has been terminated by the server

  received: (data) ->
    $('#messages').append data['message']

  speak: (message) ->
    @perform 'speak', message: message

$(document).on 'keypress', '[data-behavior~=room_speaker]', (event) ->
  if event.keyCode is 13 # return = send
    App.room.speak event.target.value
    event.target.value = ""
    event.preventDefault()
```

Using a job is more secure and performant than doing it in the controller. Active Job will take care of the work.

app/jobs/message_broadcast_job.rb

```ruby
class MessageBroadcastJob < ApplicationJob
  queue_as :default

  def perform(message)
    ActionCable.server.broadcast 'room_channel', message: render_message(message)
  end

  private
  def render_message(message)
    ApplicationController.renderer.render(partial: 'messages/message', locals: { message: message })
  end
end
```

After a new message was created in the database the job will be triggered.

app/models/message.rb

```ruby
class Message < ApplicationRecord
  after_create_commit { MessageBroadcastJob.perform_later self }
end
```

Now open a couple of browsers at http://localhost:3000 and try this basic chat application.

Templates

Once you have been working with Rails for a while, you will always make the same changes after calling `rails generate scaffold` or `rails generate model`. You are going to adapt the scaffold to your requirements. Fortunately, you can replace the Rails templates for creating the controller or model files with your own custom templates. This saves a lot of time.

I am going to show you the basic principle by using the controller and model template as an example.

 15 minutes spent optimizing a template in accordance with your requirements will save you many hours if not days of work later in every Rails project!

Scaffold Controller Template

Let's assume you want to create a scaffold User:

```
$ rails generate scaffold User first_name last_name login
     [...]
     invoke  scaffold_controller
     create    app/controllers/users_controller.rb
     [...]
$
```

The controller `app/controllers/users_controller.rb` generated by default then looks like this in Rails 5.0:

app/controllers/users_controller.rb

```ruby
class UsersController < ApplicationController
  before_action :set_user, only: [:show, :edit, :update, :destroy]

  # GET /users
  # GET /users.json
  def index
    @users = User.all
  end

  # GET /users/1
  # GET /users/1.json
  def show
  end

  # GET /users/new
  def new
    @user = User.new
  end

  # GET /users/1/edit
  def edit
  end

  # POST /users
  # POST /users.json
  def create
    @user = User.new(user_params)

    respond_to do |format|
      if @user.save
```

```
        format.html { redirect_to @user, notice: 'User was successfully created.' }
        format.json { render :show, status: :created, location: @user }
      else
        format.html { render :new }
        format.json { render json: @user.errors, status: :unprocessable_entity }
      end
    end
  end

  # PATCH/PUT /users/1
  # PATCH/PUT /users/1.json
  def update
    respond_to do |format|
      if @user.update(user_params)
        format.html { redirect_to @user, notice: 'User was successfully updated.' }
        format.json { render :show, status: :ok, location: @user }
      else
        format.html { render :edit }
        format.json { render json: @user.errors, status: :unprocessable_entity }
      end
    end
  end

  # DELETE /users/1
  # DELETE /users/1.json
  def destroy
    @user.destroy
    respond_to do |format|
      format.html { redirect_to users_url, notice: 'User was successfully destroyed.' }
      format.json { head :no_content }
    end
  end

  private
    # Use callbacks to share common setup or constraints between actions.
    def set_user
      @user = User.find(params[:id])
    end

    # Never trust parameters from the scary internet, only allow the white list through.
    def user_params
      params.require(:user).permit(:login)
    end
end
```

But if we only need HTML, no JSON and no comments then the file could also look like this:

```ruby
class UsersController < ApplicationController
  before_action :set_user, only: [:show, :edit, :update, :destroy]

  def index
    @users = User.all
  end

  def show
  end

  def new
    @user = User.new
  end

  def edit
  end

  def create
    @user = User.new(user_params)

    if @user.save
      redirect_to @user, notice: 'User was successfully created.'
    else
      render :new
    end
  end

  def update
    if @user.update(user_params)
      redirect_to @user, notice: 'User was successfully updated.'
    else
      render :edit
    end
  end

  def destroy
    @user.destroy
    redirect_to users_url, notice: 'User was successfully destroyed.'
  end

  private
    def set_user
      @user = User.find(params[:id])
    end

    def user_params
      params.require(:user).permit(:login)
    end
end
```

The original template used by `rails generate scaffold` for generating the controller can be found in the Rails Github repository at https://github.com/rails/rails/blob/5-0-stable/railties/lib/rails/generators/rails/scaffold_controller/templates/controller.rb

It is a normal ERB file that you can download and then save as new file `lib/templates/rails/scaffold_controller/controller.rb` (you may need to create the corresponding directories manually). To get the above desired result, you need to change the template as follows:

lib/templates/rails/scaffold_controller/controller.rb

```erb
<% if namespaced? -%>
require_dependency "<%= namespaced_file_path %>/application_controller"

<% end -%>
<% module_namespacing do -%>
class <%= controller_class_name %>Controller < ApplicationController
  before_action :set_<%= singular_table_name %>, only: [:show, :edit, :update, :destroy]

  def index
    @<%= plural_table_name %> = <%= orm_class.all(class_name) %>
  end

  def show
  end

  def new
    @<%= singular_table_name %> = <%= orm_class.build(class_name) %>
  end

  def edit
  end

  def create
    @<%= singular_table_name %> = <%= orm_class.build(class_name, "#{singular_table_name
}_params") %>

    if @<%= orm_instance.save %>
      redirect_to @<%= singular_table_name %>, notice: <%= "'#{human_name} was successfully
created.'" %>
    else
      render action: 'new'
    end
  end

  def update
    if @<%= orm_instance.update("#{singular_table_name}_params") %>
      redirect_to @<%= singular_table_name %>, notice: <%= "'#{human_name} was successfully
updated.'" %>
    else
      render action: 'edit'
    end
  end

  def destroy
    @<%= orm_instance.destroy %>
    redirect_to <%= index_helper %>_url, notice: <%= "'#{human_name} was successfully
destroyed.'" %>
  end

  private
    def set_<%= singular_table_name %>
      @<%= singular_table_name %> = <%= orm_class.find(class_name, "params[:id]") %>
    end

    def <%= "#{singular_table_name}_params" %>
      <%- if attributes_names.empty? -%>
      params[<%= ":#{singular_table_name}" %>]
      <%- else -%>
```

```
        params.require(<%= ":#{singular_table_name}" %>).permit(<%= attributes_names.map { |name|
  ":#{name}" }.join(', ') %>)
      <%- end -%>
    end
end
<% end -%>
```

Each time you now use `rails generate scaffold`, you get the controller in the variation you want.

Model Template

The basic idea is the same as with the controller in section "Scaffold Controller Template": it's all about adapting the model created by the Rails generator to your own needs.

The model template used by `rails generate model` and therefore also by `rails generate scaffold` can be found in the Rails Github repository at https://github.com/rails/rails/blob/5-0-stable/activerecord/lib/rails/generators/active_record/model/templates/model.rb

Save this file in your Rails project under `lib/templates/active_record/model/model.rb`. If you want to edit the method `to_s` per default, your `model.rb` could for example look like this:

lib/templates/active_record/model/model.rb

```
<% module_namespacing do -%>
class <%= class_name %> < <%= parent_class_name.classify %>
<% attributes.select(&:reference?).each do |attribute| -%>
  belongs_to :<%= attribute.name %><%= ', polymorphic: true' if attribute.polymorphic? %>
<% end -%>
<% if attributes.any?(&:password_digest?) -%>
  has_secure_password
<% end -%>
end

  def to_s
    <%- if attributes.map{ |a| a.name }.include?('name') -%>
    name
    <%- else -%>
    "<%= class_name %> #{id}"
    <%- end -%>
  end

<% end -%>
```

If you now create a new model with `rails generate model Book name number_of_pages:integer`, the file `app/models/book.rb` will look like this:

app/models/book.rb

```
class Book < ActiveRecord::Base
  def to_s
    name
  end
end
```

Appendix A: Ruby on Rails Install How-to

Development System

This chapter's installation methods described are intended for development systems. If you are looking for instructions on installing a web server in the production system, please have a look at the chapter which handles the server setup.

Both types of installation are very different.

Ruby on Rails 5.0 on Debian 8.3 (Jessie)

There are two main reasons for installing a Ruby on Rails system with RVM (Ruby Version Manager):

- You simply do not have any root rights on the system. In that case, you have no other option.
- You want to run several Rails systems that are separated cleanly, and perhaps also separate Ruby versions. This can be easily done with RVM. You can run Ruby 1.9.3 with Rails 3.2 and in parallel Ruby 2.3.0 with Rails 5.0.

 Detailed information on RVM can be found on the RVM homepage at https://rvm.io

This description assumes that you have a freshly installed Debian GNU/Linux 8.3 ("Jessie"). You will find an ISO image for the installation at http://www.debian.org. I recommend the approximately 250 MB net installation CD image. For instructions on how to install Debian-GNU/Linux, please go to http://www.debian.org/distrib/netinst.

Preparations

If you have root rights on the target system, you can use the following commands to ensure that all required programs for a successful installation of RVM are available. If you do not have root rights, you have to either hope that your admin has already installed everything you need, or send them a quick e-mail with the corresponding lines.

Login as root and update the package lists:

```
root@debian:~# apt-get update
[...]
root@debian:~#
```

 Of course, you can optionally install a SSH server on the system, so you can work on the system via SSH instead of on the console:

```
root@debian:~# apt-get -y install openssh-server
```

And now the installation of the packages required for the RVM installation:

```
root@debian:~# apt-get -y install curl patch bzip2 \
gawk g++ gcc make libc6-dev patch libreadline6-dev \
zlib1g-dev libssl-dev libyaml-dev libsqlite3-dev \
sqlite3 autoconf libgdbm-dev libncurses5-dev \
automake libtool bison pkg-config libffi-dev
[...]
root@debian:~#
```

Now is a good time to log out as root:

```
root@debian:~# exit
logout
xyz@debian:~$
```

Installing Ruby 2.3 and Ruby on Rails 5.0 with RVM

Log in with your normal user account (in our case, it's the user xyz).

RVM, Ruby, and Ruby on Rails can be installed in various ways. I recommend using the following commands and get at least one cup of tea/coffee/favorite drink:

```
xyz@debian:~$ gpg --keyserver hkp://keys.gnupg.net \
--recv-keys 409B6B1796C275462A1703113804BB82D39DC0E3
[...]
xyz@debian:~$ curl -sSL https://get.rvm.io | bash
[...]
xyz@debian:~$ source /home/xyz/.rvm/scripts/rvm
xyz@debian:~$ rvm install 2.3 --autolibs=read-only
[...]
xyz@debian:~$ gem install
[...]
xyz@debian:~$
```

 gem install rails installs the current stable Rails version. You can use the format gem install rails -v 5.0.0 to install a specific version and gem install rails --pre to install a current beta version.

RVM, Ruby 2.3 and Rails 5.0 are now installed. You can check it with the following commands.

```
xyz@debian:~$ ruby -v
ruby 2.3.0p0 (2015-12-25 revision 53290) [x86_64-linux]
xyz@debian:~$ rails -v
Rails 5.0.0
xyz@debian:~$
```

Ruby on Rails 5.0 on Windows

At http://railsinstaller.org/ there is a simple, all-inclusive Ruby on Rails installer for Windows for Ruby and Rails.

Ruby on Rails 5.0 on Mac OS X 10.11 (El Capitan)

Mac OS 10.11 includes Ruby by default. Not interesting for our purposes. We want Ruby 2.3 and Rails 5.0. To avoid interfering with the existing Ruby and Rails installation and therefore the packet management of Mac OS X, we install Ruby 2.3 and Rails 5.0 with RVM (Ruby Version Manager).

With RVM, you can install and run any number of Ruby and Rails versions as normal user (without root rights and in your home directory). So you can work in parallel on old projects that may still use Ruby 1.9.3 and new projects that use Ruby 2.3.

 Detailed information on RVM can be found at the RVM homepage at https://rvm.io/

Xcode Installation or Upgrade

Before you start installing Ruby on Rails, you must install the *latest* Apple Xcode tools on your system. The easiest way is via the Mac App Store (search for "xcode") or via the website https://developer.apple.com/xcode/

Please take care to install all the command line tools!

Installing Ruby 2.3 and Ruby on Rails 5.0 with RVM

RVM can be installed in various ways. I recommend using the following monster command (please copy it exactly) that installs the latest RVM, Ruby and Ruby on Rails in your home directory:

```
$ gpg --keyserver hkp://keys.gnupg.net \
--recv-keys 409B6B1796C275462A1703113804BB82D39DC0E3
[...]
$ curl -sSL https://get.rvm.io | bash
[...]
$
```

Now exit the current shell/terminal and open a new one for the next commands.

```
$ rvm install 2.3
[...]
$ gem install rails
[...]
$
```

 gem install rails installs the current stable Rails version. You can use the format gem install rails -v 5.0.0 to install a specific version and gem install rails --pre to install a current beta version.

RVM, Ruby 2.3 and Rails 5.0 are now fully installed. You can check it with the following commands.

```
$ ruby -v
ruby 2.3.0p0 (2015-12-25 revision 53290) [x86_64-linux]
$ rails -v
Rails 5.0.0
$
```

Appendix B: Further Rails Documentation

Here is a list of important websites on the topic Ruby on Rails:

http://guides.rubyonrails.org

A couple of very good official guides.

http://rubyonrails.org/

The project page of Ruby on Rails offers many links for further documentation. Please note: some parts of the documentation are now obsolete. Please check if what you are reading is related specifically to Rails 3.2 or to older Rails versions.

http://railscasts.com/

Ryan Bates used to publish a new screencast every Monday on a topic associated with Rails. Unfortunately he hasn't published screencasts for some time now but the page still has valuable old ones

Made in the USA
San Bernardino, CA
06 January 2017